BORN TO BE
HANGED

Praise for the Book

While tracing the making of Zulfikar Ali Bhutto—the most popular leader of his people, Dr Syeda Hameed easily identifies him as a self-destroying character in a Greek tragedy. But the chief merit of this book lies in explaining the factors contributing to his meteoric rise and the unravelling of his mind through a reading of his prison letters with Dr Mubashir Hasan's help, and how Bhutto, with a Janus like posture, tried to build a socialist castle on the foundation of Islamic ideology. The guardians of vested interest were not duped; they hanged him for shaking their throne. An eye-opener for students of Pakistan's muddled politics.

—I.A. Rehman,
Human Rights Activist and Political Analyst, Pakistan

Syeda Hameed's labour of love, spanning two decades, has flowered into a vivid portrayal of one of the most intriguing public figures of South Asia

—Asif Noorani,
Senior Journalist and Author, Pakistan

BORN TO BE
HANGED

POLITICAL BIOGRAPHY OF
ZULFIKAR ALI BHUTTO

SYEDA HAMEED

RUPA

Published by
Rupa Publications India Pvt. Ltd 2017
7/16, Ansari Road, Daryaganj
New Delhi 110002

Sales Centres:
Allahabad Bengaluru Chennai
Hyderabad Jaipur Kathmandu
Kolkata Mumbai

ISBN: 978-81-291-4967-1

Second impression 2018

10 9 8 7 6 5 4 3 2

The moral right of the author has been asserted.

Printed in India by Replika Press Pvt. Ltd, India

'I know the burden on you is heavy but this is inevitable because of the confidence I repose in you and because of your unstinted devotion to the common cause. I hope you don't mind if I keep pressing you on these matters. As time passes you will be more and more pressed but I am certain you will respond to the call and fulfil all the growing requirements.'

Letter from Zulfikar Ali Bhutto to Mubashir Hasan
11 September 1968

This book is dedicated to Dr Mubashir Hasan whose life is a testament to this prediction.

Contents

Prologue

Oh, my children, where are you?
For you too, I weep
Though I cannot see your faces
Knowing the bitter life men will make for you
In the days to come.
(Oedipus, self-blinded, addressing his children in Sophocles's
Oedipus the King, 5th Century BC)

As a student of literature, I have always thought of Zulfikar Ali
Bhutto (ZAB) as the protagonist of a Greek tragedy. Parallels
abound in the stories of Zulfikar of Larkana and Oedipus of
Thebes. Oedipus had four children; two sons—Eteocles and
Polynices, and two daughters—Antigone and Ismene. Zulfikar
had four children; two sons—Mir Murtaza and Shahnawaz, and
two daughters—Benazir and Sanam. Oedipus, when he came
to know the truth of his patricide and incest, blinded himself
and went into self-imposed exile. Zulfikar, when he realized his
flawed judgment and personal hubris, was already held in a vice,
which a virulent regime turned into the noose finally ending him.
Oedipus's sons fought over his kingdom and slew each other.
Polynices was refused burial by the state. Zulfikar's sons met a
similar end. Murtaza was bullet-showered as he was driving into
his own house and Shahnawaz was poisoned, far away from home;
the assailants of both remain untraced to date. Oedipus's daughter

Antigone was sent to death by her uncle Creon for disobeying the law of Thebes. Zulfikar's daughter Benazir was assassinated on her way back from a public meeting. Both men, larger than life, are victims despite epitomizing qualities which are the antithesis of victimhood—self-confidence, masterfulness and intensity. The Greeks would say they were cursed by the gods; ensnared by fate; their self-destruction resulted from an imbalance in the 'humours' of which they were made. Seven thousand years later, what would we say about our protagonist?

The tragic sagas of Antigone and Benazir reverberate through generations. Sophocles, in his drama, has immortalized Antigone. A parallel piece needs to be written on Benazir. Polynices and Murtaza have remained unsung. But that is another story for another time.

Sir Morrice James was Britain's High Commissioner in Islamabad in the 1960s. He had worked closely with ZAB from 1962 onwards. In his *Pakistan Chronicle*, he writes, 'Bhutto certainly had the right qualities for reaching the heights—drive, charm, imagination, a quick and penetrating mind, zest for life, eloquence, energy, strong constitution, a sense of humour and a thick skin. Such a blend is rare anywhere, and Bhutto deserved his swift rise to power'. But then he adds, 'There was—how will I put it—a rank odour of hellfire about him. It was a case of *Corruptio Optimi Pessima* (corruption of the best is the worst of all) I believe that at heart he lacked a sense of the dignity and value of other people; his own self was what counted. I sensed in him ruthlessness and a capacity for ill-doing which went far beyond what is natural.'

Finance Minister Mubashir Hasan, a loyal and close associate of ZAB, commented that the above remarks of Morrice James, 'emanate from a man with middle class mind. These are relevant for the sovereign mind only to the limited extent that their practice does not cause violent turbulence in the state to endanger it. The sovereign's highest interests are strengthening the state against foreign powers, keeping his government strong and staying in power; if possible, expanding both personal and state power. This has priority over all values and powers derived from values. Moral considerations, personal and populist values become secondary to the pursuit of power and staying in power.'

What then was the tragic flaw which led to the fall of the two protagonists, Oedipus and Zulfikar? In the Greek world, fate rules supreme. Any attempt to question or alter fate is catastrophic. Oedipus was destined to commit fratricide, incest and self-mutilation. He was warned by the oracle of his horrible destiny. Being a mortal, he defied the gods and tried to change its course; he challenged fate. This, in the eyes of Thebans and their gods was unforgivable, the flaw that led to tragedy. From 5th Century BC to 1979, several centuries had elapsed when the tragedy of ZAB unfolded. Fate was no longer the human determinant. Human species had evolved to become its own arbiter. Zulfikar's tragic flaw was his arrogance. The Greeks call it *hubris*, which, from beginning to end, emerges as his tragic flaw. Mubashir Hasan explains this, 'His tragedy lay in assuming that he could exercise sovereign power whereas he had lost almost all of it.'

Morrice James' last sentence, like the oracle at Delphi, defines the tragedy that flows from his flaw: 'Despite his gifts, I judged that one day Bhutto would destroy himself. When and how, I could not tell. In 1965, I so reported in one of my last dispatches from Pakistan as British High Commissioner. I wrote by way of clinching that Bhutto was born to be hanged. Fourteen years later that was what it turned out to be.'

At the end of the play, Sophoclean chorus speaks words that elevate tragedy. Its words are applicable to both protagonists. It, thereby, fulfils its role of transporting tragedy to the height of catharsis. We, as witnesses, transcend immediate grief when we learn about Oedipus unriddling the Theban riddle and Zulfikar bringing the wretched and ragged of Pakistan to centre stage. They both tried to solve the unsolvable, leading to their tragedy and our catharsis.

The Greek play ends with the chorus' comment; the chorus stands for the audience witnessing what transpired:

Dwellers of Thebes,
Behold, this is Oedipus,
Who unriddled the famous riddle,
And was a man most notable.
What Theban did not envy his good fortune?
Yet behold into what a whirlwind of trouble he was hurled!
Therefore, with eyes fixed on the end destined for all,
Count no one of the race of man happy,
Until he has crossed life's border free from pain.

Introduction

The time I began to think of writing about Zulfikar Ali Bhutto I had no idea of the depth and expanse of my subject. For twenty years I have lived with a man I never met. The unexplored portions of his life, his times and my discovering them made me think of a poem of John Keats, the poet most of us read in our growing years. When he read Homer, Keats wrote *On First Looking into Chapman's Homer* (Chapman translated Homer from Greek to English)

Then I felt like some watcher of the skies
When a new planet swims into his ken
Or like stout Cortez when with eagle eyes
He stared at the pacific

A new planet in the form of ZAB had swum into my personal landscape. I was the 'stout' explorer Hernan Cortez. With an 'eagle eye' I would explore the vast ocean of ZAB's life and present it to the world just as Cortez presented Mexico to Spain.

ZAB remained on my agenda throughout the ten years I served as Member of Planning Commission of India. The materials I had collected over seven years from 1997 to 2004 lined my bookshelves. But where was the time!

When I first conceived the project in late nineties, most of ZAB's close associates, with the exception of J. A. Rahim, who had passed away, were living in Pakistan or elsewhere and were willing to help. Over the years, I met a few of them and carefully preserved the notes I took at these meetings. My mind conjured images about events I had never seen. These images have foregrounded the narrative of the book.

I picked up the work full steam in 2014. Haneef Ramay, Chief Minister of Punjab for many years and Rafi Raza, Special Assistant and later Federal Minister in ZAB's Cabinet, had passed away. Also gone was Khan Abdul Wali Khan, President National Awami Party and Leader of Opposition during Bhutto years. In the 1980's I had translated his autobiography in English from a handwritten Urdu manuscript. I met him and Begum Naseem several times in the 1980's but the present book was not conceived yet. I had the privilege of sitting down with Ghulam Mustafa Khar, who was Governor and Martial Law Administrator and Chief Minister of Punjab during the Bhutto years. I had several meetings with I.A. Rehman, Pakistan's best known journalist who watched the drama of 'thanda kamra' and the story of ZAB unfold day by day. But my best friend and source of most of the knowledge I garnered was Mubashir Hasan who not only placed all his archives at my disposal but began working with me at the age of 73 and today at 93 he continues to have the same sharpness of mind he had then. He is a formidable taskmaster and relentless critic. He has read every word I have written, never allowing the slightest diversion from fact, a poetic license or flight of imagination in which I am prone to indulge. He rejects the old adage saying:

Badha bhi dete hain kuchh zeb-e-daastaan ki liye
(We exaggerate a bit to embellish the tale)

The emergence of Bangladesh coincided with the rise of Zulfikar Ali Bhutto who came to power in 1971 following the defeat of his country by India. His political agenda based on Islamic faith, democratic polity, socialist economy and confrontation with India made him beloved of Pakistani masses. Pakistan's military dictator General Yahya Khan, when he was forced to quit by the army following its defeat by India, signed on the dotted line which made ZAB the President and CMLA (Chief Martial Law Administrator). He began work the moment he left the erstwhile President's chambers. Unrelenting about executing his work plan, he made his core team work around the clock not permitting the slightest laxity. 'Bhutto would work until early hours of the morning' writes Mubashir Hasan. Within a few months he had carried out his agenda of socialist reforms. Pakistan got its Interim Constitution within four months of ZAB coming to power. And in 1973 Pakistan had its first ever Constitution passed by an elected Assembly based on adult franchise.

During the next few years, ZAB had fully consolidated his power. He emerged as a leader with an international stature and immense support of the masses. However, within a few years, his power eroded. His reliance on civil and military bureaucracy rather than on the people left him at the mercy of the former. First, he lost support in the cities where the business class became his bitter enemy. It took longer before the people of the countryside followed suit. The United States, who was never in his favour due to his socialist agenda and dreams for leadership of Islamic countries and the third world, warned him of becoming a 'horrible example'.

ZAB was overthrown in 1977 by the Chief of his Army Staff General Ziaul Haq and was executed in 1979 through a contrived judicial process described by former Chief Justice Mohammad Muneer, as judicial murder. Ziaul Haq ruled over Pakistan for 11 years with an iron fist, curbing all dissent until he got blown up in an air crash in 1988. In almost three decades since then, Pakistan's leadership has changed hands 15 times. An extremely controversial and confrontational politics is associated with the era of Zulfikar Ali Bhutto. It is therefore not surprising that, considering his towering stature, not enough has been researched and written about the tumultuous years of his accession to power culminating in, what today is best described, as regicide.

The most popular work on ZAB is Stanley Wolpert's *Zulfi Bhutto of Pakistan: His Life and Times* published in 1993 in which he has written over 100 pages about the crucial years 1972–76. But one giveaway of his bias is the dedication of his book to Ardeshir Cowasjee who Mubashir Hasan describes as 'inveterate Bhutto hater'. The most important source for me, other than oral history and archival material, was *The Mirage of Power* (published in 2000 by Oxford University Press) written by Mubashir Hasan in which ZAB's close associate writes his honest, unadorned and factual account. Fatima Bhutto's *Songs of Blood and Sword* (published in 2010 by Penguin-Viking) is a daughter's memoir which has nuggets about her grandfather's turbulent life. Rafi Raza's *Zulfikar Ali Bhutto and Pakistan 1967-1977* and Anwar H. Syed's *The Discourse and Politics of Zulfikar Ali Bhutto* shed strong objective light. A few Indian authors like Pran Chopra did great service by bringing out ZAB's memoirs of his last days at Rawalpindi Jail in *If I am Assassinated*.

Two watershed moments in writing this book need to be placed on record. First is anecdotal. An 83-year-old woman, Mubashir Hasan's mother, gave him a piece of advice, its essence being 'power is an affliction'. She was worried about her son's absence from home. The year was 1968 when PPP was gaining huge popularity. He explained to her that he was 'doing' politics to replace the present corrupt dictatorship with a 'young educated and popular leader'. 'Is he well off, does he have wife and children?' she asked. Hasan replied that he was rich and had a wife and four beautiful children. 'Then what afflicts him' she asked 'that he wants to become a king?'

My second watershed moment was when I learnt of the 17-page letter Mubashir Hasan wrote to his leader two years before he was hanged by the state. The imminent doom was evident to all his close associates. Mubashir wrote in his letter 'What is needed in Pakistan is a leadership with the willing partnership of peasant and labour through a democratic process without the intervention of persons whose interests conflicted with those of the working classes.' He wrote this letter two years after he had resigned from the Cabinet, a move which according to Rafi Raza baffled ZAB that a politician would so willingly relinquish power. Mubashir Hasan, son of a wise mother, saw the reality through the 'mirage of power'; ZAB did not.

It has taken 20 years to complete this work for which I have visited Pakistan as many times. Most of my days were spent in Lahore where all the documents were available. In Karachi I entered ZAB's mansion, 70 Clifton, with a strong sense of *deja vu*. The place was opened for me by Ghinwa Bhutto, ZAB's daughter-in-law and leader of PPP (Shaheed Bhutto) who is also one of the warmest persons I have known. The library was as grand and well-equipped as its owner. I did read a few of the documents placed there and I testify that the library has a lot for future historians and biographers.

As an endnote, I place on record that are two diametrical opposite personalities which became the subject of the major research of my life, Maulana Abul Kalam Azad and Zulfikar Ali Bhutto. Their only common point is that they were both very important world leaders who were also Muslims. (I do not think of them in the category of 'Muslim leaders' an epithet used often in intellectual discourse.) But my engagement with them created one more 'similarity'. My manuscript on Azad was rejected by Oxford University Press (OUP) India and my proposal on ZAB was rejected by Jawaharlal Nehru Memorial Fund. This double rejection forms an interesting narrative; its subtext is evident. I received both rejection letters in 1997. The next year, my Azad book was published by OUP Pakistan titled *Islamic Seal on India's Independence*. Seventeen years later OUP India proactively published the same book with the title *Maulana Azad, Islam and the Indian National Movement*. And now this book!

Ismail Guljee's 'Lapiz Zulfikar' which is featured in the photo pages of this book speaks volumes about the man. In the portrait, he is seated on a chair with a sense of ease as if he is sitting on a throne. His clothes are Awami shalwar suit, not Savile row suit and silk scarf which equally formed his wardrobe. His expression is at once thoughtful, compassionate and arrogant. It is a surrealistic work of art. In blue stone, the artist has created flesh, blood and passion. Guljee, the artist from Peshawar, who made the portrait was murdered in 2007; he understood his subject and knew how to display his many dimensions in semi-precious stone. This is its first public view. So far, it has been posheeda (hidden); not found in any real or virtual art gallery.

ZAB's story must begin. But not before I indulge myself in recalling lines from the poet Sauda which spring to my mind when I look back on 20 years of my life with Zulfikar Ali Bhutto.

Sauda Khuda ke wastey kar qissa mukhtasar,
Apni to neend ur gayi tere fasane mein.

(For God's sake shorten your tale O Sauda,
Your tale has blown away my sleep.)

Foreword

Zulfikar Ali Bhutto's presence in Lahore was always an electrifying event. He was an immensely popular person; every common Pakistani was eager to meet him, shake his hand or touch his clothes. Out on the streets or at a public meeting, he was always in danger of being crushed by mobs of admirers. Huge crowds waited to greet him at airports and railway stations. His arrival at public meetings in Lahore required meticulous arrangements to ward off physical danger. The route he would take from his hotel to the meeting place was a secret known only to one or two persons—myself or a party member, Miyan Aslam. We had to make special arrangement for his arrival or departure from a public meeting. His physical safety was our principal concern. A ring of strong party youth was always needed for his safety. Seeing him off from rallies after a public speech without being crushed by mob required meticulous preparation. He had to be encircled by a ring of strong arms locked together. A safe passage through a crushing mob of college students was another problem for his hosts. On one occasion to prevent the crush, a portable ladder was used to take him down two storeys through a window of the YMCA hall at Lahore.

How did it all start? Zulfikar Ali Bhutto (ZAB) had gained immense popularity by his speech before the Security Council in 1965 in which he had told Indian forces to get out of Kashmir. His words, 'We shall fight for a thousand years' had won the hearts of Pakistanis especially young Punjabis. It took him time to understand the reason why crowds surged to greet him. It took him time to realize that he had become a hugely popular leader of the masses.

ZAB was the youngest minister in General Ayub Khan's Cabinet after the latter staged a *Coup d'etat* in 1958. He remained his leading supporter for eight years until 1966 when President Ayub Khan signed the agreement with Lal Bahadur Shastri at Tashkent. Strongly opposed to the Tashkent Agreement, he despised Ayub Khan for signing it. When Shastri died of a heart attack at Tashkent and an assistant brought the news of his death, Bhutto was asleep. 'Sir, the bastard has died,' he reported. ZAB asked 'Which one?'

About the national political scene, ZAB and I had a close understanding. Whenever he called me early in the morning he asked 'Did you see the newspaper?' Each time I understood exactly which piece he was referring to. Generally, it was not about a political event but about a colleague making a politically foolish statement or about his own posture in a newspaper photograph.

Syeda Hameed and I have discussed almost all aspects of ZAB's career for years. In our opinion he lived and died as an outstanding individual not only among his contemporaries in Pakistan but on the international scene of the region. The author has used the lens of Greek tragedy to view his life and death. She sees him through the prism of Oedipus the King of Thebes. That is her view which also resonates with mine. Of the book which unravels the life of the man Zulfikar Ali Bhutto, I as his oldest and closest living associate, say in the words of Mirza Asadullah Khan Ghalib's lines which are inspirational and which I offer as my tribute to the author and her protagonist:

Aatey hain ghaib sey ye mazameen khayal mein
Ghalib sareer-e-khama nawa-e-sarosh hai

(These hidden themes are revealed to my mind
Movement of my pen is divine inspiration.)

—Mubashir Hasan

(Co-founder of Pakistan People's Party and a close associate of
Zulfikar Ali Bhutto)

1

The Boy from Larkana

Zulfikar Ali Bhutto was born on 5 January 1928 in Al-Murtuza in Larkana. When the news came to Sir Shahnawaz Bhutto, he was offering his Fajr (predawn) prayer. It is said that he spoke these words, 'Allah, I am grateful to you, I am your devotee. My father was your devotee and my mother is your devotee. My life is in your control and you are the highest.' He rose from his prayer mat, crossed over to the zenana and recited the azaan in the ear of his newborn. The child was called Zulfikar Ali because of his desire that when this child grows up he should slash the darkness of the world like the sword of the fourth Khalifa, Hazrat Ali, who was called Zulfikar.

An interview with Maula Bakhsh, old family retainer, was conducted in Garhi Khuda Bakhsh, 132 hours before ZAB was hanged. It was written in the journal 'Atishfishan' (Volcano) from Lahore.[1] Bakhsh reported that ancestors of the Bhutto clan came with Mohammad bin Qasim in the year AD 712. At the time Fatimids were ruling Egypt when the Bhuttos were owners of large parts of Sindh. Their earliest patriarch Doda Khan was described in one British account as 'the best and most enterprising zamindar in the whole of Sindh.'

---

[1] From the private library of ZAB at 70 Clifton.

Doda Khan had three sons—Amir Bakhsh, who was given jagir of Naudero; Khuda Bakhsh, who was given jagir of Garhi Khuda Bakhsh; and Elahi Bakhsh, who was given Pir Bakhsh Bhutto. Khuda Bakhsh was ZAB's great-grandfather. His son was Ghulam Murtaza who had two sons—Shahnawaz and Ali Gauhar Khan. Shahnawaz who was knighted and became *Sir* Shahnawaz Bhutto, was ZAB's father.

Shahnawaz was married twice. By his first wife, he had Imdad Ali Bhutto, Sikander Ali Bhutto and four daughters. By his second marriage to Begum Khursheed, he had three daughters and one son; Mumtaz Begum, Munawarul Islam, Benazir (died at age 12) and Zulfikar Ali. He had 10 children in all. Zulfikar Ali Bhutto was a child of an influential and a prominent Sindh feudal who held sway over thousands of haris (cultivators), over hundreds of hectares, and vast landholdings in interior Sindh. His mother was a Hindu woman of modest means who had converted to Islam.

Mubashir Hasan narrates an incident which occurred in the 70s in Sindh Club in Karachi. One evening, while sitting over a drink with his friends, ZAB saw Jam Sadiq Ali (later chief minister of Sindh) walk past without acknowledging his presence. 'Call him back,' ZAB was miffed. 'He walked past me without a salaam.' The man was summoned. 'Without a salaam, Sadiq? Don't you remember your father, when he attended my father's kutcheri, used to sit on the floor?' The man stood for a moment and said, 'Yes, Sahib, I remember. But he sat there because that was the best seat to watch Lakhi Bai's dance.' ZAB's mother's name before her marriage was Lakhi Bai.

His father was well respected by the people of the region. 'For generations my family had rendered distinguished services to Sindh, first in undivided India, and after partition in Pakistan,' ZAB wrote in his Writ Petition in 1969 submitted to the Lahore High Court. Opulence, and that too of Sindhi feudal, marked generations of the Bhuttos. In 1972, ZAB was asked by Khalid

Bin Sayeed, a professor from Canada, 'You were born with a silver spoon; how come you have so much compassion for the poor?' They were coming back from a dinner hosted by Qaism Patel at his residence in Karachi. 'I got it from my mother,' ZAB replied. The professor records that he saw tears rolling down his cheeks.

The family was a devotee of the shrine of sufi saint Shahbaz Qalandar at Sehwan. When Zulfikar fell seriously ill as a child, his mother prayed day and night. She attributed her son's recovery to the miracle of Shahbaz Qalandar of Sehwan Sharif. More than 40 years later, as prime minister of Pakistan, Zulfikar prayed at the same shrine, and ordered a pair of solid gold doors to be installed there.[2] ZAB was only 13 when his marriage was arranged to an older cousin, Shireen Amir Begum. She was the daughter of Ahmed Khan of Naudero, who was by far the largest landowner in the Bhutto tribe. He was the only son of Rasul Bakhsh Bhutto and was 'cursed' with three daughters and no male heir.[3] ZAB was 10 years younger than his bride. Once, Begum Khursheed's friend Begum Ansari asked her, 'Why did you get your son married to an older girl?' Her answer was, 'Don't you know who I am? If today Sir Sahib dies, they will throw me out. By marrying Zulfi to his uncle's daughter, I have held them back so that we also have some anchor in life.'[4]

In the first four years of ZAB's life, his father received many honours, which were attributed to his auspicious birth. He was given the title 'Sir' and was made the leader of the Sindhi Delegation at the Round Table Conference in London. He then entered politics at the local and national level; it is recorded that

---

[2]*Zulfi Bhutto of Pakistan: His Life and Times*, Wolpert, Stanley A., Oxford University Press, 1993. p 19.

[3]*Songs of Blood and Sword*, Fatima Bhutto, Penguin Books India 2010, p 45.

[4]*Zulfikar Ali Bhutto Sayasi Sawaneh Hayat (Vol-I)*, Rasheed Akhtar Nadvi, 1974, Islamabad: Idaara Ma'araf-e-Milli.

he shook hands with Ramsay MacDonald and would not let go of that hand until he agreed to include the separation of Sindh as an agenda at the Round Table Conference. The Government of India Act of 1935 created councils in various provinces in the Raj and elections were held in October 1937. In those days there were no political parties in Sindh, so it was an election that was open to very few. Sir Shahnawaz Bhutto stood for election from Larkana, his home town.[5] But he lost to Sheikh Abdul Majeed Sindhi, who interestingly, was the brother of the Indian leader Acharya Kripalani, and had converted to Islam.[6] Rafi Raza, (later to become Bhutto's Minister of Law) wrote that Sir Shahnawaz was the one who nurtured his ambitious son on politics; letters to him in student days conveyed the political news of Pakistan rather than family news and usual parental advice. Raza wrote that some of these letters were shown to him by ZAB, such as a long note explaining his electoral defeat by Sheikh Abdul Majeed Sindhi and his subsequent retirement from politics. He blamed members of Mumtaz Bhutto's branch of the family for his defeat, who in turn maintained that it happened because Sir Shahnawaz lived in Bombay (now Mumbai) and did not visit his rural constituency.[7] In 1947 he moved to Junagadh, a small princely state, and became the Diwan of the Nawab of Junagadh. In 1934, when Shahnawaz was inducted in the Bombay State Cabinet as the Sindh representative, the family moved to Bombay and ZAB was enrolled in Cathedral Boy's School in 1937 at the age of nine. Earlier he had been tutored at home in Larkana; this was his first formal school. He had to work hard to come up to the standard of his class fellows. Besides being a good student, he was also a fine tennis, badminton and cricket player. In the

---

[5] *Songs of Blood and Sword*, Fatima Bhutto, Penguin Books India 2010. p 43.
[6] Oral history from I.A. Rehman, Lahore, 18 July 2017.
[7] *Zulfikar Ali Bhutto and Pakistan, 1967-1977*, Rafi Raza, Oxford University Press, 1997. p 1-22.

cricket world he was very close to the great sports legend, Syed Mushtaq Ali.[8]

When he was 15 years old, he wrote a letter to a man he adored as a role model—Quaid-e-Azam, Mohammad Ali Jinnah:

Charleville Hotel, Mussourie
26 April 1943

Dear Sir,

The political situation which has taken place in the Frontier has made me so wild and angry that I have found the courage to write to you my thoughts. Musalmans should realize that Hindus can never and will never unite with us, they are the deadliest enemies of our Koran and our Prophet. We should realize that you are our leader; you Sir have brought us under one platform and one flag and the cry of every Musalman should be 'onward to Pakistan'. We have a capable leader in you and nobody can stop us, who are a nation by ourselves and India is a subcontinent. Therefore we must have our rights.

How can Sheikh Mohammad Abdullah and others such as Dr Khan Sahib call themselves Musalmans when they fall victims to Congress policy. It breaks my heart when I read their stupid speeches against the League. Are they really so ignorant or is it their idea of patriotism? It will take a million such Abdullahs in trying to convince us that our aim is wrong and even then they will not succeed because they don't realize that you have inspired us and we are proud of you.

Being still in school, I am unable to help in the establishment of our sacred land. But the time will come

---

[8]Indian cricketer and the first Indian to score a Test Century away from home, at old Trafford in Manchester in England in 1936.

when I will even sacrifice my life for Pakistan. I belong to the province of Sindh, undoubtedly Sindh is another province which is causing trouble but inshallah the day will come when Sindh will turn for the better and play a vital part in our Pakistan.

Sir, I fully realize that you are very busy and you might not have time to read a letter of a schoolboy, leave alone replying to it.

If you think that I am being very foolish then please forgive me but I simply had to write to you after reading those ignorant speeches of impractical men.

I am your follower.
Zulfikar Ali Bhutto

And then much to the ecstatic delight of the small boy came a reply! The great Quaid-e-Azam wrote him a personal letter from his residence at Mount Pleasant Road Bombay on 1 May 1943:

I was very glad to read your letter of 26th April and to note that you have been following the various political events. I would advise you, if you are interested in politics, to make a thorough study of it. But, don't neglect your education, and when you have completed your student's career, I have no doubt that you will be better qualified if you study thoroughly the political problems of India, when you enter the struggle of life.

Signed:
M.A. Jinnah

His politics was being moulded, as his letter shows. Firm conviction about Sheikh Mohammad Abdullah and Dr Khan Sahib's betrayal of the cause of Muslims remained deeply embedded in his heart.

Zulfikar spent his adolescence between two Sindhs: Larkana,

which later became Pakistan, and Bombay, the capital of Sindh in India. India was still one country when Zulfikar left home to begin his undergraduate studies at the University of California at Berkeley. Partition was imminent but still not there. The country ZAB left would be broken into two by the time of his return. Some of his detractors would later insist that he was still legally an Indian citizen. That was rightly trashed as a politically-motived lie and counter arguments were written in a pamphlet widely circulated by his supporters. But ZAB's very identity was impacted by the shifting boundaries of his subcontinent. It was in Bombay, on the eve of his departure to California, that he first read Marx, and his privileged existence faced its first challenge. He was born a feudal master, a zamindar, and no one could ever imagine that he would become the nemesis of capitalist aggression. He later said that it was his reading of Marx that stirred a shift in his attitude towards the feudalism that his generation took for granted. Decades later, on 1 March 1972, as president he announced a programme of land reforms whereby the maximum amount of land that may be held by one family was reduced from 500 irrigated or 1000 unirrigated acres to 150 irrigated or 300 unirrigated acres. And on 5 January 1977, New Land Reforms again reduced the maximum land held by one family to 100 irrigated or 200 unirrigated acres. Mubashir Hasan says, 'Bhutto himself donated 38,000 acres of his land.'[9] His granddaughter Fatima Bhutto writes, 'When speaking of the government's land reforms, in which he surrendered his own land (mainly the land in Jacobabad, fought for and won by Doda Khan), he said, "I'll lose still more, my children will lose still more… I've felt no fear of giving up what I own ever since the day I read Marx."'[10]

---

[9]Interview with the author in July 2017. Confirmed by Mr I.A. Rehman.

[10]*Songs of Blood and Sword*, Fatima Bhutto. Penguin Books India 2010. p. 46.

Piloo Mody[11] was one of his closest friends in school. Mody penned down several anecdotes of their schooldays in his book, *Zulfi, My Friend* (1973). He records that once in 1945, he with his cousin, Jehangir Mugaseth and Zulfi, went on a holiday to Mussoorie and stayed at the Charleville Hotel. Whenever they were served pudding after dinner, Jehangir and Zulfi emptied it out and packed it for later hunger pangs of growing boys!

Besides Mushtaq Ali, 'Emperor of Cricket', who he greatly admired, ZAB's greatest icon was Mohammad Ali Jinnah. In this matter he followed his father, who was a staunch believer in the Quaid and his two-nation theory. ZAB had Hindu friends whose ideal was Mahatma Gandhi but this difference did not stand in the way of their friendship. When the news of Gandhi's assassination broke, Mody was his guest in California. It was ZAB who gave him solace at that time of great distress. In 1948, he joined University of California, Los Angeles (UCLA) and after one year he transferred to Berkeley. There he graduated in Political Science and again shared a room with Piloo Mody. Both friends were highly competitive, devoted most of their time to studies and were students of the famous Professor Lipski. ZAB studied International Law and Political Science. A lecture he gave on heritage of Islamic Civilization made the proposition that Islamic countries should adopt socialism. His inspiration, he said, came from no less than the sunnah of the Prophet; it is recorded that whenever the Prophet sat for a meal, he shared his frugal table with the hungry and needy. Islam and socialism were therefore aligned since its inception.

Next was Christ Church, Oxford, where he received an LLB, followed by LLM and an M.Sc (honours) in Political Science. There

---

[11]An Indian architect, politician and one of the founding members of the Swatantra Party. Elected to the 4th and 5th Lok Sabhas, he served in the Rajya Sabha from 1978 until his death.

were friends who looked back and remembered: 'His lively and energetic mind would seek out a host of subjects, asking, learning and remembering everything in minute detail on a wide variety of topics, ranging over history, literature, politics, philosophy [...] Zulfi had a very perceptive mind, a phenomenal memory and an insatiable thirst for knowledge.'[12] Upon completing his degree, he was called to the bar at Lincoln's Inn. There his extraordinary academic record got him lectureship in International Law in the University of Southampton. It was then that he received news that his father was critically ill and without a second thought he returned to Pakistan. That was 1953; six years into partition. Next, he returned to Karachi to practise law at the Dingomal's Chambers (West Pakistan High Court, Karachi) and at the same time began teaching constitutional law in Sindh Muslim Law College, Karachi.[13] Highly intelligent, well-read and ambitious, his legal acumen spread and the Chief Justice, an Englishman named Constantine, paid ZAB rich tributes, and predicted a very bright future for him in the legal profession.[14]

In 1954, a new formula was devised to integrate all the provinces and principalities of West Pakistan into 'one unit' under one administration, which would then elect exactly as many members to a new National Assembly as East Pakistan.[15] Its purpose was to diminish the differences between the two unequal wings of Pakistan which were separated from each other by more than a thousand miles. On 30 September 1955, the Assembly passed the Bill merging 310,000 square miles into a

[12]*Zulfi My Friend*, Piloo Mody, Paramount Publishers, January, 1973. p 26.

[13]Wolpert, Stanley A. Zulfi Bhutto of Pakistan: His Life and Times. New York: Oxford University Press, 1993. p 42–43.

[14]*Zulfi My Friend*, Piloo Mody, Paramount Publishers, January 1973. p 34.

[15]One Unit scheme continued until General Yahya Khan dissolved it on 1 July 1970.

single province, with Lahore as its provincial capital. West Pakistan had formerly comprised three Governor's provinces, one Chief Commissioner's province, a number of states that had acceded to Pakistan, and the tribal areas. The result of the new Bill was to unify these various units into one province to be known as West Pakistan.

This clever idea would, in fact, disenfranchise almost 20 per cent of East Pakistan's population, thus stripping that region of its national majority status. The smaller provinces of the west also felt cheated, for they would now become political cyphers of the Punjabi majority under whose unitary umbrella they were to be integrated. ZAB found this scheme unacceptable and argued that it would instead only 'augment disintegration'.[16] When the Chief Minister of Sindh, Muhammad Ayub Khuhro, learnt this, he was enraged and wanted to get ZAB arrested. But his friends advised him against it because it would mean making enemies of the entire clan of Bhuttos.

ZAB's political journey began when the President of Pakistan Iskander Mirza[17] came for a hunting trip to Larkana. Mirza and Sir Shahnawaz were old friends and he had been a regular guest at Al-Murtuza. He was greatly impressed with ZAB's quick wit and sharp grasp of politics and diplomacy. So, in 1955, he proposed his name for the delegation which was to go to United Nations (UN) to represent Pakistan. But Chaudhry Mohammad Ali, who was then Secretary General of Government of Pakistan scuttled the idea. It was again on the recommendation of Iskander Mirza and Prime Minister Huseyn Shaheed Suhrawardy[18] that, in 1957,

---

[16]*Zulfi Bhutto of Pakistan: His Life and Times*, Wolpert, Stanley A., Oxford University Press, 1993. p 47–48.

[17]An East Pakistan politician who served as the first President of Pakistan, elected in this capacity in 1956 and was dismissed in 1959.

[18]Suhrawardy was from a prominent Bengali Muslim family. He became the second Prime Minister of Pakistan in September 1956. He joined Awami League

he was made a member of Pakistan's delegation to the UN. At the age of 29, Bhutto addressed the Sixth Conference of the UN on 25 October 1957 on 'Defining Aggression'.

He referred to the speech of representative of Belgium about the miraculous achievements of modern science and the need to keep our social sciences in rhythm else they would face the danger of becoming effete. While agreeing with his premise he argued that this was a double-edged argument. 'If modern man can launch a sputnik, he can also define aggression.' He said that he could not only define aggression but also circumvent, subvert and abuse it. Then he dealt his master stroke before the largely First World delegates, who must have listened to his words, open-mouthed. 'A definition, under these circumstances, would literally mean the presentation of our civilization on a uranium platter to a would-be aggressor, to a twentieth century Chengiz Khan or Attila; a would-be world dictator who would most certainly find the means to distort and mutilate the definition for his own wicked and gruesome ambitions'.

Later, as a participant at the International Conference in Geneva, Switzerland in March 1958, ZAB made five presentations over two weeks. Almost in tears and his voice charged with emotion, he spoke for mankind with the bold declaration: 'The High Seas are free to all,' a speech which is still regarded as one of the best on the subject. World leaders were amazed to see this young man who was speaking from the depth of his convictions, not just as a representative of Pakistan but as a citizen of the world. He was telling them that the UN was not fulfilling its mandate as it could not see the difference between war for aggression and war for protection.

Prime Minister Huseyn Shaheed Suhrawardy, recognizing

---

in 1952, a party that would later launch East Pakistan's Six Points, demanding virtual autonomy, under the lead of his disciple, Sheikh Mujibur Rahman.

young Bhutto's potential, used to ask him to join his party whenever Bhutto visited him at his home. It was on one of these visits to Suhrawardy's home that he first met Sheikh Mujibur Rahman.[19]

Iskander Mirza wanted him for the Cabinet but ZAB asked that he be named by Ayub Khan, because he could see the writing was on the wall for Iskander! So it was on Ayub Khan's behest that he became, on 27 October 1958, the youngest Federal Cabinet member in the history of Pakistan at the age of 30. Over the next few years he held key portfolios of Minister of Commerce, Minister of Information, Minister of National Reconstruction, Minister of Fuel, Power and Natural Resources before becoming the Foreign Minister. In 1960, he was the first minister to lead a delegation to Moscow to conclude the Russo-Pakistani joint venture in oil exploration in Balochistan. As a result of this, the Soviet government floated a long-term loan of 30 million dollars for this joint venture.

Bhutto wrote later, 'I went to Moscow to conduct negotiations with the Soviet Union for an oil agreement. I mention this fact because it marked the point at which our relations with the Soviet Union, most unsatisfactory until then, began to improve.'[20]

By the eve of his 33rd birthday, ZAB had become Pakistan's second-most experienced adviser to Ayub Khan on foreign affairs. His UN experience had helped him to focus his global vision more sharply, convincing him that for a world 'dominated by the great powers and filled with the fear of a nuclear holocaust, the umbrella of a World Organization was the best protector of smaller non-nuclear states.'[21]

---

[19]As told by Mubashir Hasan.

[20]Peter Niesewand's article titled 'A vain autocrat who gave his nation confidence' published by The Guardian on 5 April 1979.

[21]Zulfi Bhutto of Pakistan: His Life and Times, Wolpert, Stanley A., New York, Oxford University Press, 1993. p 66.

On 8 September 1951, ZAB married Nusrat Isphahani, whose family had moved from Isphahan (Iran) to Bombay and then moved to Karachi after partition. Within few months, her family had bought a place near the Bhutto's at 23 Clifton. Nusrat was born and schooled in Bombay.[22] Her father founded Bombay's Isphahani Soap Factory. Both Sir Shahnawaz and Begum Khursheed were not happy at their son marrying an 'outsider'. But ZAB was determined and they were married in a secret ceremony attended by two of his close friends, Nusrat's two sisters, and a Maulvi to perform the nikah. Two days later, Sir Shahnawaz hosted a reception for his son and his wife.[23]

Begum Nusrat Bhutto wrote a Foreword to *Siyasi Sawaneh Hayat* (political biography of ZAB) written by Rasheed Akhtar Nadvi which begins with a description of their family life. She writes that she was very close to her parents-in-law who treated her more like a daughter than a daughter-in-law. Devout followers of Islam, she recalls how generous they were with distributing charity among the poor and the deprived.

For the first couple of years after marriage, Nusrat writes, she lived with her in-laws since ZAB was in London. After that, she divided her time between Larkana and Karachi. She narrates how kind ZAB was to his servants and cultivators, and how fiercely loyal they were to him. Their first child Benazir was born on 21 June 1953 when ZAB was 25 and she was 24. Their second child Ghulam Murtaza was born on 18 September 1954. He was the first male child in the family after 20 years, so there was a big celebration. The third child, Sanam Seema was born on 24 August 1956 and the fourth son, Shahnawaz on 21 November 1958. This was also the year ZAB took the oath of office as the Minister of Commerce in the Ayub Khan Cabinet.

---

[22] Ibid. p 38-39.
[23] *Songs of Blood and Sword*, Fatima Bhutto, Penguin Books India 2010.

Regarding their children, she said that ZAB expressed more affection for his daughters than his sons. 'When I asked him why, he said, "I love my sons equally, but I don't express it in case they become spoilt with excessive love. I want them to be able to face life's trials with grit. I don't want my children to be brought up like little princes; I want them to consider themselves ordinary humans and not deserving special treatment. I want them to understand problems of the common man by identifying with them."'

The next generation was to receive from their father the values which he had imbibed from his parents. This is evident in the lines he wrote on the exquisite copies of the Quran, which he presented to both his sons when they were leaving home for higher studies.[24]

For Mir Murtaza
Mir My Son,

Take with you the last message of God to mankind. Howsoever you have been brought up, howsoever you might think today, the day will come when Islam will put its final seal. Do not be swayed or influenced in any other direction, when Allah has shown through his message the real direction.

Best of luck my son, may God guide you. I am always with you, wherever you go and wherever you are.

Love,
Papa
September 2, 1972

---

[24]Taken from 70 Clifton library.

For Shahnawaz
My youngest born son,
    I am giving you the best message of God for you to
follow as the only path for there is no other path both for
this world and the world hereafter. It will guide you more
clearly than any of the books you will read in the course
of your higher studies. It is the highest study. There are
other paths also. Look at them but take your steps only
in this chosen path if you want to serve man. Satisfy your
aims and earn the blessings of your parents and mankind.

Zulfikar Ali Bhutto
August 24, 1976

Nusrat was asked about ZAB's state of mind after he returned home from Tashkent and went into seclusion. She said, 'I have never seen him as worried as he was at the time, he was the most disappointed man. When I persisted in asking the reason he told me the bitter truth, "In Tashkent, Ayub Khan sold Pakistan. He did not uphold the dignity of a nation nor did he show any self respect." He then began pacing up and down and mumbled to himself, "I will not be able to work with Ayub, because he has not only disgraced himself but the entire country." He kept repeating this one sentence, "I will not be able to work with Ayub Khan again. He did not listen to me and inflicted this despicable agreement on the country. How can I get along with this traitor?"'

Nadvi then asked her, 'What was his state of mind when he was removed from office in June 1966 through compulsory leave?' She answered, smiling, 'He was very happy, I found him like a prisoner who had just been freed from jail.'

Few days after ZAB was dismissed, he and Begum Nusrat went for a three-month tour of Europe; that is when they devised their future road map. He began to draw a blueprint for a new party.

2

Rise of the Star

At the age of 15, ZAB wrote a letter to Quaid-e-Azam Mohammad Ali Jinnah on 26 April 1943. His anger at the events in the Frontier and Kashmir spilt on the paper. The events, he wrote, were the pro-India stance of Dr Khan Sahib and Sheikh Mohammad Abdullah. 'How can Sheikh Mohammad Abdullah and Dr Khan Sahib call themselves musalmans when they fall victim to Congress policy? It breaks my heart when I listen to their stupid speeches against the League. Are they really so ignorant or is it their idea of patriotism?' In one stroke, he condemned pro-India movement of Red Shirts and 'Indian stooges' like Sheikh Mohammad Abdullah of Kashmir, calling them 'ignorant speeches of impractical men.'

Deep distrust of the 'other' was embedded in the mind of this teenager. The letter seems to spit out the words. 'Musalmans should realise that Hindus can never, will never unite with us. They are the deadliest enemies of our Koran and our Prophet.' The 15-year-old was studying at Cathedral School, Bombay. He had Parsi friends, like Piloo Mody but must have rubbed shoulders with Hindu boys as well.

He then offers himself to his one and only leader, 'The time will come when I will even sacrifice my life for Pakistan.' He affirms his strong belief that Sindh 'will one day play a vital role in the birth of Pakistan.'

These childhood expressions later on were to become the foundation of his popularity when the country was at its most vulnerable—first having lost the 1965 war to India and later when Ayub Khan and Lal Bahadur Shastri signed the Tashkent Agreement in 1966. Next was the war of 1971 which led to the fall of Dacca on 16 December. The country was stung with even more humiliation.

For the two countries, the 18 intervening years following Independence and partition, 1947–1965, were filled with extreme tension and enmity. There were divided families on both sides. Difficulties of travel were mounting; in the early days, permission from District Commissioner was the only required document needed for travel. Soon special passport and later international passport was introduced. In the aftermath of the India-Pakistan war of 1965, many Pakistanis became anxious about the future of their country. There was widespread economic hardship in daily life. There was scarcity of coal, water, weapons; India had not paid Pakistan's share of the Consolidated Fund. India's refusal after partition to part with what a resource-starved Pakistan regarded as its meagre share of financial assets and military equipment was deplored by no one less than Mahatma Gandhi.[25] Pakistan was deprived of salt pans, which India had in plenty. East Pakistan had all the jute cultivation but its market and trade was not in Dacca; it was in Calcutta, a factor which paralyzed East Pakistan. The battle over the accession of the Muslim majority state of Kashmir in 1948 (which was to be cut into half by a ceasefire line) sealed the feud. Not including the communal slaughter occasioned by partition, it would be only the first round of bloodletting between

---

[25]For details of the conflict at partition over the division of military assets, see *The Defence of Pakistan: An Historical Perspective*, Ayesha Jalal, (paper presented at a conference at Oxford University, October 1984).

India and Pakistan. Both states embarked on a collision course which was to become a permanent feature of their relationship in the years ahead. India, because of its greater economic resources and an industrial base as well as a vibrant political movement led by the Congress Party, was better able to absorb the costs of such ventures, Pakistan was not.

ZAB wrote *Confrontation with India*[26] at the time he was in thick of politics. His bitterness as reflected in the letter to Quaid-e-Azam now covered a much wider canvas. 'At the time of partition, Pakistan had lost Gurdaspur, Ferozpur and certain disputed parts of Punjab as well as valuable territories in the East, notably Assam and Tripura. Likewise in district Amritsar, Muslim majority areas that we lost, spread from Lahore to the suburbs of Amritsar... It has taken 20 years and two wars to establish the separate entity of our state with its population of over 120 million, and yet there are people who still lament the partition of the sub-continent, portraying Pakistan as prodigal son who will someday return to the bosom of Bharat Mata... India wants breathing space in which to deal firmly with dissident elements. She would like to crush the Nagas and Mizos, who are close to East Pakistan, suppress the South and the Sikhs, contain pockets of discontent in Rajputana and break the spirit of 60 million Indian Muslims.'

ZAB's resentment against what he sees as India's hegemony recurs throughout his writings and speeches. His deep-rooted hurt at Pakistan's weak responses and capitulation to India became the trigger which catapulted him into the political arena. It played out in the theatre of war in 1965.

India-Pak skirmishes reached Srinagar between 10–13 August 1965. Government of India issued strong protest against Pakistan violating the Line of Control. As Pakistan's Foreign Minister,

---

[26]The book lies in 70 Clifton Library

ZAB denied the charge in strong words. On 16 August 1965, Pakistan entered Kargil and conflicts occurred in Chhamb, Medhar, Poonch, Uri and Thethwal. Pakistani armies advanced till Joriyan. On 6 September 1965, India crossed the international border and opened war fronts in Sialkot, Lahore and Sindh. The 1965 war began.

ZAB did not, publicly at least, take the credit for starting the war with India in 1965. However, as subsequent disclosures were to reveal, he was the chief proponent of a forward policy directed at forcing India's hand over Kashmir. Thus, in accordance with 'Operation Gibraltar' in August 1965, Pakistan had infiltrated trained 'guerrillas' into Kashmir whose task was to provoke an armed uprising in the troubled valley.[27] Unhappily for ZAB, 'Gibraltar' was an unqualified fiasco. The Indian forces had responded in full measure not only to meet Pakistan's offensive in Kashmir, but had escalated the conflict by launching an attack against Pakistan itself. While Ayub Khan favoured limited and short military adventure, he had no desire for a full-scale war which neither the US nor the Soviet Union would support despite their own differences. The war would only give satisfaction to China. Thus, the 17-day war was brought to an abrupt end in September.

Fifty years after the 1965 war, at the age of 92, Dr Mubashir Hasan speaks with sharp recall of his deep personal feelings as eyewitness to the India-Pakistan war:

'The 1965 war between India and Pakistan was to leave a deep imprint on the psyche of the people of Pakistan, especially along the eastern border of the country. I too was profoundly affected. The Indian army was within 12 miles of my home; I could hear the booming of the guns and regretted the inadequate preparation

---

[27] Altaf Gauhar, 'Foreword' in M. Asghar Khan's, *The First Round: Indo-Pakistan War, 1965* (London, 1979)

of the Pakistan Army. While I was opposed to the regime of the military dictator, Field Marshal Ayub Khan, I offered my services to the Commander-in-Chief, General Musa Khan for war duty, an offer which he declined.'

ZAB's speech as Pakistan's foreign minister at the emergency meeting of the UN Security Council on 22 September 1965 launched his star on Pakistan's political firmament. He began by asserting that Pakistan was a small country. 'You have only to look at a map of the world and see our size to be aware of our resources and our ability.' He defines India as a 'great monster', always 'given to aggression'. He recounts its aggression against Junagadh, Manavadar, Mongrol, Hyderabad and Goa. 'Pakistan, according to Indian leaders, is its enemy number one. We have always known that India is determined to annihilate Pakistan.'

At the UNSC meeting, ZAB announced the cessation of hostilities by Pakistani forces. But before making the announcement, he made sure that he had put across what was his deepest conviction. 'We are resolved to fight for our honour, to fight for Pakistan, because we are victims of aggression. Aggression has been committed against the soil of Pakistan. Irrespective of our size, irrespective of our resources, we have the resolve, we have the will to fight because ours is a just cause. Ours is a righteous cause'. He went on to speak words which would echo in the region for decades. 'We will wage a war for a thousand years, a war of defence.'

With these lines, he raised the stature of his country and made the world sit up in grudging admiration of the grit of this fiery orator from a country which was on the discard list of most nations: 'This is the last chance for the Security Council to put all its force, all its energy, all its moral responsibility behind a fair and equitable and honorable solution of the Jammu and Kashmir dispute. History does not wait for councils, organizations or institutions, just as it does not wait for individuals... Let me tell the Security Council on behalf of my Government, that if now, after this last chance that we are giving the Security Council, it does not put its full force, full moral responsibility and full weight behind an equitable and honourable settlement of the Jammu and Kashmir dispute, Pakistan will have to leave the United Nations. In leaving the United Nations Pakistan will be fulfilling the Charter of the United Nations.'[28]

He then stated the reason why Pakistan was created; its basic principle was to bring about a permanent settlement between the two major communities. 'For seven hundred years we sought to achieve equilibrium between the people of the two major communities, and we believed eventually that the only way to live in lasting peace with India was to establish our homeland, to establish a country smaller in area, but nevertheless capable of having a relationship, a modus vivendi, with a great and powerful neighbour. That was one of the prime factors responsible for the creation of Pakistan.' He gave example of Sweden and Norway, which had to separate to get closer. By the same token, he explained, 'a separate country, Pakistan, would enable a permanent peace, a permanent understanding, between the people of both countries.'

He spoke of the limited resources of both the countries, which need to be deployed for development of the people. 'It is not the law of God that people in Asia and Africa should be poor... We want to break the barriers of poverty—we want to give our people a better life, we want our children to have a better future.'

He speaks of his country's respect and regard for people of India and its hope that separation would have brought them closer. The basic principle that areas occupied by Muslim majority would form Pakistan, he said, was accepted by the Indian leaders. 'All

---

[28]Speech delivered at the UN Security Council on 22 September 1965 on Kashmir Issue.

we ask is to live in peace, friendship and goodwill with India on the basis of the understanding and agreements which the Indian Government and the Indian leaders themselves solemnly pledged to my people and my country.'

Passionately appealling to stop the war of aggression, he said, 'Today we are fighting a war, a war imposed on us by India, a naked predatory unwarranted aggression by 450 million people against 100 million people, a war of chauvinism and aggrandizement by a mighty neighbour against a small country. We do not want to be exterminated... But today our cities are being bombed indiscriminately by the might of India...'

He later asked India to honour its commitments, pledges and promises to the people of Pakistan. Having said that, he came to the unresolved issue of Jammu and Kashmir. Perhaps this is one of the most iconic speeches by any foreign minister at the UN Security Council. ZAB uttered these words to representatives of world powers. The following statements echo Bhutto's frustration at the negligence of the world towards Pakistan while it was confronting India during the 1965 war.

'Jammu and Kashmir is not an integral part of India and has never been an integral part of India. It is a disputed territory between India and Pakistan. It is more a part of Pakistan than it can ever be of India, with all its eloquence and with all its extravagance with words. The people of Jammu and Kashmir are part of the people of Pakistan in blood, in flesh, in life—kith and kin of ours, in culture, in geography, in history and in every way and in every form... We will wage a war for 1,000 years, a war of defence. I told that to the Security Council a year ago when that body, in all its wisdom and in all its power, was not prepared to give us a resolution... But the world must know that the 100 million people of Pakistan will never abandon their pledges and promises. The Indians may abandon their pledges and promises—we shall never abandon ours. Irrespective of our size and resources, we shall fight to the end.'

The anger which was simmering all through the speech burst out and his words hit hard both India and UN. 'We are grateful to all of you for whatever you have done to uphold the cause of justice, because, finally and ultimately, justice must prevail. We believe, more than ever, that justice is bound to prevail for the people of Jammu and Kashmir. Five million people must have the right to decide their own future. Why should they be made an exception?'

The debate tossed up the issue to heights beyond the sky which stretched over the UN dome when he asked, 'Should the whole phenomenon of self-determination, stretching from Asia and Africa, apply to the whole world except to the people of Jammu and Kashmir? Are they some outcastes of an Indian society? Are they some untouchable pariahs that they should not be given the right of self-determination, that they should not be allowed to have the right to their own future? The whole world believes in the right of self-determination. Must it be denied to the people of Jammu and Kashmir merely because power must prevail over principle? Power shall never prevail over principle. Finally and ultimately, principle must prevail over power. This is a Christian concept, it is an Islamic concept, and it is a civilized concept.'

He then avers that in this matter India was isolated with the whole of Asia and Africa supporting the right of self-determination of the people of Kashmir. Listing the countries which support Pakistan, he said, 'On the one hand, you have the whole world arrayed on the side of the cause of right and justice and morality, and, on the other hand, you have a war machine, an arrogant and chauvinistic state breaking its pledges, breaking its promises and wanting to destroy the will and the spirit of a people. The will and spirit of our people can never be destroyed. Let me tell you: you can have one ceasefire, you can have another ceasefire, but the 100 million people of Pakistan shall face extermination rather than forsake their principles or allow their principles to be negated and destroyed by sheer force and power.'

The President's message was lying untouched on his desk, he did not once look at it while he spoke. There was total silence in the Security Council. But the time had come when, having exonerated himself, he would read what was written by his head of state. 'I have the honour to transmit the following message from the President of Pakistan, which I received from Rawalpindi at 2 o'clock (which, is 11 o' clock W.P.S.T.) today (22 September 1965):

> Pakistan considers Security Council Resolution 211 of 20 September as unsatisfactory. However, in the interest of international peace and in order to enable the Security Council to evolve a self-executing procedure, which will lead to an honourable settlement of the root cause of the present conflict—namely, the Jammu and Kashmir dispute—I have issued the following order to the Pakistan armed forces. They will stop fighting as from 12.05 hours West Pakistan Time today. As from that time they will not fire on enemy forces unless fired upon, provided the Indian Government issues similar orders to its armed forces. Please accept, Excellences, the assurances of my highest consideration.

Anyone else in this situation would have concluded his speech at this point, not ZAB. It was an extraordinary display of confidence fuelled by anger, which made him continue, drawing the Security Council's attention to its own cardinal weakness. After reading the message, he continued, 'But a cessation of hostilities is not enough. The Security Council—the most important organ of the United Nations—must now address itself to the heart of the problem. For 18 years it has played and toyed with the future of Kashmir. It can no longer make a plaything or a toy out of five million people. It is the moral responsibility of the Security Council to address itself to a meaningful, a lasting solution of the problem of Jammu and Kashmir.'

He reminded the Security Council that the last time he was here it was not prepared to give Pakistan a piece of paper called a resolution. The Security Council had called it a dead and dormant issue. 'This can never be a dead issue, it can never be dormant.'

The speech to UNSC was followed six days later on 28 September by a much longer speech to the General Assembly which focused on the Kashmir dispute. First he laid down the basic principle; ceasefire this time must lead to a final settlement of the grave political problem underlying the conflict of the future of the State of Jammu and Kashmir.

He gave historical precedents of self-determination such as Morocco, Tunisia and Algeria expressly based on the principle of ascertaining and respecting the wishes of the people involved. To deny people their right to choose their own destiny as India denies it to the people of Jammu and Kashmir, the excuse given is that they are building multiracial or multireligious societies and if they permit self-determination of one group or area their whole State may disintegrate. In pleading this excuse, they try to exploit the fear of dismemberment among many sovereign States.

He then quoted words of one of the foremost Indian ideologues, Jayaprakash Narayan which vindicate his argument,

> If we are so sure of the verdict of the people of Kashmir, why are we so opposed to giving them another opportunity to reiterate it? The answer given is that this would start the process of disintegration of India. Few things that have been said in the course of this controversy are more silly than this one. The assumption behind the argument is that the States of India are held together by force and not by the sentiment of a common nationality. It is an assumption that makes a mockery of the Indian nation and a tyrant of the Indian State.

He referred to the United Nations Commission for India and Pakistan. He said that the plan embodied in the Commission (UNCIP) resolutions of 13 August 1948 and 5 January 1949 provided for a ceasefire and the demarcation of a ceasefire line; the demilitarization of the state of Jammu and Kashmir; and a free and impartial plebiscite under the auspices of the UN to determine the question of the accession of the State to India or Pakistan. It was upon acceptance of both resolutions by India and Pakistan that hostilities ceased on 1 January 1949. Then, as now, the ceasefire was meant to be a prelude to a permanent settlement, which was to be achieved through a plebiscite under UN auspices after a synchronized withdrawal of forces.

Confronting India's stand, he said that the whole history of the Jammu and Kashmir dispute is India's exploitation of the ceasefire, the first part of the agreement, for evading the implementation of the other two parts, rather than facilitating them.

'But the non-performance of an agreement by one party cannot render it invalid or obsolete. If it did, there would be no order in international life and the entire basis of the United Nations Charter would be undermined. Even though the agreement embodied in the two United Nations resolutions was not implemented by India, the Security Council repeatedly made clear its binding nature as an agreement and affirmed that its provisions were recognised and accepted by both India and Pakistan.'

ZAB's speech at the UN changed the history of Pakistan. Emerging as a national hero, he became immensely popular, especially in those districts where Indian bombs had fallen during the 1965 war. 'His speech was delivered on the world stage, which stunned the most powerful countries,' says Mubashir Hasan.

In January 1966, a few months after ZAB's speech at the UN, India and Pakistan met at Tashkent under the watchful eye of the Russian President. The Indian delegation was headed by Lal Bahadur Shastri and the Pakistan delegation by Ayub Khan.

The venue of the meeting was a hotel in Tashkent, Uzbekistan. There is a Pakistan Archives photo of General Ayub Khan and Lal Bahadur Shastri; behind them is a third figure, a glum-faced Zulfikar Ali Bhutto.

Newspaper *Mashriq* in Pakistan reported: 'When Pakistan rejected the Indian compromise formula, Presidents Kosygin and Ayub held a discussion, the content of which was not revealed. Bhutto being the greatest impediment to this agreement was excluded from this meeting. Everybody knew that Bhutto was very unhappy with Tashkent.'

Kuldip Nayar, resident editor of *The Statesman*, reported: 'Bhutto was in a sour mood from the beginning. All the Pakistan delegates greeted Shastri's inaugural speech with loud cheers, Bhutto, however, sat passively with his arms crossed.' He wrote how ZAB was kept at a distance throughout by Ayub. After the inaugural speech, when the three leaders walked out to meet in a private room, ZAB tried to join them, but with a motion of his eye Ayub stopped him. Anger was large on the foreign minister's face. He insisted that Kashmir be included for the reason that no peace between India and Pakistan was possible until this was settled. None of his suggestions were taken on board.

ZAB threatened to return to Pakistan and take the nation into confidence. His plea to Ayub Khan was to the effect, 'Accept my resignation and let me go back to Larkana; and I cannot work with you anymore.' Being placed in a very tight spot, Ayub Khan pleaded with him not to resign or leave. He said, 'If you resign at this time, the opposition will take advantage and there will be a chaos in the country with the result that both India and Russia will intervene.' Under great stress, ZAB stayed back for a day in Tashkent, but could no longer continue in Rawalpindi. He returned home to Larkana.

Pakistan Times reported ZAB's statement which was issued from his home. 'Although the Tashkent declaration has resumed the dialogue between India and Pakistan but no amount of platitudes can substitute or detract from the imperative need for a permanent settlement of the tragic dispute over Jammu & Kashmir.'

A year after ZAB left Ayub Khan's government, he wrote his book, *The Myth of Independence*. The dispute over Kashmir, he argued, was no ordinary territorial dispute. If Pakistan were to settle for peace without securing the right of self-determination for the people of Kashmir, it would be the first step in the establishment of Indian hegemony in South Asia, with smaller states reduced to the status of Indian satellites.[29]

It was the emotion behind the glum face which ultimately made ZAB Quaid-e-Awam (Leader of masses). His popularity soared when he alleged appeasement at the 1966 peace treaty signed at Tashkent by President Ayub Khan of Pakistan and Indian Prime Minister Lal Bahadur Shastri. Serious irreconcilable differences surfaced between the foreign minister and president of Pakistan.

Mubashir Hasan recalls, 'At Tashkent, ZAB put up his resistance to the discussion and commitment leading to the agreement through body language, which was accusatory throughout.' What Bhutto used here has been described as 'emotional nuance'. Floyd Henry Allport, the father of Social Psychology describes emotional nuance 'as an attitude to feel and react in a highly specific fashion towards another human being.'[30]

Syeda Sara Abbas wrote in her paper titled 'Deliberative Oratory in the Darkest Hour: Style Analysis of Zulfikar Ali Bhutto's speech at the Security Council': 'Using emotional nuance shows a deep understanding of the audience, message and purpose

---

[29] *The Myth of Independence*, Zulfikar Ali Bhutto (Oxford University Press, 1969).
[30] *Social Psychology*, Allport, Floyd Henry, Routledge/Thoemmes. 1994: 96. Web. 30 July 2010.

because it is tailored to each individual. The audience may feel that the speaker is addressing them individually. It is interesting to see how and why Bhutto used emotional nuance. His words reflected the ambivalent relationship between India and Pakistan from the Pakistani viewpoint. She further writes about Bhutto's understanding of his audience, message and purpose in campaign discourse. How expertly he played to his audience's expectations! He knew how to cajole his audience and used emotional nuances to communicate with them at several levels.

Husain Haqqani writes that both countries needed peace before they could progress but, Bhutto like most Pakistanis particularly felt 'that India had not truly recognized partition.'[31]

Several scholars have written about Bhutto's spectacular grip on discourse. Anwar H. Syed writes that 'Bhutto's discourse was his legacy and that his conduct was a mirror in which Pakistanis could view themselves.'[32] Syed Zulfikar Gilani writes that 'his discourse cultivated his audience's need for identity and for a redeemer or messiah.'[33] Akmal Hussain writes that 'Bhutto cultivated his charisma and encouraged audience participation through rhetorical questions and rhythm.'[34]

Tashkent runs as a theme throughout the Pakistan People's Party (PPP) era. ZAB was against Ayub Khan, whose hurried peace with India and the entire apparatus was evident from his sullen body language and sulking stance. On 1 January 1969, when ZAB was in prison, J.A. Rahim, the acting chairman of

---

[31] *Pakistan: Between the Mosque and Military*, Husain Haqqani, Washington D.C.:Carnegie Endowment for International Peace: 2005. 87, 88-90.

[32] The Discourse and Politics of Zulfikar Ali Bhutto, Anwar H. Syed, Palgrave Macmillan, 1992, p 253–259.

[33] 'Z.A. Bhutto's leadership: A psycho-social view', Gilani, Syed Zulfikar, Contemporary South Asia Vol. 3 (1994). 232. Web. 30 Jan., 2010.

[34] Akmal Hussain, 'Charismatic Leadership and Pakistan's Politics'. *Economic and Political Weekly*, January 1989. p 136-137.

PPP, wrote to Dr Mubashir Hasan about Tashkent: 'The positive demand should be voiced that the Tashkent Declaration should be repudiated because the President's signature was obtained under duress... Another point to be noted, had it not been for ZAB's opposition to Tashkent Declaration, Government of Pakistan would, by this time, have buried the right of self determination of the people of Kashmir. Mr Bhutto has been thrown in jail because he may have revealed the truth about Tashkent and also because he is President Ayub Khan's most powerful rival in the coming elections'. Again in January 1969 he wrote that it will be three years since signing of the 'shameful Tashkent Declaration, it is an anniversary of national shame.'

The popular sentiments at the time were, 'Break the chains of Tashkent,' 'Repudiate Tashkent Declaration,' and 'No to Tashkent'.

About 50 years after 1965 Indo-Pak war, in 2014, Mubashir Hasan wrote its oral history in the form of a small book *Awami Leader* which he dedicated to the 'innocent awam' of Pakistan. It was his political theory about what were the ingredients of a mass leader. It analyzed four mass leaders—Gandhi, Jinnah, Mujibur Rahman and ZAB. These South Asian leaders were ranged alongside each other to determine what constituted their appeal to millions. His theory was that these men reached the pinnacle only after they had scoured public consciousness and discovered what the masses were willing to die for. What they discovered may or may not have matched their personal belief but they had found the key to the hearts of the masses. Their next move was to find its best expression which could move the awam to tears, embed their imprint on their hearts, and thereby impel their adoration. Their journey as Awami Leaders would thus kick-start.

Mubashir Hasan recalls the one and only time he was face-to-face with Mohammad Ali Jinnah. It was 23 March 1940. A jalsa was arranged at Minto Park (now Jinnah Park) at which the

Pakistan Resolution was passed. There were impassioned speeches by all big leaders. At its conclusion, Mubashir Hasan and his friend Hameed Nizami, founder of the fortnightly *Nawa-i-Waqt* which was launched that very day, were collecting papers from the table at which the leaders had sat. As a souvenir, they picked up the pad on which Mr Jinnah had made some marks. What they saw at that moment was history in the making. Quaid-e-Azam was thumping an activist's back while getting down from the stage with these immortal words, 'So... you have your Pakistan now... Are you happy?' Jinnah had discovered and targetted the fire that had been blazing in their hearts for 83 years. He was the Awami leader standing on the pinnacle.

In 2012, Mubashir Hasan got interviews conducted in Lahore with people from a cross section of the city who expressed the popular feelings at the time. The predominant sentiment was public disillusionment with Ayub Khan's Tashkent betrayal. 'Ayub Khan's time had ended Bhutto's had begun,' said Raja Riaz, who was lifelong PPP activist. After his speech at United Nations he was acclaimed in streets as the undisputed national leader. Munno Bhai, the popular leftist columnist, felt that during 1965 war, for the first and probably last time, people of the country were united. They had first believed Ayub Khan's propaganda that, in a few days, the green hilali parcham (crescent flag) would be hoisted over Red Fort. In September 1965, Ayub Khan had given a slogan in the name of Islam, '*Kis quom ko lalkara hai/ Jiska Kalma la Ilaah Illallah.*' 'Pure fallacy, wishful thinking.' Munno Bhai spat, 'We went to UN for ceasefire and then came Tashkent. Ayub Khan signed the agreement ignoring the vehement protest of his Foreign Minister.' These two blows hit hard evoking howls of protest which were expressed by Munno Bhai. 'He was a wise, incisive leader, who had seen Ayub Khan trample public sentiment by signing Tashkent. He sensed his growing mass appeal especially after his landmark anti-India UN speech, when the black and white camera captured his storming out of the UN. He was about to be anointed as hero and king.' ZAB's informal manner of public address during which he would be simply dressed in a shalwar suit, a scarf thrown around his neck, his sleeves rolled up became a hallmark, which won hearts of the people.

The book is the most authentic record of the common public sentiment during those tumultuous days. At the pitch of the 1965 war, people wanted to form a citizen's militia.[35] Ayub Khan, whose popularity had plummeted, momentarily gained ground because he spoke to the nation promising confrontation with India. But Sufi Iftikhar, humble PPP worker, recalled the rapt attention with which people listened to ZAB on radio broadcast. 'It was as if he was giving voice to the emotions which were surging in our hearts. Tashkent was the greatest betrayal, it was Bhutto who gave us a glimmer of hope.' These twin follies of ceasefire and Tashkent Agreement stripped Ayub Khan of all support; in public perception he became 'murderer of aspirations'. Communist leader, Mushtaq Ahmed Raj said, 'ZAB understood what people wanted. Outwardly he seemed to support the US but at heart he was a communist. When Ayub Khan declared ceasefire, lightning struck us and then…came the moment when ZAB spoke at UN Security Council. It brought him on a massive wave to the gullies of Pakistan as its Awami Leader'. Many years later, in February 2017, Mubashir Hasan explained his leader's strategy, 'Bhutto Sahib spoke at length against India; he actually concealed the

---

[35]Citizen's militia was to crop up time and again in the context of Pakistan's lack of strategic depth vis-a-vis India. On 3 January 1969, J.A. Rahim was to write to Mubashir Hasan in the context of the popular demand for Citizen's Army or Citizen's Militia. 'If the thin line of defence is overrun, the whole country will fall prey to a hostile army just because there is no geographic depth which can be utilized by Pakistan forces to regroup. If, however, the people were armed, the enemy will be faced with resistance everywhere, the nation could fight back. The militia makes up for the lack of depth.'

presidential offer of peace which he had received from Islamabad. It was at the end of the historic speech that he transmitted the order. He had thereby exonerated himself from the blame.'

'In Lahore, the air resounded with cries of "Crush India"', Mushtaq Ahmed Raj continued, 'People were marching towards Wagah. The General still continued to mislead the populace as if the nation was at the cusp of victory. ZAB took siyasat to the gullies and mohallas thereby giving importance and dignity to us. People were sick of Ayub Khan's false bravado. Many times over the next several months ZAB made public declarations that he would expose the secret of Tashkent. His promise raised very high expectations; people kept urging him but he never made any revelation'.

'Future belonged to ZAB. He was the hope of the masses; when he had arrived from Pindi to Lahore, the massive crowds, which received him, were not mobilized by the party, they had come entirely on their own. He never let the masses down. That is why even Himalaya wept when they hanged this man.' Kamran Islam, lifelong worker and keen observer, spoke these words. 'In Punjab he exuded the Punjabi style; he began what was called "tharra siyasat" (bazaar politics).'

Waliur Rahman, trade unionist, recounted how hundreds used to crowd around the radio listening to his speeches; their understanding was limited but their clapping was limitless. He said, 'At the UN when he declared 1000-years war he had become our hero.' Senior journalist and editor Masood Ashar declared, 'There never was a leader of his calibre. Highly educated and intelligent, he towered above all.' Abdur Rauf Malik said, 'There was one section of the military, which blessed the "messiah" and wanted to see the end of Ayub Khan.'

Tariq Waheed's expression was poetic, 'Bhutto, anchor of our dying hope. Lodestar of our desires.' Zahid Islam, political activist from old times talked of the youthful minister taking full advantage of 'Crush India' slogan. 'It was we who were "crushed" post Tashkent but Bhutto played his masterstroke by declaring a 1000-year war.' President of hawker's union Roozi Khan said, 'There was apprehension about what Ayub Khan would do in Tashkent. Generals don't understand politics. They are unable to configure roundtables. Only Bhutto knew his politics but he was ignored at Tashkent; Ayub Khan was actually in awe of his Foreign Minister's abilities.' Ghulam Rasool Rahi, party worker in Baghbanpura said that people saw him as a ray of hope. 'This man', they averred, 'will represent our sentiments in the corridors of power.'

His speech won acclaim from all over Pakistan. M.A. Azam from Dacca was eloquent in praise of ZAB's performance at the UN: 'One of the greatest heroes of the war and of peace is our Foreign Minister, ZAB. Hats off to this brave son of Pakistan. At this decisive hour of the nation, Mr Bhutto has risen to an unprecedented height. He has raised the prestige of Pakistan at home and abroad. The war has been a proud rediscovery of self for every Pakistani. Our peace will be a glorious rediscovery for our diplomatic leader, ZAB.'[36]

ZAB was eloquent but also had the ability to state everything in few simple sentences. His speeches at the UN in 1965 and 1971 reflected the sentiment of his people, their anger, frustration and anxiety about the future of the country and the urgent need to define the role they could play in improving their social and economic condition. His fiery speech, almost single-handedly, dragged Pakistan back its feet and restored the nation's morale. In the words of Peter Niesewand, 'Bhutto was, to them (masses) a world statesman who gave Pakistan confidence and respectability, a man who ensured, that when he spoke, world leaders listened.'[37]

---

[36] *Zulfikar Ali Bhutto Sayasi Sawaneh Hayat* (Vol-I), Rasheed Akhtar Nadvi, 1974, Islamabad: Idaara Ma'araf-e-Milli.

[37] Peter Niesewand's article titled 'A vain autocrat who gave his nation confidence' published on 5 April 1979 by the Guardian.

Lawrence Ziring[38] rightly argues that 'Bhutto happened to be at the right place at the right time in a third world country where the political culture guaranteed the rise of single leader.' Then came the 1971 war between India and Pakistan. Pakistan suffered a fatal fracture followed by genocide, civil war, migration and territorial reconfiguration. This national trauma finds expression in ZAB's statement at the UNSC on 12 December and 15 December 1971. This statement is the cry of a wounded country drawing in a few word-strokes a stark image of the national viewpoint. It brings forward the major complexities of the event. Pakistan termed the war as an Indian-Russian conspiracy, not a local movement. 'This binary view is reflected in ZAB's statement', writes Syeda Sara Abbas.[39]

His passionate speech in UNSC on 15 December 1971 is remembered as his 'Farewell Speech to the UN Security Council' in which he lashes out at the actions of the Council for neglecting the pleas of Pakistan to explain their position on the fall of Dacca.

First the extraordinary conditions in which Bhutto made his statement before the UN need to be assessed. By the time ZAB addressed the Security Council on 12 December 1971, it had become clear that developments in East Pakistan had taken place far faster than he had anticipated or was given to understand Pakistan was dismembered and considerable territory on the western front was overrun and occupied by India. Moreover, Pakistan at this point was a country without a viable government, money, international policy or even a constitution.

This situation was complex because it involved gross human rights violations plus a territorial conflict between two long-standing enemies. East Pakistan was neither a colonial territory

[38]Lawrence Ziring, 'The Campaign before the Storm' Asian Survey. Vol 17, No. 7. (Jul.1977): 582. Web. Apr.15, 2010. Lawrence Ziring is also the author of 'Pakistan in the twentieth century: a political history'.

[39]'Deliberative Oratory in the Darkest Hour' by Syeda Sara Abbas.

nor a separate nation. However the violations of murder, rape and arson were severe enough to deem it an international crisis. Because of war crimes, the issue came back to the Council. Abbas further says that the movement between the two forums, the General Assembly and the Security Council, revealed a dismal understanding and weak handling of the war on Pakistan's side. Pakistani generals drew analogies between 1965 and 1971 and expected the war would end inconclusively as in 1965. They neglected diplomatic channels until the last week. Rafi Raza, who accompanied Bhutto to the Security Council, says they came too late. Bhutto arrived at the UN on 10 December when the Pakistan Army began suffering reversals and the Soviet Union began to appeal for a hearing for the Bangladeshi representatives[40]. ZAB appealed to the council to condemn Indian aggression and order a ceasefire. US and China, Pakistan's allies, did little to help. Meanwhile, back in the Security Council, the members proposed new resolutions that revealed Pakistan's deteriorating position. The three new draft resolutions, the Polish, the Russian and the Anglo-French recommended a ceasefire with troop withdrawal and power handed over to East Pakistanis. Pakistan's choices were grim—it could accept any resolution or wait for the army to surrender. Finally, on 15 December, ZAB requested the president of Security Council to convene a special session where, in the words of Khalid Hasan[41], he 'made the most emotional, though well-prepared, speech of his career.' The fall of Dacca the next day put an end to all the deliberations.

The 15 December 1971 statement was made in extraordinary conditions because of Pakistan's position and Bhutto's own status. Pakistan was not only on the losing side but was poised to lose

---

[40]*Zulfikar Ali Bhutto and Pakistan 1967-1977*, Rafi Raza, Oxford University Press, p 118.
[41]Khalid Hasan, 'Did Bhutto break up Pakistan?'

half its territory. It would face dismemberment similar to that experienced by the Ottoman Empire in 1921 and Germany in 1945 and would be divided in two smaller countries. Territorial dismemberment would accompany military surrender and national humiliation. Pakistan would suffer the disgrace of the biggest surrender in military history and 93,000 men would be taken as prisoners of war. The war meant the end of united Pakistan. There was also the problem of breaking such news to a deeply emotional public that had believed in the invincibility of its armed forces and in the superiority of its culture. There was also the problem of Bhutto's own status. Unlike Swaran Singh, his Indian counterpart, he was both diplomat and leader and both roles were in direct conflict. Husain Haqqani argues that Bhutto's trip to the UN was arranged by the Army to put a civilian façade on a military debacle. The Inter Services Intelligence (ISI) realized that schism was inevitable and they would need a charismatic, civilian scapegoat to blame for the break-up of Pakistan.[42] Bhutto was a deputy prime minister of a martial law regime that itself lacked legitimacy. Ironically, he had no fiat and had been almost recalled on his way to New York.[43]

On 12 December 1971, ZAB said, 'The real trouble started not with what happened in Dacca on 24 March or 26 March. The real, fundamental trouble started when the Treaty (Indo-Soviet Treaty)[44] was concluded and we had to face a new India, supported by the power, the prestige, the spirit, the resources, the technology and the arms of the Soviet Union.'

---

[42]*Pakistan: Between the Mosque and Military,* Husain Haqqani, Washington D.C.: Carnegie Endowment for International Peace: 2005. 87, 88-90. Web. Aug. 15, 2010.

[43]*Zulfikar Ali Bhutto and Pakistan 1967-1977,* Rafi Raza, p 122

[44]The Indo-Soviet Treaty of Peace, Friendship and Cooperation was a treaty signed between India and the Soviet Union in August 1971 that specified mutual strategic cooperation. The treaty was later adopted to the Indo-Bangladesh Treaty of Friendship and Cooperation in 1972.

He then asks, 'I would really like to know what crime or what wrong Pakistan has committed against the Soviet Union that my country should be dismembered. Because the Soviet Union has bad relations with China? China's relations with the Soviet Union are their relations... We do not want to have good relations with China at the cost of the Soviet Union, nor do we want to have good relations with the Soviet Union at the cost of China. But as a result of our good relations with China, we are being not only penalized, but treated in a fashion in which limb by limb we are being taken apart. This is unprecedented... Why should we be the victims? Why should we get into this nutcracker? The trouble is that we belong to Asia.'

He urged leaders of the world to stand by their principles. About France, which had abstained from taking sides, ZAB said, 'The relations between Pakistan and France have been so good that we are really pained by France's present attitude in claiming that they are working behind the scenes. When there is no scene left, where will "behind the scenes" be? France must take a positive moral position for national unity and integrity. We are not enemies of France; we are good friends of France. As far as we are concerned, Mr Permanent Representative, the die has been cast. You must cast your die. Sometimes there will be the east wind; sometimes there will be the west wind. Do not go by the east wind; do not go by the west wind. Go by a principle. The principle is that Pakistan is a united, sovereign state, and an attempt is now being made to dismember Pakistan by physical force.'

He went on, 'India's Foreign Minister said that West Pakistan had exploited East Pakistan—the resources and the riches of East Pakistan—and that that is basically the reason why we have come to the present situation. This is a very fundamental question. Exploitation is not a phenomenon of individuals or regions. Exploitation takes place as the result of a social system.

It is the social system that exploits. And the same social system basically prevails in India and Pakistan. As much as they are making efforts in India to change their social system, we are also doing in our country because we believe that our present social systems are basically exploitative. The political party which I lead contends that there was exploitation, that East Pakistan had been exploited, as well as regions in the west, but by the social system. The struggle was really related to the social system. We are not denying that there were problems. But we do not say that this means that our country should be destroyed and dismembered by another country.'

There is amazing sagacity in the manner in which he turns the argument about exploitation on its head. Its root causes, he avers, were identical in both countries, the fossilized social systems within which exploitation is embedded. And then comes his master stroke, his reference to his own political party, PPP, which negates and derides this social system.

He continues, 'A basic unalterable principle of international law is non-interference in the internal affairs of other countries. Article 2, paragraph 7 of the Charter speaks of non-interference in the internal affairs of states. It says:

> Nothing contained in the present Charter shall authorize the United Nations to intervene in matters which are essentially within the domestic jurisdiction of any state or shall require Members to submit such matters to settlement under the present Charter...

Now this is a Charter obligation. But the Indian Foreign Minister spoke for an hour and fifteen minutes... His whole speech was devoted to the internal affairs of Pakistan. I am glad he raised those questions even though it constituted interference in Pakistan's essentially domestic matters. It was as if I were to talk about the DMK movement in Madras, about the Nagas' or the Mizos' struggle for independence, about the plight of poor Bhutan and Sikkim, or about the many other matters that plague India. What is sauce for the goose is sauce for the gander. The consequences will come to the surface soon. It is up to India. If India thinks that Pakistan is going to be dismembered, the process is not going to stop there. The germ is going to spread, and it is going to spread very fast.'

Having played his trump card in referring to the DMK, Nagas, Mizos, Sikkim and Bhutan, India's Achilles' heel, he warns that dismemberment won't stop with Pakistan. The germ will spread!

'However, I will not choose to talk about the internal problems of India. Interference in the internal affairs of another country offends not only the Charter principle, it also violates the Bandung principles.'

On 15 December 1971, ZAB, with his voice often breaking, told the Council that his 11-year-old son called him from Pakistan to say, 'Don't come back with a document of surrender...' ZAB continued, 'I felt that it was imperative for me to come here and to seek justice from the Security Council. But I must say that the Security Council has denied my country that justice. From the moment I arrived we have been caught by dilatory tactics.'

His face streaked with tears, he walked out of the Security Council after accusing it of 'legalizing aggression'. His parting words to the Council, before he ripped up his notes, pushed back his chair and rose, were:

Mr President, I am not a rat. I've never ratted in my life. I have faced assassination attempts, I've faced imprisonment. Today I am not ratting, but I am leaving your Security Council. I find it disgraceful to my person and to my country to remain here a moment longer. Impose any decision, have a treaty worse than Versailles, legalize aggression, legalize occupation—I will not be a party to it. We will fight. My country harkens for me. Why should I waste my time here in the Security Council? I will not be a party to the ignominious surrender of part of my country. You can take your Security Council; here you are. I am going.

The *New York Times* reported that, as Bhutto walked out, the delegates around the circular table watched in stunned silence. *The Washington Times* called it 'living theatre'. *The Sunday Telegraph* said Britain should have supported India instead of remaining neutral, which was ironically one of Bhutto's points as well.

ZAB's speeches in the UN Security Council on 22 September 1965 and 15 December 1971 have become the subject of many researchers studying the art of public speaking. Syeda Sara Abbas argues that the statement of ZAB at the UN is a clash of two discourses—the scholarly and the theatrical as he was trying to communicate with 'two' distinct audiences simultaneously; the international community and the Pakistani nation. As a diplomat, he appealed to the western audience and the international community (in this case, the direct audience) to order a ceasefire so a small country with varied ethnic groups could defend itself. He used scholarly themes laced with rhetorical wordplay for this audience. This was a logical appeal that reached out to smaller countries with heterogeneous populations in the post-colonial era. As a political figure, he tried to mentally prepare his voters for the reality of dismemberment and military defeat so that they would absolve him of blame. He used theatrical, hyperbolic themes to connect indirectly to Pakistani audience. Bhutto must have made his statement keeping in mind the emotional needs of his Pakistan listeners.

The undated letter written by him to Mubashir Hasan from Sahiwal prison sometime between December 1968 and January 1969 reveals his understanding of the psychology of his people, as he explained to Mubashir Hasan: 'Please understand the psychology of our masses. They are simple people. They do not have a sustaining capacity. They are equally awed by the crisis. They are a forgiving people. They would like to see an end of the crisis. Any statement that gives impression to the contrary will be misunderstood by them.'

The following lines from 1971 are an example of the theatrical discourse that was spoken in the UN but addressed to his indirect audience—the people of gullies and mohallas of Pakistan: 'For four days we have been deliberating here. For four days the Security Council has procrastinated. Why? Because the object was for Dacca to fall. That was the object. It was quite clear to me from the beginning. All right, so what if Dacca falls? So what if the whole of East Pakistan falls? So what if the whole of West Pakistan falls? So what if our state is obliterated? We will build a new Pakistan. We will build a better Pakistan. We will build a greater Pakistan...'

The direct audience for the statement were the members of the Security Council, international press and its readers across the globe. Media reports of mass killings and thousands of refugees had transformed the conflict from an internal issue to a global one where the superpowers picked sides in glaring view of the international press. Its indirect audience, the people of West Pakistan, received the only message which mattered to them, that finally, irretrievably, East Pakistan was lost. Giving the audience this shattering news was tough as the state-controlled press had all along reported glorious victories. For the East Pakistanis, however, the message was totally different. It conveyed that Bhutto continued to fight for his country despite his repugnance for the mistakes made by the army. He was the father who, with a brave face, covered their shame.

This might have been his greatest challenge in communicating with a disparate, vast audience. However, his statement established his sincerity and also his own reputation as a thinker and orator.

Abbas writes, 'He was a representative of a small country on the brink of extinction and his own position was shaky. Yet he gave advice and orders as if he was the one in power: "You will be turning the medium sized and small countries into the harlots of the world. You cannot do that. (15 December 1971)."'
In her analysis, Abbas looks at the mind play going on. She writes that Bhutto was more successful with his indirect audience, the Pakistanis. Though theatrical, deeply personal and hyperbolic, the statement served their emotional needs. He told them what they wanted to hear, which was that Pakistan would survive. They wanted to blame someone—India, Russia or an international conspiracy—for the near-death experience. Bhutto gave them that blame object. His statement told the world that Pakistan possessed organic, popular and forceful leadership that was as anomalous as the nation. The Pakistani press played up the theatrical, florid side of his statement and Bhutto came to power in a burst of popularity.

Another fine point made by Abbas is that in some ways Bhutto may have been too successful in his rhetorical aims with the Pakistani audience, since he may have deflected attention away from the true events behind the fall of Dacca so that later it became difficult for Pakistanis to believe in the genocide unleashed by the Pakistani army. 'The genocide was remembered euphemistically as military action, the suffering of war refugees was eclipsed by the capture of prisoners of war... Bhutto projected himself as a human microcosm of the country. At that moment in the Security Council he was Pakistan with all its rage, prejudices and complexities. No Pakistani leader would have dared to use such rhetoric against the superpowers on their own turf. It is also doubtful that any other discourse would have satisfied the Pakistani people in their darkest hour.'

3

The Founding Convention 1967

The Tashkent Agreement was signed on 10 January 1966 by India's Prime Minister Lal Bahadur Shastri (who died the next day) and Pakistan's President Ayub Khan. The agreement was mediated by Soviet Premier Alexei Kosygin in Tashkent. The parties agreed to withdraw all armed forces to positions held before 5 August 1965; to restore diplomatic relations; and to discuss economic, refugee, and other questions. The 17-day war between Pakistan and India had ended on 22 September 1965 with a ceasefire secured by the UN Security Council.

The agreement was criticized both in India and Pakistan. Criticizing the agreement, ZAB called it a humiliation, and expressed his unwillingness to continue to work with Ayub Khan. He was asked by Ayub Khan to go on compulsory leave, which he was more than willing to do. As he rode on a train from Rawalpindi to Karachi, and then to Larkana, he discovered the depth of affection in which he was held by the people of West Pakistan. Large crowds came to greet him at stops on the way. The scene at the railway station in Lahore, where Bhutto was to break the journey for lunch with the Nawab of Kalabagh, was enough to turn any politician's head.

A large number of people were swarming over the platform, the carriage roof, and bridges and the people were spilling on to the road outside. As the train approached the station they ran forward to garland him, clasp and kiss his hands. Thousands of students and well-wishers had flocked to see him. They lifted him on their shoulders and carried him out shouting slogans like 'Bhutto Zindabad' (Long live Bhutto) and surprisingly, anti-Ayub slogans as well. Their affection, warmth and enthusiasm so moved him that tears poured down his face as he was carried out of the station.[45]

This massive demonstration of public acclaim, repeated at Karachi and Larkana, confirmed his charisma and potential power, and eventually determined his future course of action.

Ayub Khan tried to steer ZAB away by granting him licenses, offering him lands and loans to establish industries.[46] Bhutto refused to offer the assurances they wanted. Beginning in February 1967, Ayub Khan's ministers began denigrating his personal integrity and his role as a minister, and the civil administration concertedly disrupted his public meetings.[47] These attacks may have aroused Bhutto to the need for a political organization in launching a more effective counter-attack. His friends and admirers on the political left urged him to form a new party of

---

[45]*Zulfikar Ali Bhutto Sayasi Sawaneh Hayat* (Vol-I), Rasheed Akhtar Nadvi, 1974, Islamabad: Idaara Ma'araf-e-Milli, pp. 349-55. Similar account of Bhutto's reception can be seen in *Bhutto: A Political Biography,* Salman Taseer, (New Delhi: Vikas Publishing House, 1980), pp 76-77, *The Discourse of Politics of Zulifikar Ali Bhutto,* Anwar H. Syed, Macmillan Press Ltd, p 59.

[46]Bhutto himself later provided an account of these offers and threats in his 'Affidavit' in the Lahore High Court on 5 February 1969, reproduced in *Awakening the People: Statements, Articles, Speeches 1966-1969* (Rawalpindi: Pakistan Publication, n.d.). p 212-14.

[47]In one such case in Lahore government agents flooded the meeting ground where Bhutto was addressing a crowd and snapped overhead electric cables which fell in the water. As a result, many people in the audience received electric shocks. See *Zulfikar Ali Bhutto Sayasi Sawaneh Hayat (Volume-I).* Rasheed Akhtar Nadvi, 1974. Islamabad: Adaara Ma'araf-e-Milli, pp 387-8.

his own. Thus the Pakistan People's Party was born. Mubashir Hasan said that the decision to convince ZAB that he should make a party was taken in a meeting at Paris between him and J.A. Rahim in the autumn of 1966 when the Bhuttos were on a tour of Europe. That was one of the several reasons, Rahim claimed, that the party was his brainchild.

In his book, Rafi Raza wrote, 'Towards the middle of 1967, Mubashir Hasan and Rahim presented to ZAB the principles they had formulated for a new socialist party. ZAB was conscious that no party with a socialist program had made headway in Pakistan. He saw the merits of their views but was uncertain of the viability of socialism as a vehicle for change in West Pakistan's traditional society. In the 1960's, world-wide, progressive forces were looking towards socialism. In Pakistan, the disarray of the left offered opportunities for creating orderliness and, moreover, it was mainly leftists who had responded to ZAB.'[48]

Raza writes about the original nucleus which helped him flesh out the PPP; J.A. Rahim, Mubashir Hasan, Mumtaz Ali Bhutto, Ghulam Mustafa Khar, Mairaj Mohammad Khan and Hayat Mohammad Khan Sherpao. 'They were a curious mix, each talented in a different way. This was no elitist or distinct group as in other parties; they came from diverse classes, cultures and academic backgrounds. Rahim was a former officer of the Indian Civil Service and senior diplomat who had fallen out with Ayub Khan and was living for a while "penuriously" in Paris, his pension nowhere in sight. He helped ZAB, on leaving government, to write *The Myth of Independence*.[49] Most significantly, he provided the intellectual framework and content for the proposed party. He was supported by Mubashir Hasan, a staunch leftist from

---

[48]*Zulfikar Ali Bhutto and Pakistan 1967-1977*, Rafi Raza, Oxford University Press, p 4.
[49]*The Myth of Independence*, Zulfikar Ali Bhutto, Oxford University Press, 1969.

Lahore, who had an American doctorate in engineering. Mumtaz Ali Bhutto was a barrister and had been a member of the National Assembly since 1965. Khar, a young landlord from Muzaffargarh in the Punjab, who was elected to the National Assembly at the age of 25 in 1962, became an ardent follower of ZAB. Mairaj Mohammad Khan was a Karachi student leader, an outstanding leftist orator and agitator. Hayat Sherpao[50] came from a Muslim League family in the NWFP, a fiery young speaker who hero-worshipped his new leader. Differences were apparent, even in terms of language. Rahim and Mumtaz, both Oxbridge-educated, mainly spoke English; Mubashir was equally fluent in Urdu and English; the other three were more at ease in Urdu.'

This political team, Raza writes, was probably the best balanced and most competent ever in Pakistan. Notwithstanding their inexperience and the inevitable weak links resulting from the need to represent various interests and regions, it included party stalwarts, good orators, and educated young talent who were mostly in their mid- to late-thirties except Rahim and Mahmud Ali Qasuri who were in their sixties. ZAB was one of the few in his mid-forties.[51]

These men were attracted by ZAB's dynamism, intelligence and charisma. A good team was formed, to be joined by others, though it had no one of prominence in the early days. They were all frequent visitors at 70 Clifton where free and frank discussions flowed in an informal setting.[52]

The stage was now set for the first big moment for the yet-to-be-born party. Amidst government-inspired rumours and sense

---

[50]Hayat Mohammad Sherpao Khan was assassinated on 8 February 1975 by an explosive device in a tape-recorder while speaking at Peshawar University. Bhutto's hand was suspected.

[51]*Zulfikar Ali Bhutto and Pakistan 1967-1977*, Rafi Raza, Oxford University Press, p 145.

[52]Ibid, page 4-5.

of disquiet, a convention was held. No place such as YMCA hall was available for holding the convention, so it had to be held at Dr Mubashir Hasan's residence at 4K Gulberg, Lahore.

'Democrats, friends of the downtrodden, men and women of goodwill and patriots, were invited to join in the convention held on 30 November and 1 December 1967.

Mubashir Hasan writes in his book *The Mirage of Power*: 'By 1966, I had scaled down my lucrative practice as a consulting engineer to dedicate myself to social and political work. A group of like-minded, educated men and women in their thirties met every month at my house for one year discussing social, political and ideological issues. It was 1967 when we ended up with framing a manifesto for a new political venture based on radical socio-economic change. Simultaneously, ZAB announced his intention to form a new political party. Our group discussed with Bhutto and his ideological mentor, J.A. Rahim, the aims and objectives of his party-to-be-announced. Upon reaching agreement, Bhutto and Rahim invited our group to join hands in launching the new party.'

Three other names for the party were suggested—'People's Progressive Party,' 'People's Party,' and 'Socialist Party of Pakistan.' It was finally named Pakistan People's Party.'[53]

The agenda of the Founding Convention was carefully drafted by Rahim and Mubashir Hasan duly approved by the Chair. The military had clamped section 144. Public areas were out of reckoning. The PPP Convention had to be held at a private venue.

PAKISTAN PEOPLE'S PARTY CONVENTION, LAHORE

Dates:	Thursday, 30 November and Friday, 1 December 1967
Place:	4K Gulberg, Main Boulevard, Opposite Auriga Cinema

---

[53]Interview with Mubashir Hasan at Lahore 17 July 2017.

Registration Fee: Rs 20 only
Enquiries: Malik Aslam Hayat, Dev Samaj Road, Phone 3062
Admission: Yellow Cards should be presented at the Gate

PROGRAMME

30 November 1967

9:15 a.m. to 10:15 a.m.   **Registration of Participants**

10:15 a.m. to 1:00 p.m.   **FIRST SESSION**
1. Recitation from the Holy Quran
2. Poems by Mr Aslam Gurdaspuri and Mr Halim Raza
3. Address of welcome by Malik Aslam Hayat
4. Speech by Mr Zulfikar Ali Bhutto
5. Formation of Steering Committee
6. Presentation of Draft Declaration
7. General Discussion

3 p.m. to 6 p.m.   **SECOND SESSION**
1. General Discussion
2. Formation of the following Committees by the Steering Committee
   (a) Resolution Committee
   (b) Constitution Committee
   (c) Draft Declaration Committee

1 December 1967

10 a.m. to 12:30 p.m.   **THIRD SESSION**
1. Resolutions
2. Discussions

3 p.m. to 5:30 p.m.   **FOURTH SESSION**
1. Endorsement of:
   (a) Resolutions
   (b) Constitution

(c) Draft Declaration
2. Announcement of the following Committees
   (a) Organising Committee
   (b) Principles Committee

6 P.M. PRESS CONFERENCE BY MR ZULFIKAR ALI BHUTTO

'Lahore has the privilege of being the birth place of some of the greatest personalities. It is the land of Datta Ganj Bakhsh and the mausoleum of Qutubuddin Aibak. When Sahabuddin Ghori and Qutubuddin Aibak together defeated Prithviraj in the battlefield of Terawari, they had gone there from Lahore. Lahore is the city of Jehangir, Lahore has Akbar's Fort, Lahore has Aurangzeb's Shahi Masjid, Lahore is the resting place of Hazrat Miyan Mir. And Lahore is the place where Mohammad Ali Jinnah's Lahore resolution was passed. Finally, Lahore was the place where the PPP convention changed Pakistani course of history on the first December 1967.'[54]

'Lahore was also the capital of India for 14 years during the rule of Emperor Akbar,' adds Mubashir Hasan. In Lahore then, on the sprawling lawns of Mubashir Hasan's home, a shamiana was pitched with 500 chairs; people from all over West Pakistan trickled in from early morning of 30 November 1967. ZAB, dressed in a light grey suit, sat on the dais quietly, looking at the slowly growing audience. He was trying to read their deepest feelings that brought them here. Records of his speech on this occasion may be in media reports, although media was under close watch. The excerpts from his speech below are from his political biography:

'I have addressed national and international gatherings at the critical times, when we were at war and peace, but today I

---

[54] *Zulfikar Ali Bhutto Sayasi Sawaneh Hayat (Vol-I)*. Rasheed Akhtar Nadvi, 1974. Islamabad: Idaara Ma'araf-e-Milli.

address you on the most crucial day of my life. It is very difficult for me to speak today.'

He proceeded by taking stock of national life for the last 20 years of Pakistan's existence. Identifying the core malaise, he said that common people were never taken into confidence. 'A small group of ruling elite became arbiters of destiny of 120 million. Rulers ran the country to serve their private ends. Instead of working for the masses, they worked for the small group of economic czars of Pakistan.'

He spoke of the Defence of Pakistan Rules (formerly Defence of India Act 1939) which have been imposed to curb freedom of speech. He said that the first task of PPP would be to remove all the obstacles between the party and the public, and forge a direct connection. The party would learn from the masses and masses would learn from the party. 'And when we are one with the masses, then, hand in hand, we will march towards our destiny. People must understand that PPP has only been established to end their deprivation and bring prosperity.' For two hours his speech held the audience in a spell.

Four committees were established. The prominent members of the committees were J.A. Rahim, Mubashir Hasan, Mir Rasool Bakhsh Talpur, Sheikh Mohammad Rashid, Mairaj Mohammad Khan, Hayat Mohammad Sherpao, Haq Nawaz Gandapur, Ashiq Alim, Begum Abaad Ahmad Khan, Ahmad Raza Khan and Khurshid Hasan Mir. There were two poets in the gathering— Aslam Gurdaspuri and Dr Halim Raza. There were two Maulanas Maulvi Mohammad Sayeed and Qazi Qudratullah. Mustafa Khar and Mumtaz Bhutto did not join any committee due to apprehension that they would be disqualified from the National Assembly membership.

Raza writes, 'Once it was decided to form a new party, ZAB planned ahead meticulously. He could see the broad picture and seldom forgot a detail. Rahim and he were a curious couple, essentially complementary in the early days. Rahim provided the ideology and ZAB the pragmatism and popular appeal. Their different approaches were exemplified in the Foundation Meeting... Most Pakistanis today are not familiar with the Foundation Documents. The documents provide a basis for understanding the forces unleashed by the PPP, its motivation, and ZAB's ideas and actions. The Interim Constitution of the Party was finalized in a hurry by Rahim during the Convention with its four slogans:

Islam is our Faith;
Democracy is our Polity;
Socialism is our Economy;
All Power to the People.'[55]

Rahim had drafted the manifesto that was finalized in consultation with Mubashir Hasan and had it printed in October 1966. From Paris, he wrote to Bhutto, 'In the words of the Chinese oracle I Ching, "The ablution has been made, but not yet the sacrifice". The manifesto has been printed and herewith the Movement has been launched. I will go on with the work according to the plans... We expect you to act on your part. There is no point in keeping silent. The people must be taught that there is an alternative to the present regime of corruption. The manifesto is the guide.' Rahim believed that he and ZAB were, indeed, about to inaugurate an era of idealism and selflessness for Pakistan. 'We expect you to keep firmly to its sixteen doctrines. When dealing with politicians, who will come to you to bargain for themselves, please do not compromise on the doctrines. Without the Doctrine the Movement is nothing.'[56]

---

[55]Interview in Lahore on 17 July 2017, Mubashir Hasan said that 'All Power to the People' was taken from Soviet Union's 'All power to the Soviets'.
[56]*Zulfi Bhutto of Pakistan: His Life and Times*, Stanley Wolpert. p 111.

In his biography of ZAB, Stanley Wolpert writes about ZAB's core team. 'J.A. Rahim and socialist Dr Mubashir Hasan were to serve as the ideological parents of the PPP's doctrine. They were both theoreticians, the only doctrinaire intellectuals among the new party's activist founding fathers, each in his own way a world remote from Zulfikar Ali Bhutto, yet both wise enough to appreciate that Bhutto alone had the wealth as well as the charisma and popular vote-getting appeal to give their radical doctrines any chance of winning mass support in the conservative polity... From its conception, then, the Peoples Party was a unique and unstable blend of the right and left wings of West Pakistan's leadership spectrum, for Zulfi, Mumtaz, Khar, and Jatoi could hardly be accused of harboring any radical-socialist leanings, nor could barristers Rafi Raza, or Hafeez Pirzada, who early joined them. Mubashir, on the other hand, could never be accused of feudal or reactionary proclivities. Rahim was more difficult to label, sometimes as radical as Mubashir, at other times more reactionary, or authoritarian, than Zulfi.'

'I am now working on an elaboration of the program that can make a reality of 'Mass Mobilization,' wrote Rahim to his leader. 'If I can manage it, I shall have it printed as a brochure.' He closed his letter to Bhutto with 'You must take the lead now.'[57]

The new party's ideological and programmatic positions were first set forth in a series of papers called the *Foundation Documents*[58].

The Foundation Documents

Resolution passed by the PPP in their Lahore convention:

1. Name of the party

---

[57]Ibid, p 111.
[58]The documents provide a basis for understanding the forces unleashed by the PPP, its motivation, and ZAB's ideas and actions.

2. Flag of the party
3. Why a New Party?
4. Why Socialism is necessary in Islamic state of Pakistan
5. Basic Rule
6. Economic Reform
7. Declaration of the Unity of the People
8. Jammu & Kashmir
9. Relations with Assam
10. Six Points Answered

The Urdu version was composed in an elegant literary style, representing a blend of Islamic, socialistic and liberal democratic values and vocabulary. The second part of Document 7 (pp. 64-68) is especially noteworthy for its scriptural style of poetic prose. The documents, purporting to be ZAB's covenant with the people, spelled out the party's analysis of Pakistan's developmental journey during the previous regimes, the rationale for its coming into being, its basic principles and commitments, and its case for socialism. [59]

Raza wrote that of the ten Foundation Meeting Documents, ZAB drafted 'Why a New Party?', Mubashir Hasan drafted 'Declaration of the Unity of the People' and Rahim drafted the rest. [60]

Mubashir Hasan endorsed Raza that ZAB had written some documents, and J.A. Rahim, the party's secretary general and ideologue, wrote the rest. The Urdu version was written by himself and Haneef Ramay. [61]

[59] Anwar H. Syed, The Discourse of Politics of Zulifikar Ali Bhutto, Macmillan Press Ltd, p 61.
[60] Zulfikar Ali Bhutto and Pakistan 1967-1977, Rafi Raza, Oxford University Press,, p 5.
[61] Haneef Ramay later became the Chief Minister of Punjab. He belonged to the influential Arian community.

The most important was Document 4 which asserted that socialism alone could cure Pakistan's economic and political crisis. But the road to socialism need not be the same for all; each nation's peculiar circumstances, values, and usages would influence its design. Pakistan must have its own kind of socialism, accommodating its religious and cultural values. Social justice and the establishment of a classless society were declared the party's guiding principles. There were a huge number of programmatic commitments as well; a constitutional democratic order based on universal adult franchise; civil rights and liberties; full remuneration to peasants and workers for their labour; further elimination of feudalism and landlordism; encouragement of self-help projects and voluntary cooperative farming; development of nationwide unions in certain industries; minimum wages and the workers' right to strike; free healthcare for peasants and workers; reorganization of education to bring about a classless society; encouragement of regional languages expressing the people's cultural personality. Freedom of belief and expression, press, organizations, and assembly were upfront. Islam received a place of high honour in the value system projected in the documents. This was easily done since some of the major socialist values—egalitarianism and outlawry of exploitation—were suited to be preeminently Islamic values.[62]

ZAB was careful to avoid widespread hostility in the name of Islam just as he was launching PPP. He carefully calibrated it as an agent of social change, not as maker of revolution. The documents were written without any revolutionary or militant vocabulary. Exploitative capitalism was to be demolished; image built was that of a progressive nation builder with promise of humane and civil conduct.

---

[62] *The Discourse of Politics of Zulifikar Ali Bhutto,* Anwar H. Syed, Macmillan Press Ltd, p 62-63.

Rafi Raza writes that Rahim's ideological thrust was expressed in the opening words of the document, 'Why Socialism is necessary for Pakistan': 'To put it in one sentence, the aim of the party is the transformation of Pakistan into a socialist society'. The 'Declaration of Principles' reiterated this as the 'objective', and called for fundamental changes: the nationalization of finance and key sectors of industry, the removal of the 'final remnants of the feudal system', and the strengthening of trade unions. It also sought the abolition of illiteracy, equal rights for women, the separation of the Executive from the Judiciary, and academic freedom.

The flag of the party was designed and explained by J.A. Rahim:

> The flag of the Party is a tricolor divided in equal vertical segments. The middle containing a crescent and star symbol. The arrangement of the colored fields in the order, black and green from mast to free end, has been determined primarily for aesthetic reasons.

The three colours—red, black and green belong to Muslim history. The flag of the PPP is the symbol of the struggle for social and economic justice, freedom, rights of the workers and peasants, and for the attainment of a classless society. The colours chosen belong to the tradition of the Muslims who created a homeland for themselves in this subcontinent. The flag marks their unity while it also proclaims their revolutionary future, the achievement of their socialist ideals, under the leadership of the PPP.

ZAB addressed the first of the four sessions on the problems facing the country: corruption, exploitation, fundamental rights, Jammu and Kashmir, Vietnam and American influence in Pakistan. The Document he contributed, 'Why a New Party?' referred to the 'conservative' and 'progressive' forces finding their 'respective unities', followed by the national unity of all opposition parties in order to launch a constitutional struggle for the restoration of democracy. The new party 'would form a bridge between the existing conflicting interests and give a lead in reconciling the historical dichotomies of the opposition'.

In the fourth and concluding session on the afternoon of 1 December 1967, the party was officially named and formed. It also formally adopted the Party flag.

ZAB was ready for battle. Leading from the front, ZAB was the right man in the right place at the right time. His aspirations, grasp and reach had been evident for several years. It had got public airing when he was appointed to Ayub Khan's cabinet. His straight talk at the two sessions at UN defined his Indian policy which over the years would be moulded with circumstances but would remain unchanged at the core. He saw India as a Leviathan ready to devour smaller entities within its catchment area. In this context, I came across a letter written by him a few days after the Founding Convention which more than any single document reveals the vision, the grasp, the anger and bluntness which distinguished him from any other leader in the history of Pakistan. It was addressed to S.M. Yousuf, Secretary, Ministry of Foreign Affairs, one of the most senior bureaucrats.[63] Its trigger was a statement made by the ministry in response to a statement issued by PPP. His contempt for the supine stand taken by the government spilt all over the pages. The letter ended with the question addressed to Yousuf which was directed at the ministry; but which also was written to shame the entire Government of Pakistan: 'Finally, may I ask an experienced civil servant like you whether it was really necessary for the spokesman of the Foreign Office, who happens to be an official, to make personal attacks on me in the course of that deplorable manifestation of political weakness and immaturity?'

The background of the above invective was a statement issued

---

[63]Copy of the letter is with the author

by MFA on 15 December 1967, clarifying that Pakistan has no claim on Indian territory. This clarification was the result of a declaration by ZAB that Assam must have a special status with Pakistan. He writes to Yousuf that first of all, his statement made no territorial claim—it only referred to having a relationship with Assam of a kind that France has with Quebec in Canada. It was this factual claim that led the Pakistan bureaucrats to take 'supine positions' and abandon 'one powerful lever after another'. He warns them of adverse circumstances if natural rights are surrendered to India in the quest of buying peace.

Then he speaks words which reflect the vision of a statesman who looks at the big picture—South Asia in a global context and East Pakistan's symbolic relations with Assam.

'Can it be denied,' he writes, 'that it is from Assam that hundreds of thousands of Muslims are being forcibly pushed out into East Pakistan? There seems to be no end to this tragic exodus which the Government of Pakistan has failed to prevent all these years. The Indians call the unfortunate victims "infiltrators" and Pakistan calls it "eviction". Thus, these ill-fated victims are neither Indian nor Pakistani but have acquired, by their miserable plight, a special status which requires special attention.'

Then he speaks of the struggle of a large section of Assam against Indian domination. With the same fervour, he points at the struggle of the Nagas and Mizos against Indian aggression. ZAB has the distinction of being the first South Asian leader to the best of my knowledge who spoke for Mizos and Nagas; people who are always forgotten in the political melee by 'mainstream' powers which surround them. 'Must we not have sympathy with the Mizos, the Nagas and others who are struggling to assert their right of self-determination and who have never accepted the status of Indian nationals?' He draws an analogy with the struggle of the Nagas for a 'third nation' with the struggle of Muslims to carve a second state. Both struggles, he writes, were against 'Hindus'.

Then he decries the policy of favouring West Wing over East Wing. 'If we demand self-determination for Jammu and Kashmir and pay no heed at all to what is going on next door to East Pakistan it would mean taking a position unfavorable to one wing of the country. Kashmir is contiguous to West Pakistan but the problem is a national one. Why should a serious problem, getting more menacing and directly affecting East Pakistan, be regarded as merely regional if any attention is paid to it at all? This question is all the more pertinent in view of the mounting inter-wing tensions caused by discriminatory policies like the one being pursued in this matter.' He writes, 'It is a high moral obligation on our part to sympathize with the people of Assam. The only restraining influence on this obligation would arise out of India's willingness to make amends on each and every outstanding dispute. A passive policy short of these minimum terms would end not in reconciliation but capitulation.'

He then recounts ways in which 'India has shamelessly interfered in Pakistan's internal affairs...particularly in East Pakistan, so much so that, as Foreign Minister, I was compelled to close the Indian Mission at Rajshahi.' He speaks of authentic knowledge of India's plans to wreck the economy of East Pakistan by the Farrakha project and by massive evictions of Muslims from Assam. 'Despite Pakistan's one sided gestures and unilateral concessions India pays scant attention to your pleadings and has turned a deaf ear to your entreaties for better relations. This is so because the only answer to pressure is counter-pressure, which you are not prepared to understand and use.'

Then he squares with the issue of Kashmir which he fears Pakistan will surrender in the name of 'reason or peace'. He deplores that Pakistan welcomed the US offer of arbitration. 'This has happened because the surrender of one basic right entails the surrender of all other rights'.

He then indicts the government for refuting the very carefully crafted declaration of PPP thereby harming national interest. 'Quite apart from these wider considerations, it should have been expedient from the narrow view point of diplomatic negotiating capacity for Government to take advantage of the divergent views of political influences and press them into service in the defence of national interests. This is exactly what India has done so successfully in dealing with Pakistan.'

He believes only PPP can salvage the country from 'quagmire' into which it is being pulled by people like S.M. Yousuf. In a letter to Aslam Hayat written on 16 June 1968, well before he was thrown in prison for 'sedition', he writes:

> 'Inshallah success is bound to come to us because we alone are in a position to salvage the country from its quagmire. See how miserably the government's policy of Capitulation to India has failed. The Muslims of India are being subjected to greater waves of terror and intimidation, their lives and properties have become more insecure while a systematic campaign of extermination is being waged by India... The follies of the government have led us to a path of despair and humiliation.'

The letter is a classic example of his wisdom and empathy— qualities for which history has never given him credit.

4

Sahiwal: The Writ Petition

It was 7 November 1968. ZAB arrived in Rawalpindi from Sherpao[64]. On the road, a large crowd of students from the Gordon College Polytechnic greeted him. At the Intercontinental Hotel, he learnt that the police had opened fire at students resulting in the death of one student, Abdul Hamid. He was also told that students were insisting on taking the body to President's house and wanted him to lead their procession. His first thought was to persuade the students to exercise restraint so he sent some party men to the campus. But they could not meet the students because police had sealed the institution. So he left for Pindi Gheb to offer condolences to the family of Abdul Hamid.

In Rawalpindi, it was decided that he would reach Lahore by train. Mubashir Hasan and a colleague Miyan Aslam left Pindi a day earlier to make arrangements. They informed the press that ZAB would arrive at Lahore station at 2 p.m. However, the train was delayed due to large crowd of people gathering at various stations. As the train pulled into the station milling with one lakh people, the question was how to take him off, considering the crush of people. Mubashir Hasan brought his VW Beetle right onto the railway platform. Driving in reverse, he slid it right

---

[64]Sherpao is in the North West Frontier Province.

up to his compartment until he was 3-feet away from the door. ZAB climbed in the front seat. People were all over the car, on the bumper, roof and bonnet. They were shouting and panting with joy. Only when he shook hundreds of hands, they agreed to give way to the car.

Mubashir Hasan drove him to InterContinental Hotel for a cup of tea and thereafter to his house at 4K Gulberg where the historic founding convention of PPP had been held a year ago. Mustafa Khar, who had driven from Rawalpindi was sent for the night to Haneef Ramay's house. Lahore Party workers kept coming to see their leader. They were served glasses of sherbet by Mubashir Hasan's old-time help, Omar. An elaborate dinner was laid out for the group—Mustafa Khar, Mumtaz Bhutto, Amir Bakhsh Bhutto and a few others.

ZAB stayed at Mubashir Hasan's house for a few nights. On 13 November, it was late night by the time he retired to the master bedroom. The sound of AC subdued all external sounds including grunts, growls and grating of security persons at the gate. The police had surrounded the house from all sides. It was very late when Mubashir Hasan and his wife Dr Zeenat, who were wide awake in the study room, heard a firm knock which was ominous and heart-stopping.

A man in uniform was standing at the front door; other figures were visible behind him. 'We have come to arrest Mr Bhutto,' they said when Mubashir Hasan opened the door. 'He has just gone to sleep,' Mubashir Hasan said softly. 'Sir, please. Please wake him up. These are our orders, please.' Reluctantly, he went to the door and only knocked once. Immediately came the answer 'Ask them to wait.' It was clear that the man inside had not slept either. From the store, Dr Zeenat, took out a new razai and a couple of new pillows. The bedding was rolled up. An attendant came out of the bedroom with a small suitcase.

'I am ready,' Bhutto said to his hosts. Husband and wife stood silently as the two small belongings were loaded on the police van. Then Mr Bhutto came out on the driveway, stepped quickly into the back seat and slammed the door shut.

In the next few minutes, they came for Mumtaz Bhutto and Amir Bakhsh, both being close relatives of the chief. Beddings were found for them, placed in the van, which briskly took them away. Finally, it was Mubashir Hasan's turn. 'Dr Sahib you are also under arrest.' In one hour, the house had emptied out and the police force dispersed. 'What a bleak November night,' Dr Zeenat thought as she locked the door of the house, which had just witnessed the making of history.

They went to separate jails. ZAB to Mianwali, Mumtaz to Sahiwal and Mubashir Hasan to Gujarat. Amir Bakhsh was sent home. Later, ZAB told Mubashir Hasan, 'I slept all the way to Mianwali.'

The forty-year-old prince from feudal Sindh was being driven to jail for the first time in his life and he slept! Slept all the way to Mianwali, a sleepy town in Punjab, where he was initially kept for a few days before being moved to join the others in Sahiwal. Total term served was three months and two days. He was finally moved to Borstal Jail, Lahore where the hearing was held and Writ Petition filed. The division bench included Justice Maulvi Mushtaq Hussain and Justice Mohammad Gul. ZAB's wife and three children plus core group members of PPP were present at the hearings.

The court first listened to the Home Secretary who also submitted the special branch police report and the governor's directive explaining the reason for the arrest. Answering one of the questions, the Secretary admitted that a student of Polytechnic Institute was killed on 7 November in the police firing. Outside the court, there was a huge crowd shouting 'Bhutto Zindabad'. On the second day, when the court convened, advocate Mahmud Ali Qasuri on behalf of ZAB examined the Home Secretary.

In the third session on 13 January, the Home Secretary was examined again. On 23 January, the Advocate General submitted a request that since he had not read ZAB's writ petition, the case be postponed. The court agreed.

ZAB wrote many letters from prison. Some of them have survived in the private papers of Mubashir Hasan. They form a historical record, which is crucial to understanding ZAB and his era. They will be presented in a separate chapter.

The document which captures the political history of the period, is the Writ Petition (No. 1794 of 1968), which was prepared word for word by ZAB. It was filed in the High Court of West Pakistan, Lahore. The entire petition forms an Annexure to the book. A brief of its contents is presented below.

The petitioner was Begum Nusrat Bhutto versus the respondent, Government of West Pakistan. The Affidavit was of the Detenu Mr Zulfikar Ali Bhutto in Support of the Petition.

'I, Zulfikar Ali, s/o Late Sir Shahnawaz Khan Bhutto, Muslim, adult, resident of Larkana, at present in detention at the Borstal Jail, Lahore, West Pakistan, on solemn affirmation state as hereinafter: That I am the detenu in the above writ petition filed by my wife Begum Nusrat Bhutto the petitioner challenging the order of my detention dated 12-11-1968 passed by the Governor of West Pakistan under rule 32 of the Defence of Pakistan Rules.'

He avers that the mass stir in the country was due to gross economic mismanagement and corruption of the government; it was not caused by him or his party. 'Economic mismanagement is the most potent factor of political discontent.' He asserts that there must be something brittle about the government if its edifice crumbles by his one-week tour. 'The people acclaimed me not because I was putting a plan of violence into action but because I represented their feelings when I declared that corruption had reached a nadir, that the students were in chains, that the people were in agony and that the conditions had become intolerable.'

Then he reveals the real reason for his arrest—Tashkent Declaration. If he were to reveal its truth it would explain not only why he quit government but also his persecution and detention. He calls the face of the regime fatigued and says that signs of decomposition are writ large over it. He denies planning violence of any kind; it is the government which perpetrates violence. 'Government has employed force capriciously. Everywhere the blood of innocents has watered the land, sometimes in Balochistan and sometimes in East Pakistan. On occasion, it is in the Punjab and Sindh; on others, in the ramparts of our northern regions'.

He then dwells on 'incompetent rulers' who do not understand how the mainsprings of history move. They place blame for their incompetencies on people they least like. 'If the students give trouble, they imagine there must be somebody inciting them.' So they believe all is well and there are a few 'agitators' and 'rabble rousers' who are leading 'the ignorant and illiterate people astray'.

He gives two reasons why government has subjected him to 'grotesque harassment' and finally prison. First, it was dreaded that he would reveal the truth of Tashkent to the people. Second, he was Ayub Khan's most powerful rival for President and enjoyed public confidence. He then deplores the arrests and torture of his party men which followed his arrest.

Next, he recounts few instances of government's attempts to thwart his public appearances and political rallies by any and every means. He gives details of events which immediately preceded his arrest. That part of the affidavit is given verbatim below.

'On my arrival in Rawalpindi by car from Sherpao on the 7 November 1968, I was greeted on the road by a large crowd of students of the Polytechnic, a couple of miles ahead of their institution because the police had closed the highway leading to it. When I arrived at the Hotel Intercontinental, I found the whole Mall area thick with teargas smoke. I was told that a number of students who, having come out of the Gordon College in a procession to protest against the seizure of their purchases at Landi Kotal, had gathered in the lawns of the Hotel Continental, from where, without any provocation, they were suddenly and mercilessly beaten up and chased away. About one and a half hours after my arrival in the hotel, I received a telephone call from the Polytechnic informing me that the police had opened fire there resulting in the death of a student Abdul Hamid. I was told that the students were insisting on taking the body in a procession to the President's House. I advised the students to do nothing that might aggravate the situation. I fervently appealed to them to restrain their feelings and not to exacerbate the tension. I tried to send some of my party men to the Polytechnic Institute to explain to them the need for discipline in a crisis created by the Government. They were unable to meet the students because the Institution was sealed off by the police. On 8 November I left Rawalpindi by car at about 3:00 p.m. for Pindi Gheb to offer condolences to the family of Abdul Hamid. Mr Khurshid Hassan Meer, Advocate, the Chairman of PPP Rawalpindi District accompanied me. The following morning he was arrested in an arson case alleged to have occurred at Rawalpindi after 3:00 p.m on 8 November 1968. When he was granted bail by the Session Judge which was confirmed by the High Court later, he was again detained on 10 November under an order rescinded during the hearing of his writ petition. This briefly indicates the Government's attitude towards my party and my party-men. A member of the Principles Committee of my party, Dr Mubashir Hasan was arrested on the ground that he was "creating disaffection against the Government." Two influential members of the National Assembly one of whom is a relative and the other a friend, were arrested merely because they were seen in the Gordon College, Rawalpindi. In this fashion, a sweep of arbitrary arrests was made on 13 November and subsequently.'

The above is followed by a description of the arrest itself. This has been recounted as narrated by Mubashir Hasan.

Next, he describes the condition of his cell. The description assumes importance because it became the sticking point on which the bench hauled up the home secretary for the rotten treatment meted out to him in contravention of jail rules for political prisoners of his standing.

'I was confined in an old cell full of rats and mosquitoes, the charpoy was tied to a chain. There was an adjoining little room meant for toilet purposes. But it was so dirty that it was repulsive to enter it. The food consisted of two chappatis made of red wheat with dal which had stones in it or two tiny pieces of meat. A strong light shone for 24 hours through my stay there, making sleep at night extremely difficult. I was kept in solitary confinement. When I learnt that the High Court had granted my lawyers permission to meet me I immediately asked for some paper to enable me to make notes for my meeting with them. Despite my repeated requests writing paper was not given to me until the afternoon of 18 November. My letters and telegrams were not delivered to me. Except for *Pakistan Times* and *Mashriq*, I was not provided with any other newspapers. As the Hon'ble High Court ordered that all detainees should be kept in one jail, on the evening of 18 November I was taken to Sahiwal where I arrived in the early hours of 19 November.

Makeshift arrangements were made at Sahiwal for my detention where I continued to be kept in solitary confinement. Here, instead of the rats the room was full of bats and, to avoid them, I had to sleep with a towel over my face. The mosquitoes and flies were in legions. The bathroom was separate from the cell and was shared with others. The practice in jail is to provide Class I and II detenus with a convict for personal service. The convict provided to me was told that he would be skinned alive if he spoke to me. Unlike at Mianwali, this man was not even provided with a kitchen knife to prepare my meals. Again unlike Mianwali, where my cell was locked at about 8:00 in the evening, the warden came to lock me in at 5:00 in the evening. The food was as inedible and insufficient as at Mianwali. I showed the two tiny pieces of meat constituting my meals to Sheikh Rashid, Advocate, when under orders of the High Court he interviewed me. Contrary to law, I was not permitted the use of a radio or to make private arrangements for my meals. I addressed about five or six applications to the authorities protesting against the illegal conditions of my detention which were neither controverted nor was any action taken on them.'

He then tries to shame the government for treatment of someone who had been a minister for eight years, especially Foreign Affairs Minister during the war. He quotes the praise Bertrand Russell lavished on him in a letter to *The Economist* (20 August 1966) defending him against their attack on him. On 3 September 1966, *The Economist* published an anti-ZAB article, 'Ayub's Rival'. Repudiating its line, Bertrand Russell wrote, 'Your attack on Mr Bhutto (20 August 1966) should be placed in context. Mr Bhutto's sin in western eyes is that he was an important figure in conceiving an independent policy for Pakistan, placing it in the context of Afro-Asia and outside the rank of countries which are dominated by the United States. The fate of national leaders who respond to needs of their people is increasingly clear, unless they find the means to resist the pressures applied to them, in which case journals such as *The Economist* attach unpleasant labels to them. Mr Bhutto is a national leader of his country in the tradition of Jinnah, and the storm of prolonged applause which he receives is not restricted to London. There are many who wish him well and who admire his role in working for an independent policy for his country consonant with the social aspirations of the peoples of Africa, Asia and Latin America.'

He then quotes President Ahmad Soekarno, who while conferring the Order of the Republic of Indonesia at a ceremony in the Mardeka Palace in Jakarta on 20 April 1966, said that it was an honour for him to confer the order on him in recognition of his 'great services to the friendship of Indonesia and Pakistan.' He concluded by saying that ZAB was 'a great freedom-fighter and great worker for Afro-Asian solidarity'.

He also quotes President Mikoyan of the Soviet Union who, in April 1965, praised ZAB's services to Pakistan at a meeting in the Kremlin, in the presence of the Soviet and Pakistan delegations. 'He told President Ayub Khan that "Mr Bhutto is a remarkably intelligent person" and that his "youth and energy were a tremendous source of strength to President Ayub Khan and to Pakistan."'

Finally, he reminds the court that at the age of 34 in August 1964, the high order of Hilal-e-Pakistan was conferred upon him. 'While conferring the award in the presence of Muslim League leaders assembled at the President's guest-house at Rawalpindi, President Ayub Khan advised the youth of Pakistan to emulate me.'

He accuses the government of putting him in jail after it was convinced that he would not relent on his political convictions. Elaborating this, he quotes the Home Secretary's note to the Governor, 'Mr ZAB had chosen to be on the warpath. For the furtherance of his vindictive designs against the present regime he has been publicly talking of violence, bloodshed and revenge.' Before demolishing the charge of this sarkari spokesperson, he makes a well-placed argument to disarm his most entrenched critics. Refering to the poison administered to him by the regime, he invokes the story of the Athenian philosopher Socrates. For his sin of speaking the truth he was made to drink a cup of poison. This point could not have been lost on the Pakistan intelligentsia or even the middle class. Urdu poetry is replete with references to 'Suqrat' and 'zehr ka pyala'. ('Socrates' and 'poison cup').

'My Lords, in the year 399 before the Christian Era, Athenian Rulers condemned a philosopher to death for having led astray the youth of the city. Socrates was given hemlock to drink.'

He writes that his Hyderabad speech was made *raison d'être* for the charge. But the circumstances prove, beyond doubt, that it was his threat to disclose Tashkent and his decision to contest election which unnerved the government. For this reason, the Home Secretary Ayub Awan was sent to meet him in Sindh to ask if his Hyderabad announcement was irrevocable. The government's desperation at losing its grip on power was evident in the false criminal cases built against him with government servants as approvers. Disqualifying him from taking part by getting him convicted in a criminal court was their game plan.

He asks why he was not arrested on the night after the Hyderabad speech. After all, 'a man who preaches bloodshed, revolution and overthrow of the government' is not allowed to continue his mission from one part of the country to another.

He questions President Ayub Khan, invoking the motto of Quaid-e-Azam—Unity, Faith and Discipline. He reminds the court and the people of his country of the hypocrisy of this call when given by this regime, 'Are the people being asked to unite against adult franchise and fundamental rights in defence of emergency laws or to expand the economic empire of the 20 families with the sweat of their united labour? In the same spirit, is it discipline addressed to a free people? Dictatorship has its own discipline. Section 144, the Defence of Pakistan Rules, the Security Laws and the Criminal Law Amendment Act provide a tautological basis of discipline. Is the appeal for discipline to be that of the graveyard, a silent quiescence to the denial of rights, a servile obedience to the regime's personal mandate?'

His hardest blow aims at a government, which is 'allergic' to the word 'revolution' when its whole structure is based on force. He recounts instances of bloodshed, the opposition threatened with death, student leader of Rawalpindi beaten up by thugs, banner bearing the 'Kalma' torn to shreds 'as if Pakistan was a Jan Sangh state'. The final word of this historic Writ Petition is his philosophy, his dream for Pakistan.

'The issues that confront Pakistan reach beyond the limitations of time and space. They come once in an epoch to make or mar, they wade across the horizons of the ugly moment and give the future a beautiful image—a future in which Pakistan is a formidable fortress of the millat of Islam, serving oppressed mankind everywhere, never relenting until it has liquidated the last vestige of aggression in Kashmir and liberated Baitul Maqaddas'.

On 7 February, after the prosecution had completed its argument, ZAB suddenly requested that he be allowed to withdraw his Writ Petition. Simultaneously, he issued a notice that unless the government lifts the emergency within one week, he will go on a fast unto death. He explained the reason for withdrawing his Writ Petition. Asserting that he was ready to sacrifice his life to save the rights of the awam, he declared, 'As a protest, I asked to withdraw my Writ and announce that if the emergency is not lifted in a week, I will fast unto death.'

In an unexpected move, the court responded by ordering ZAB to proceed to Larkana and remain there under house arrest. The reason for this turnaround can be read into what ZAB calls the 'regime's dread of the people'. It was a dread both ways—ZAB in prison meant mass protest and ZAB's freedom meant mass rejection of the regime.

The account of his journey on Khyber Mail from Kot Lakhpat station Lahore to Larkana is given in detail in Nadvi's political biography of ZAB. On 11 February, Bhutto was sent from Lahore to Rohri and by special train further, from Rohri to Larkana. Mustafa Khar accompanied him. He had travelled many times on trains, but this was the first time he was travelling as a prisoner. A huge crowd waited wherever the train stopped. At the Multan camp, the station resounded with sounds of 'Bhutto Zindabad' but being under arrest, he could not come out of the compartment to greet the crowds. At Rohri station, where he reached at dead of night, he was transferred to a special train, which took him home to Al-Murtuza. The crowds knew that they would only catch a glimpse of him since he was now under house arrest. Nonetheless, they came in hordes all day and stood outside the gates chanting 'Bhutto jiye hazaron saal'.

At the end of the day, Abdul Waheed Katpar, Chair of PPP Sindh, announced that Mustafa Khar, Mumtaz Bhutto, Chakar Ali Janjui, Nisar Mohammad Khan, and himself, all would fast unto death alongwith ZAB and thousands across the country would follow. Media reported that Mubashir Hasan and Hayat Sherpao from Lahore and Peshawar respectively would join the fast followed by Mir Rasool Bakhsh Talpur.

At the time when Larkana was resounding with cries of 'Bhutto jiye hazaron saal', the special bench of Lahore High Court gave its judgment. It accepted ZAB's request to withdraw his petition. But in public interest, it condemned the government for the inhuman treatment meted out to ZAB in Sahiwal and Mianwali jails. The court condemned Ministry of Interior via its Joint Secretary for giving false evidence. Both the ministries of Justice and Interior were grilled by the Bench. The situation was further aggravated by the announcement of fast unto death. The fast was therefore less than four hours old when the government announced ZAB's freedom and the freedom of all those who had been arrested across the country under Defence of Pakistan Rules. Nervousness of the regime had reached a breaking point.

As soon as the announcement was made, people were overjoyed. Inside Al-Murtuza, ZAB was lying down observing the fast when he got the news. He came outside and spoke to the massive gathering which surrounded his house, 'The government has decided to release me. This was exactly as expected. But my fast unto death was not for my freedom. My fast was for lifting of the martial law.'

The delirious crowd then rushed inside the haveli. Lifting him on their shoulders, they took him to the national stadium where he made a resounding speech in which he stated that the government's offer of talks is futile; talks will never be successful unless he from West Pakistan and Mujibur Rahman from East Pakistan are included.

He trashed the regime's offer to dialogue with political leaders while showering common people with their bullets: 'It is a strange logic of the government that on the one hand, it is trying to create dialogue with political representatives and on the other, guns are being fired in parts of the country. This is exactly like the "ceasefire" in Vietnam while bullets are raining. The country is still operating under Black Laws and oppression of every kind exists. Tongues have been silenced. When atmosphere for talks is blocked, any dialogue becomes impossible.'

The essence of his speech was his disdain for being invited by the government for the round table discussions. His main thrust was that the people have to taste freedom, and this time he promised that they would. He said he could envision the change; the awakening was universal and they would now fight for their rights. Newspaper *Jang* in Lahore and *Dawn* in Karachi reported this stunning speech.

When ZAB was urging this mammoth gathering to reclaim its rights, a story was being filed from Rawalpindi by the correspondent of *Dawn* Karachi. It was President Ayub announcing that from 17 February 1969, martial law would be lifted and basic democratic rights of citizens would be restored.

On 17 February 1969 PPP was fourteen and a half months old. This was exactly the amount of time it took ZAB to demolish the military rule and liberate the people. The next day, when he started his journey from Larkana station, it was 2 a.m. on 18 February. A huge crowd raised the slogan 'zalimo javab do, khoon ka hisab do' (Oppressors, give the answers and accountability for the bloodshed). At Kotri station, the crowds were from all sections, but mostly cultivators and haris. Media described how his voice was choked with tears at the devotion of the masses. The train moved on to Jhamb Pir, Jung Shahi, Dhabchi and finally reached the Karachi cantonment. Everywhere the crowds were unprecedented.

From the station they took him on their shoulders to a beautifully decorated truck which headed for the Mazar of Quaid-e-Azam. Standing on this truck he sometimes joined his wrists as if bound in chains, and then yanked them apart to signify breaking of chains. With him in the truck were Mir Rasool Bakhsh, Talpur and Mustafa Khar. At the Mazar, he addressed the crowd for 15 minutes. The essence of his speech was to promise that whatever he did from that day on, would be with the permission and concurrence of people of Pakistan. By people he did not mean the landlords, the capitalists, the propertied, government servants and industrialists. What he meant were the cultivators, the labourers and students. He reiterated the principle of his party: Islam. 'We created the country on the basis of Islam because we want to live as Muslims and die as Muslims, it is equally our duty to struggle for 50 lakhs Muslims in Kashmir and freedom of Baitul Maqqadas from Israel.'

The plan was to take him from Jinnah's Mazaar to Liaqatabad, but it had become late so he could not go. Meanwhile, in Liaqatabad, the government's goondas indulged in loot and arson leading to injury of innocent citizens.

The invitation from Ayub Khan was waiting for a round table conference. ZAB laid down ten basic conditions for attending the conference:[65]

1. Government should lift restrictions on the Press.

---

[65]*Zulfikar Ali Bhutto Sayasi Sawaneh Hayat* (Vol-I), Rasheed Akhtar Nadvi, 1974, Islamabad: Idaara Ma'araf-e-Milli, p 667.

2. Having admitted the need to address problems of the underdeveloped areas, the President should consult opposition parties of those regions on the same.

3. In addressing complaints of the students, their representatives should be taken into confidence; no law should be made without including them.

4. Immediate release of political prisoners, labourers, leaders and students.

5. Government should announce compensation for families of those who have been killed by State forces and compensate those who have been injured.

6. Inquiry by a High Court judge or any high official on the atrocities and desecration of mosques by government servants.

7. High Court judge to investigate the causes of the 7 November firing in Rawalpindi and Naushera which led to this atrocity.

8. Political Party Act should be struck down and none but small landowners be allowed to sell public land.

9. Restrictions on trade unions' right to strike be lifted and negotiations should start with labour leaders.

Finally the momentous point,

10. Agartala Conspiracy Case[66] against Sheikh Mujibur Rahman be dropped forthwith.

For ZAB, the conference was of secondary importance. His priority was to visit Sheikh Mujib and Maulana Bhashani in Dacca to reach an understanding. He travelled to Dacca where to a press query he declared that if East Pakistan nominates its

---

[66]The Agartala Conspiracy Case, named after its venue, Agartala, was about the alleged conspiracy of East Pakistan leaders with India against West Pakistan for which Mujibur Rahman and other leaders, including some military personnel, were brought to trial in 1967.

own candidate for President he will abdicate in his favour.

Then he launched his extensive tour; criss-crossing the country. From Karachi, he went to Dera Ismail Khan (DI Khan), district of NWFP. Then to Kulachi, where thousands awaited him; with tears in his eyes he saw the wretched condition of the farmers and cultivators. He turned to his friend Haq Nawaz Gandapur who had accompanied him and asked him to bear witness. 'When PPP comes into power,' he thundered, 'your miseries will end; I promise you will get insaaf, you will get livelihood, you will benefit from Islamic socialism.' At Tank, he was similarly welcomed. When he returned to base that evening, he addressed a gathering of PPP workers and spoke for the first time in public about the notorious Tashkent Agreement. In September 1968, when Ayub was on a tour of US, the media there had cornered him and questioned him on breaking the promise he had made to the US President by sending Zulfikar Ali Bhutto to the UN. Then he revealed to his party workers that when the Security Council was going to discuss Pakistan-India war, Ayub wanted to send S.M. Zafar instead of him, his own Foreign Minister. Why? Because US President had asked him to drop the idea of sending ZAB. In Tashkent, when Ayub Khan tried to persuade Shastri to first resolve Kashmir, Shastri said to Ayub Khan, 'My country did not give me mandate to talk about resolving Kashmir, so I will not speak about it.' So ZAB turned to Ayub Khan and asked him to do the exact opposite, raise the issue of Kashmir because 'your people have also not given you the mandate to kill it'. He then added, 'Ayub Khan scolded me and said, "I know better than you." But I insisted that he was thwarting the will of people of Pakistan. At this point he threatened me, "If you interfere in my decision, I will ruin you."'

'Despite this threat,' ZAB told his workers 'I declared war against Ayub Khan.'

5

Letters from Prison

Among many letters ZAB would have written, I had access to 17 letters, which he wrote from time to time, most of them to Mubashir Hasan. The most important ones were from Sahiwal. Numerous sheets of neat handwritten letters from there are hallmark of this period. The letters he wrote to Mubashir Hasan were neat and precise, every line ran straight from left to right. Sitting on his bunk in a dim-lit cell, his pen moved effortlessly on the page. Literature abounds in letters written from prison. Political prisoners have written the best prose in their solitary confinement. Jawaharlal Nehru's best writing emanated from prison. Maulana Abul Kalam Azad wrote the best epistolary Urdu prose from Ahmednagar prison. At the time they wrote letters, there was no thought of sharing them with the world. In both cases, they reached the world through careful collectors and archivists who saw their value for future generations.

ZAB's letters are filled with directions, disappointments and blame. 'The party cannot be run by telephone calls between Rahim and you from Karachi to Lahore,' he writes. 'It requires regular meetings and consultations. A crisis cannot be faced in this fashion. Rifts have increased and even people like Chaudhry

Mohammad Ali[67] have begun to attack us openly. He is too timid a person to attack a strong opposition party in the midst of a crisis unless he thinks it is safe. He would never have dared to do it if I were not in jail and you people had saved the party from dissension.'

Temptation to produce the content verbatim had to be overcome in favour of arranging the contents subject wise. They were written between November 1968 and early 1969; the period is significant because while he was in prison his popularity graph was rising everyday while contrary political forces were hard at work to discredit him in every way. The tiger was inside the cage caught in a paroxysm of emotions, some of which found expression in letters secretly sent to his comrades.

'Feudal and the Bottle'

It was several weeks after all PPP stalwarts, except ZAB, had been released.[68] A man arrived at Mubashir Hasan's house and said, 'I have come from Sahiwal with a message. He has asked for a bottle.' They all knew the meaning of 'a bottle'. But no one knew this man, they were suspicious of this being a sarkari trap to mix poison in the drink; so the man was sternly asked to leave. Mubashir, Mumtaz and Mustafa confided their suspicion to one another. The man returned with the same message three times, the last time, he carried the boss's handwritten letter. One of the lines made the three friends wince—'No one understands me except Mustafa.' So the 'bottle' was sent by special arrangement through their comrade Rao Sattar[69], a lawyer and a small landlord from Mewat. In his letter dated 4 December 1968, ZAB cautions Rao Sattar against arousing slightest suspicion that letters were being

---

[67]One of the Pakistan Democratic Movement leaders.

[68]By end of December 1968 most of the arrested PPP leaders were released.

[69]Later when PPP came into office, Sattar was appointed Senator.

smuggled from jail. 'There should be no suspicion. It is our duty to protect him (informer).'

When ZAB was released, the three M's[70] asked him how he was able to make the man do this high-risk work. The boss smiled. 'When I reached the cell, I threw a 100-rupee note on the floor and asked him to pick it up. He crawled to grab it. From then onwards, he became my slave and mole.'

It was not until much later that the real story of the mole was discovered. After forming the government, Mustafa Khar, acutely suspicious, summoned this man who was later discovered to be an Intelligence Agent. 'What was your game?' He spat the words at him. He could see these words had terrified him to the core. He cried, crawled and squealed, in a bid to save his life. 'Sir I had the Superintendent Jail's permission for all my trips back and forth. They all were intelligence agents making fools of Bhutto Sahib and all of you, his closest friends.' It was later proved that whatever the man carried back and forth was with the General's personal permission.

Tragedy of the trusting feudal was evident so early in the game. His 100-rupee note never worked. His misplaced trust in the coterie headed by Zia also did not work. He was duped to death when he thought he would outwit them all! It was he who was ultimately tricked; yanked out of life itself.

Blaming 'President's Men'

News used to trickle inside his cell, sometimes out of context, which made ZAB very tense and unhappy. He blamed his men · outside who were unable to take control and often made mistakes at his cost. One such incident was the Party announcing his candidature for President in the forthcoming presidential elections against Ayub Khan under the hated Basic Democracy (BD)

---

[70]Mustafa Khar, Mumtaz Bhutto and Mubashir Hasan.

system[71]. Mubashir Hasan recollected the circumstances behind this announcement; its aftermath is recorded in letters ZAB wrote during his confinement.

Rahim told his colleagues, 'I am very worried about his life. Ayub has announced election. I want to announce that he will be the candidate for President.' Rahim was afraid that Ayub Khan could harm ZAB. To save him, Rahim wanted to place him on the highest rung. Nothing could be safer than pitching him as a rival to Ayub Khan. Even the President will be afraid of touching him once he is placed on that pinnacle. The risk was that this could be viewed as betrayal of the boycott decision of the opposition parties in protest against the laws Ayub Khan had proclaimed for elections. Rahim convinced his colleagues that, to save ZAB, this would have to be done.

ZAB's friend, the lawyer, Abdul Wahid Katpar went to meet him in Sahiwal jail. He had been deputed to take his permission to announce his candidature. 'When he returned he was jubilant and told us in a dramatic way that ZAB had agreed,' Mubashir Hasan said. The next day Rahim held a press conference to announce that ZAB will be the Party's presidential candidate. In his speech before Bar Association Lahore on 28 December 1968, Rahim spoke as acting Chair of the party, 'There is no doubt that the events of the last two months—especially what has been happening since the arrest of ZAB on 13 November 1968—manifest the resolve of the people of Pakistan to end the regime that came to power with the

---

[71]An indirect system of democracy used by Ayub Khan to strengthen and legitimize his presidency 'democratically'. It was a four-tiered arrangement with 80,000 primary units, half each from East and West Pakistan, to be elected at the grass roots level. Ayub's nominated Cabinet resolved that a vote of confidence in the President be held among these 80,000 members by way of a referendum and, if the majority were in the affirmative, 'he should also be deemed to have been elected President of Pakistan for the first term of office under the Constitution to be so made'.

promulgation of martial law in 1958. The political movement in which the whole population of the country is participating today is a veritable referendum. The PPP is convinced that ZAB, who possesses preeminently the necessary qualities of a great leader is in fact the people's choice, being the acknowledged champion of their rights and enjoying the enthusiastic loyalty and affection of all classes of population. We consider that the moment has arrived when it would be wrong to make people wait any longer.'

'The honor has fallen to my lot as the acting Chairman of PPP, to announce today that the party presents to the judgment of the people of Pakistan the candidature of Mr Zulfikar Ali Bhutto to the Presidentship of Pakistan. Bhutto zindabad. Pakistan zindabad.'

Suddenly, opposition vultures descended. Adverse press reaction ensued. Political parties attacked him saying that he was taking part in an indirect election. Holding the method undemocratic, they criticized the decision as tantamount to accepting the Basic Democracy system. 'It is betrayal of people!' they claimed. Inside the jail, ZAB was furious.

'Why did Rahim do this?'

'You had agreed,' they tried to argue.

'No. I gave no permission'.

The triumph on Katpar's face when he spoke the words 'he has agreed' flashed before the three pairs of eyes. But there was nothing left for them to say after that.

From prison, ZAB wrote a scathing letter blaming his colleagues for messing up at the cost of discrediting him and the party. He overlooked the fact that he had agreed; perhaps he thought that they could have been more cautious:

'There might have been very good reasons for announcing my candidature and I can see some of these reasons even from jail, but I should have been properly consulted. If I could write to you on so many important matters, why could you not use the same source to contact me on this most important decision and given your reasons for it in order to obtain my consent? It could have been fair to me and it would not have caused the complications which have arisen. You should not forget that at Hyderabad I made a specific declaration about the election. Your decision, whatever the reason, has given the opposition cause to attack me for breaking my word. The procedure adopted was wrong and if I may say so, immoral. Not even an effort or a show was made to consult others like Nuruzzaman[72] in East Pakistan. Please do not forget that procedure is as important as substance in such matters. Now that the decision was taken in a wrong fashion it is being exploited by the opposition and the government. Within the Party, the agent provocateurs and government agents have found a cause for a rift. They must be handled firmly.

'What makes Rahim think that Ayub Khan is going to abdicate and invite him to form a national coalition government? We must sound credible. My directions have been violated once before. This is the second instance.'[73]

He continues in the same tone: 'Press conferences have become very fashionable. A few days of mysterious silence would not have harmed our interests. You have a perfectly good and moral alibi. Your line should be that you can say nothing until your leader is released. PPP should now concentrate on my release only, not because I want to come out of jail but because unless I am out of jail the crisis cannot be resolved and the party held together.'

This part of the correspondence is remarkable for its candour and bluntness. It is indicative of the deep trust and camaraderie which is confident of being understood and accepted in the right spirit. No posturing or formal niceties exist between him and his core group.

---

[72]Nuruzzaman was PPP President in East Pakistan.
[73]ZAB's letter to Mubashir Hasan, which is with the author.

In the next reference to this, in another undated letter, he mellows and presents a strategy to turn this very 'harmful' announcement to an advantage for the party.

'Although I was not consulted, the decision about the elections has advantages and disadvantages. The main disadvantage is that it has divided the opposition and confused the people. It has contradicted my Hyderabad Declaration and affected the movement. The advantage can be that it has given PPP an initiative, which if not properly utilized can damage us, but if properly utilized, it can place us in a commanding position. The decision prevented the Pakistan Democratic Movement (PDM) from cheating us. They tried to capture the movement which we started and also the future laurels. The decision had the advantage of exploiting my detention to our benefit. The fact that it was made by the Party while I was in jail, gives us the freedom for an honourable compromise which we can bargain to our advantage. Without at all giving the impression that we are going back on the decision, our statements should also be so worded so as not to give the impression of being irrevocably final—neither going back nor that it is unalterably final. This will give us the necessary flexibility for striking a favourable bargain and make the negotiations credible. If we give the impression that we have made the announcement for ulterior purposes, we will strike a bad bargain and suffer in reputation. In other words the Party's decision is final subject to my approval'.

Analyzing the convergence between two ostensibly opposite concepts—boycott and contest, he says, 'You know all the reasons for contesting the elections. It is a better decision than boycott. But let Ayub Khan be under pressure from both sides—participation and boycott. The opposition unity can come from both pressures because basically there is no contradiction between boycott and participation if the object is to remove the regime. The regime can be removed by elections and by a boycott which launches a movement. Both streams can combine to intensify the movement. The movement gathers momentum when a date and a target are set for its realization. The pinpointing comes better with election objective. Without an election how can a movement last, especially if it is to be peaceful? And how can a peaceful movement overthrow a dictatorship? If elections are boycotted because they are undemocratic, how can the movement be democratic and legal and yet achieve its objective? The movement can only succeed if it becomes violent and illegal. The PDM has boycotted the election because they are illegal. Then how can it support an illegal movement? How can it defy 144, and if it does not defy 144 how can it create a movement to dislodge the regime? This is the basic contradiction in the boycott of the election and in a peaceful movement. Do we have the resources, the army, the press, and the tradition to launch a serious and a successful movement for an indefinite period?'

His extraordinary ability to justify the most contradicting proposition is evident from the above argument. Boycott and participation are two sides of the same coin, if the objective is to remove the regime.

He then expresses his apprehension that public will become fed up and begin blaming the opposition, thereby giving oxygen to the dying military regime. So it is advisable to let Ayub Khan remain pressured from both sides. The formula he gives is for the two streams, election and boycott, to merge at an agreed point into a movement for democracy. 'There is no contradiction between election decision and boycott. Both were ways of confronting the regime. Election to change the regime, boycott to get concessions.'

When he takes a third look at the sequence of events, he swings across to declare that it was a good idea after all. 'Events are proving that our decision was correct. The movement was not contingent on our decision to contest or boycott. It confirmed both decisions for the simple reason that both decisions challenged the government. The regime was hemmed in from both sides.' Mubashir Hasan sees in these letters ZAB's moods swing from extreme unhappiness to grudging acceptance. He found himself in a lonely role of single-handedly analyzing and resolving the contradictions between boycotting and taking part. My own sense is that he did not want elections to be boycotted. He used the phrase that when a gladiator has to come in the ring he must fight. One can't be a gladiator and not fight. This view was opposed both by right and left wing who believed in boycott as an effective weapon against Ayub Khan. Non-participation, they said, would show the hollowness of the election process.

People and Politics: Instructions from Jail

While ZAB was in Jail, Mubashir Hasan kept sending him notes/ reports on the current political developments. Against each of these typewritten paras, ZAB made comments in his beautiful tiny handwriting in the form of marginal notes. I had access to one such document written on several foolscap sheets. In the top margin he wrote, 'All important points have been dealt marginally. Please see overleaf for separate instructions.' The note was marked to Mubashir, Mumtaz, Mustafa, Hayat, wife and Rahim.

Two uppermost concerns of ZAB and his team were opposition strategies and the party's own position on all matters. Therefore, Mubashir Hasan reported that on 16 December 1968, PDM leaders (Miyan Tufail Mohammad, Chaudhry Mohammad Ali, Miyan Mumtaz Daultana) addressed a press conference at Karachi to announce that in January an East Pakistani will be nominated for President at Dacca. Tufail, acting chief of the Jamaat-e-Islami (JI), condemned PPP with 'words which were manifestly pointed at us.' ZAB's marginal instruction read: 'Let his (Tufail's) speech be exploited fully. How can there be unity when Jamaat-e-Islami prefers government (Ayub Khan) to socialists? Onus of disunity is entirely on them.'

Mubashir Hasan further reported to ZAB that on 19 December, Mustafa Khar and he had a confidential talk with Air Marshall Asghar Khan[74]. They told him that by announcing or by not contradicting the announcement attributed to him (that an East Pakistani will be the opposition candidate) he had damaged the cause of the party. As a result of the discussions he was made to agree that he would on that day announce that the choice of the candidate should be in three stages. First, decision to take part in elections, second, agreement on platform, and third, choice of a national candidate. He was told that in the circumstances then prevailing (i.e. Bhashani's[75] six points), PPP would not attend the conference. Asghar Khan stated that he would not go to Dacca either.

ZAB's comment on this was that PPP should retain Asghar Khan's cooperation. He asked them to tell him that nothing can happen without PPP's cooperation. He should be made to realize the party's strength and appreciate that politics was more complicated than mere wishes for unity. ZAB feared that Asghar was getting more and more exploited by old reactionary politicians and Ulema. In the long run this would damage his image with the people as well as with the armed forces. 'The armed forces hate the old politicians. He is not a member of PDM and yet he has endorsed its Dacca decision about boycott and says that he is morally bound by it. How is he morally bound by it?' ZAB instructed his colleagues to meet Asghar Khan for a serious heart to heart talk and to keep him on their side. If this was not possible they should keep him in the middle, and not with PDM. Asghar

---

[74]Asghar Khan, Air Marshal (retd), was a Kashmiri who gained popularity among the masses by supporting ZAB. The longer ZAB was detained, the more time Asghar Khan got to get popular. This resulted in Asghar Khan's dreaming of himself replacing ZAB.

[75]Abdul Hamid Khan Bhashani was a Mullah turned communist. He was very popular among the people of East Pakistan.

had come into politics and remained independent to keep in the middle like a bridge. He was not doing that by his statements or by his associations.

Mubashir Hasan then wrote that 20 days earlier Maulana Bhashani had told Rahim of the government's plan and of the possibility of negotiation with Ayub Khan. On the morning after Qasuri's dinner and Rahim's meeting with Nawabzada Nasrullah Khan[76], the announcement was made. Every party member mentioned earlier wholeheartedly supported it. No one had any other suggestion.

ZAB commented that Ayub Khan would gain more from this than from compromise with PDM. 'When it comes to the survival of a dictator, he can make economic concessions more rashly than political concessions. For the latter he uses power, in the former he has to improve the social conditions. Only a fool like Ayub Khan and his advisers will not understand this.'

Mubashir Hasan's next point was that Qasuri reacted most violently as if he had been hurt personally. Chaudhry Mohammad Ali, Qasuri, Tufail, Abdul Salam (Pro-PDM Awami League) came out strongly against the announcement of ZAB as presidential candidate. *Pakistan Observer, Pakistan Times, Nawa-i-Waqt* and *Awaz* wrote editorials against it in varying degrees of disapproval. Among the second string leaders, Suleimani MNA, Mahbubuzaman, Aijazuddin, Faqui spoke. Nurulamin, Morshed and Daultana (right wing) also spoke.

ZAB commented that they had given Qasuri good reason. 'You kept him in the dark and went to the other extreme by giving him contrary impression. Confidence is lost and not gained by such behaviour.'

Mubashir Hasan wrote that the above were the only adverse

---

[76]He was the opposition leader and the convener of the Democratic Action Committee (DAC), an eight party opposition alliance.

reactions. All these happened in an atmosphere of great hope for the coming monolithic solidarity of the opposition in an unreal atmosphere. ZAB's comment on this was 'why should you rejoice over throwing a cat among the pigeons?'

The note continues that deliberations began on the 2nd and Mubashir Hasan reached Dacca on the same day. The entire East Pakistan recognized in one voice that the credit of the movement in the west went to PPP. *Holiday* wrote that due to Rahim's announcement, yet another 'Palace intrigue' was averted. As a result of the announcement, Bhashani and Mujib's group (hereafter referred as Awami League) were invited to attend PDM talks. Both refused. NAP (Qasuri) also balked.

A new plan was chalked out. Qasuri played host to informal talks for unity of movement where PDM, Awami League and Ulema were invited. Awami League had an opportunity for revenge. (They disclosed this in a series of meetings with Mubashir and PPP workers). 'These despicable leaders, Nawabzada, Mohammad Ali, Daultana etc. must be humbled,' ZAB wrote.

He further commented that they (rightists) hate Mujib's sight, they hate his own sight and they must be taught a lesson. 'I and Mujibur Rahman are the only two who matter and the only two who created the conditions for them to become "Bade Sahibs" again. I wish only if Mujib realized how important it was for him to unite with me. Everything will be solved if this happens.'

In this context, it may be recalled here that two months before his imprisonment when ZAB had visited Dacca on 31 August 1968, he released a press statement about the importance of giving genuine autonomy to the people of East Pakistan. This statement was distorted by the press. ZAB's Statement,[77] dated 1 September 1968, was issued to counter that distortion.

---

[77] Handwritten copy of the statement was part of Mubashir Hasan archives. The writing on Pale blue paper was ZAB's and at the end were a few handwritten lines by Mubashir Hasan.

'A part of the Pakistan Press International (PPI) report on Mr Zulfikar Ali Bhutto's press conference in Dacca on 31 August 1968 is tendencious and false. It is aimed at creating confusion and misunderstanding by attributing words to him which he did not utter. Mr Bhutto said that the demand of people of East Pakistan for autonomy was universal and that the geographical composition of the country had made it inescapable. For this reason it was essential to concede genuine autonomy to East Pakistan, otherwise national unity would be seriously endangered.'

Handwritten by Mubashir Hasan, the following was appended at the end of the page.

'This false reporting is part of the government campaign to mislead the people about the party and its chairman. In this connection, the press is being given fictitious names of people who are claiming to have left the party to join another party. The names that have been announced do not belong to PPP.'

Mubashir Hasan makes the next point. They (Awami League) became the 'controllers' and said that these people would have to come to Mujib's house and sign the document. PDM swallowed all that was thrust down its throat and Awami League interpreted this as even swallowing of the six points. Bhashani never turned up. Conference scheduled for three days dragged on for six full days. From active aggressive boycott, PDM climbed down to mere 'non-participation'. All parties except perhaps Awami League had strong opposition within it for contesting elections.

ZAB's response to Mubashir Hasan's point was to call it an 'empty victory' for Awami League. 'Only upstarts would be happy. Awami League's interpretation is wrong that PDM has swallowed six points. Opposite is more correct. Six points have been weakened and that is good. It should now make it easier for us to negotiate with Awami League over head of PDM.'

Within the PDM, Mubashir Hasan wrote that M. Anwer

(lawyer), Malik Ghulam Jilani[78], and Nawabzada Nasrullah attacked PPP violently. Daultana opposed PPP firmly but politely. This report evoked an angry response. He was appalled that not only Jilani but the 'despicable' Rafique of Awami League of West Pakistan attacked him violently in the past and again on 10 January. 'He attacked me violently and called me a "raw hand", the Daultana line. I think my family should shift from Jilani's house without making a scene. It would cause unnecessary confusion'.

Mubashir Hasan then wrote that had Qasuri wanted, PPP would have been present at the Unity of Movement talks (Awami League and Jamiatul Ulema were already in favour). He (Qasuri) did not play fair. All the time he demanded the withdrawal of candidature. ZAB retorted, 'You also gave him unnecessary provocation, but never mind. If we play our cards properly we will still gain but… if we play our cards properly.'

Mubashir Hasan continues, 'But for Aslam Hayat[79], the announcement has been hailed by the party everywhere. As days passed it became firmer and firmer conviction of the writer (Mubashir Hasan) that the decision was correct. ZAB replied, "He (Hayat) behaved like a coward in jail. His statement has caused damage. He is a very small man."'

Mubashir Hasan continued 'Awami League promised that it is prepared to enter into bilateral agreement with PPP. ZAB wrote in the margin that he was all for it. Mubashir Hasan then wrote that *Holiday* group recommended that Bhashani will also do the same. PPP realizes that its strength is its movement for which no

---

[78] A businessman who was given a government land to breed horses, Ghulam Jilani had a rich, large and very hospitable home in Lahore. At the time Begum Nusrat Bhutto was staying there.

[79] Hayat was President of Lahore District Bar Association. For the PPP convention in Lahore in 1967, he looked most suitable to ZAB to chair the organizing committee. However, Mubashir Hasan feels that Hayat did not prove strong enough to face government's opposition.

effort is being spared to the best of (our) ability. ZAB again wrote, "Alright but watch him (Bhashani), once bitten twice shy. Awami League, PPP and Bhashani alliance is ideal. Next, Awami League and PPP alliance but not on the basis of six points. Next, PPP and Bhashani. He asked Mubashir Hasan to informally associate Kaiser Rashid[80] with all the negotiations in East Pakistan since he knows the province well and has good judgment. "Keep *Holiday* happy.'"

Mubashir Hasan wrote that Awami League claims that PDM had swallowed six points. ZAB wrote in the margin that it was not a correct claim. 'As I have said, the opposite is correct.'

Mubashir Hasan wrote, 'Asghar Khan who appeared at Dacca (contrary to his promise) gave a statement to the press or was wrongly reported, against his private statement. ZAB commented that he had dealt with as point No. 2. 'He should be on our side, but if that is not possible he should not (be allowed to) become a tool of the reactionaries, a direction in which he is moving.'

ZAB's complaints about party leaders are then directed to Mubashir Hasan. He writes that in each case they are not delivering the results he expects from them. 'Literature is not being promoted. This is most disappointing. What about funds? Mohammad Ameen[81] etc? You must assert on this vital point.'

He expresses his disappointment that despite knowing Majid Nizami[82], Mubashir Hasan was doing nothing about *Nawa-i-Waqt*. He feels they have the trump card but are not using it for some reason. Majid Nizami, he says should be spoken to and be

---

[80]Foreign Service, aristocratic family of East Pakistan and a friend of ZAB. He resigned and lived as a Dacca elite.

[81]Ameen, a crorepati and the biggest exporter of cotton, owned Crescent Group of Industries. Mohammad Bashir was his brother. Since he was Mubashir Hasan's friend, Bhutto wanted them tapped for funds but Mubashir Hasan refused knowing their right wing leanings.

[82]Majid Nizami was a hardcore reactionary. 'How could ZAB expect him to support socialist agenda of PPP?' Mubashir Hasan asked.

told that PPP was a nationalist party without which there was no future. Finally, he complains about no reply to any of his letters, 'You should not have taken such a detached attitude.'

The Caged Tiger: Frustrations in Prison

'I have sent exhaustive instructions on political matters to my wife. If these were being followed properly with variations demanded by the situation outside and by new developments, none of you would be in doubt of any matter. I have sent a full blue print and worked on it night and day. Judging from the way my statement before the Court has been prepared, I am sorry to say that the attention that I expected to all these important matters leaves a great deal to be desired. I was most disappointed with the attention given to my statement. I wrote pages and pages on what should be done, what amendment should be made, what gaps should be filled, who should correct it, when I should see the first draft, but all that was in vain. It was related to my liberty and to my country's future, I repeatedly stressed its supreme importance, but despite all that it was handed over to Qasuri[83] and, contrary to my instructions, kept there unattended. Nobody even bothered to find out whether it had been typed or vetted. Qasuri is a very busy man besides he is a politician of another party with deep differences of views with us and yet the most important political statement in my own handwriting was left with him against my expressed wishes.'

ZAB continues to scold them for their carelessness. 'I had said that he should see only the legal draft of the Writ Petition after Rahim had vetted the draft. This was not done. Thank God he was too busy to see it earlier. So many important passages are left out of it. I do not know if Mr Rahim had omitted them or

---

[83]Mubashir Hasan explained that Qasuri was ZAB's legal advisor; but his politics was totally different from theirs, he belonged to a different political party.

there is some other reason. Now, there is no way to check either.' Qasuri's affiliation with ZAB is complex and contradictory. He was his friend and lawyer handling his case at a crucial stage. While ZAB was in prison, he wrote a brilliant Writ Petition running into 68 foolscap pages, which was to be submitted in the court. As his lawyer, Qasuri was to handle it. It lay in his office without Rahim having vetted it. ZAB's anger at this casual treatment of a matter of life and death erupted in the note.

'In my general discussions on political matters, I had in particular sent important specific instructions for the following: (i) Mr J.A Rahim, (ii) Dr Mubashir Hasan (iii) Mumtaz Ali (iv) Ghulam Mustafa (v) Mohammad Hayat (vi) Ali Ahmed Talpur (vii) Katpar. I hope the instructions have been properly conveyed and complied with.'

'I have no information on the literature of the party—the pamphlet. "Thus Spake the General" is still in cold storage. The Kashmir paper which Mohammad Akmut[84] gave me in Karachi and which I asked Z. Hasan (my typist) to re-type and keep in my office has not been given to Mr Rahim although I had written over six weeks ago to hand it over to him. I gave Safdar Sheikh Rs. 600 for a book on my sayings on Kashmir but nobody has bothered to tell me what has happened. Dr Mubashir was given a cheque on 11 November. Amanullah's book is still not out and yet you want me to be a presidential candidate! I have written repeatedly on these matters but not a word have I had on this or any other matter on which I have written.'

Anger is evident as also his effort to sound reasonable. For example: 'My directions have been violated once before. This is the second instance…If Nusrat does not have time to send me a radio, please get one on credit from a shop and I will settle the account when I see her or come out. Why don't you people put

---

[84]A Kashmiri activist living in New York.

yourself in my place? Events are moving very fast. I am completely without news. I want to know what is happening. For three days, I have been crying hoarse for a radio not because I love one but because I want to be kept informed...'[85]

'Please ask Mubashir to ask my wife to send me a bottle of 'Evian' water which has finished. I need it urgently. Also *Time, Newsweek, Life, Esquire*...all these things I have asked for previously.'[86]

Arrogance, imperiousness, childishness, feudal pride and condescension, underpin the narrative that comes from the mind of a genius; the genius who feels that the others, all very well-intentioned and bright, still don't measure up to his standards.

In his 29 January 1969 letter to Mubashir Hasan, there is frustration born out of helplessness. 'Please tell my wife to send me a good short wave battery radio immediately. She should also send me Rs. 200 and one bottle of my medicine; the one you sent me earlier has been spilled by someone.'

'I want to see either Ghulam Mustafa or Mumtaz. Only they seem to understand my mind. It is a great pity that the opportunity is not being seized properly. It is most frustrating... Sorry for writing so harshly but I have to in your interest and the interest of the party and country.'[87]

The feeling that his colleagues were slackening in their work never left him for a moment. 'You people made the announcement about the election a month ago but have done nothing to explain it to the people. The other parties have taken advantage of this

---

[85]Letter from prison to Mubashir Hasan (date not specified). Copy of the letter is with the author.

[86]Letter dated 4 December 1968 from Sahiwal prison to Rao Sattar, Lawyer of Sahiwal and small landlord from Mewat. He looked after ZAB while he was in Sahiwal Jail.

[87]Letter from prison to Mubashir Hasan (date not specified). Copy of the letter is with the author.

vacuum. Ziauddin Ahmad Suleri[88] has said in today's *Pakistan Times* that the President is going to invite the opposition for discussions. I have predicted this in my article.'[89]

Mubashir Hasan's comment on the above is that Ayub Khan was in constant touch with right wing opposition. Suleri played a double game; he was with political opposition as well as with Ayub Khan.

Then there is yet another reference to the Asghar Khan story that runs throughout the narrative of ZAB and PPP. Mubashir Hasan explained that Asghar Khan had started his career by supporting ZAB and demanding his release from his first imprisonment. The stance that he took attracted a huge following. While he basked in ZAB's popularity, he assumed that the popularity was for him. That is how he first entered politics. ZAB instructed his colleagues that when Asghar Khan toured Sindh, Mumtaz and Katpar should be with him. 'We should maintain our dignity and show our strength in Sindh. Let him see how popular we are everywhere. He should hold a very big and successful meeting in Larkana. Mumtaz Ali should ask him to stay with us. In Hyderabad he should be prevailed to stay in Mir Rasool Talpur's house. He should be well looked after.'[90]

His confidence in Asghar Khan began to wear out when other facts were revealed.

'I saw the report of Asghar Khan and Murshid's speeches to

---

[88]Also known as Z.A. Suleri. He was appointed·as editor of the *Pakistan Times* in 1966. He wrote in support of military governments, capitalism and several articles against PPP during the general elections held in 1970. Subsequently, he was removed by Prime Minister ZAB from the *Pakistan Times* and was thrown in jail after he had penned an article against socialism.

[89]Letter to Mubashir Hasan dated 29 January 1969. Copy of the letter is with the author.

[90]Letter to Rao Sattar from prison. Date not specified. Copy of the letter is with the author

the Sylhet Bar Association. It was rather dogmatic for Asghar to say that the East Pakistan Parties should nominate a presidential candidate and all the parties of West Pakistan will support the nomination. He has given them a "carte blanche". This is not good politics in the first place and secondly he had no authority to make such a blanket statement on behalf of anyone.'[91]

Mubashir Hasan has a store of memories about Asghar Khan which he shared with me. By supporting ZAB and condemning Ayub Khan for putting him in jail, Asghar Khan became popular. Then some 'unimaginable' incidents occurred. Asghar told Mubashir Hasan that he had received a letter from ZAB saying that he had made him acting president of PPP while he was in jail. Mubashir Hasan was shocked. He asked ZAB why he had done such a thing. His answer was a single instruction, 'Take that letter back from him.' 'I tried several times to take the letter,' Mubashir Hasan says. 'One day Asghar came to address a meeting at which I was present. I asked him where was that letter? He said, "Yaar, somebody took it out of my pocket." The meeting was at Mai Lado mosque in Lahore and there was a big crowd.' It is possible, Mubashir Hasan averred, that he may have lost something from his pocket. 'But I didn't trust him. Everyone trusted him, except me.'

Run with the Hare and Hunt with the Hounds

Instructions issued from prison show his anxiety not to entirely alienate the right wing parties. Unlike Rahim and to a great extent Mubashir Hasan, ZAB preferred to remain left of centre. His equivocation would later lead to despair, dismantlement and disaster. This piece written from prison was an earlier expression of this tendency.

---

[91]Letter to Mubashir Hasan date not specified. Copy of the letter is with the author.

'The Party must maintain its nationalist and socialist image. It is not a tomb of the Communist Party... You must make up your minds. Do you want to get destroyed by opening two fronts? Can you fight Ayub and the Jamiat at the same time? Have you the strength to survive a two pronged attack? Do you want to make Indonesia out of Pakistan? Please be patient. Do not be impetuous. Do not get provoked. Swallow some bitter pills. Build your strength, unite the left and then think of other battles after the defeat of this regime. Some of the utterances of our leaders are being exploited by the opposition and the government. People are getting the impression that we are "extremist" in a bad sense. This is because we use communist jargon and talk irresponsibly about guerillas. Please remember that Islam is the fount of this state. We are progressive Muslims not reactionaries but we are not communists either. Indiscreet remarks can do us permanent damage. Besides we rarely bother to see before whom we utter them. Our boys should avoid slogans which divide the opposition.'

Rahim would have winced at the phrase 'we are not communists either'. Were these lines of ZAB a wake up call for him, for Mubashir Hasan, for Sheikh Rashid and for Mairaj Mohammad Khan?

ZAB then issues instructions about how his party leaders should deal with Maulana Maudoodi[92]. 'I want Dr Mubashir to meet Maudoodi on my behalf. He should remind him of my meetings with him in Lahore in June or July. At that meeting Maudoodi had said there should be a gentlemen's agreement, that we should not attack each other. I told him that I have never attacked him or his party, and that my Party's first principle is the ideology of Islam. In contrast, his party leaders had repeatedly attacked my party and me. This tirade has continued and even

---

[92]Also known as Abul Ala Maudoodi. He was the founder of the Jamaat-e-Islami. He and his party were generating support for an Islamic state in Pakistan.

increased, leading to slogans and counter slogans and now even clashes have begun. The Maulana should be asked frankly whether he wants to have it out with the party, which is Islamic and socialistic in character, as well as with the communists. He should be told about the Tufail's (JI) remarks in Karachi on 16 December and what he has repeatedly said in private that they would rather have Ayub than have me. How can they reconcile his remarks and action with their demands for unity in opposition? He should be approached in a spirit of confidence, and as an act of statesmanship rather than as if we are frightened or worried. After the meeting, Dr Mubashir should suggest a joint statement calling on followers of both parties to avoid getting exploited by government agents and that there can be no differences over the basic ideology of both parties, which is Islam. If he does not agree to such a joint statement then Dr Mubashir should write a letter to him confirming what transpired in the meeting and that he made a suggestion of a joint statement which he rejected. The letter should also mention his original promise to me about a gentleman's agreement, which his party consistently violated when he was in London. We would then consider whether the letter should be published how and when. This will then throw the others on his party and show them that we are not anti-Islamic, an impression which is wrong but which is gaining currency partly due to the hostile propaganda and partly due to some impossible utterances and elements in our own party.'

In analyzing this directive, Mubashir Hasan said that ZAB was asking for the impossible. He added that Jamaat-e-Islami had many Ayub Khan's men who worked as his secret agents; outwardly they would oppose Ayub Khan but secretly work under his orders. He did not recall following ZAB's directive and going to see Maudoodi; he deliberately ignored this instruction because he wanted no contact with Maudoodi. ZAB could not get Maudoodi on his side perhaps because he did not want to understand the huge chasm between himself and Maudoodi. There were statements of his Secretary General J.A. Rahim who wanted to convert Pakistan into a socialist nation. That was also his own statement at the founding convention that a socialist government was the best possible option for Pakistan since it meant economic and social justice and an end of feudalism and capitalist exploitation. Rahim had ridiculed Maudoodi on many occasions. One such instance was his title 'Abul A'la; A'la is God and Abul means 'father'. Put together, the title means 'Father of God' wrote Rahim. 'Maudoodi had the temerity to give himself this appellation!' The other compelling reason for both Mubashir Hasan and Rahim's aversion was Maudoodi being a sworn enemy of socialism.

From these materials and discussions around them emerges the complex called ZAB. The man wanted to fight Ayub Khan by adopting a Janus[93] posture where he would not be criticized by the left or the right. In his foundation and policy documents, his clear stand was for a socialist Pakistan. This point, however, was worded in a manner that Islam and socialism were not mentioned together in one paragraph. He tried to find a way of becoming the undisputed leader by not criticizing right wing parties such as Muslim League, Nizam-e-Islam of Chaudhry Mohammad Ali, Tonga Party of Nawabzada Nasrullah, and Jamaat-e-Islami of Maudoodi, at the same time upholding all the principles on which PPP was formed.

In undated letter[94] to Mubashir Hasan from Sahiwal prison, he dismisses the thought of a forward bloc in a revolutionary party. 'There cannot be a forward bloc in a revolutionary party. A forward bloc can exist only in a conservative and a reactionary party like Ayub's Muslim League. In a revolutionary party it is

---

[93] An ancient Roman deity, guardian of doorways and gates and protector of the state in time of war. He is usually represented with two faces, so that he looks both forward and backward.

[94] Copy of the undated letter is with the author.

nothing but a counter revolution to create a forward bloc. I would not tolerate counter revolutionary tendency.'

Later on, this very aversion would result in the undoing of Mairaj Mohammad Khan.

'This was an impossible situation,' Mubashir Hasan said, 'Lahore was highly anti right-wing parties. Slogans in the street were 'Sau Yahoodi Ek Maudoodi' (one Maudoodi is equal to 100 enemies of Islam, occupiers of Baitul Muqqadas). Today, Mubashir Hasan speaks with deep conviction when he says that ultimately it was the combined evil of Maudoodi and Ziaul Haq, which killed his leader.

From the prison cell, the instructions came fast.

'I want Mumtaz and Mustafa to meet Daultana.[95] They should tell him that I had always tried to cooperate with him. I have always held him in high esteem. I had never attacked him publicly and privately although they cannot say the same for him. They have not been authorized to raise the past but to tell him that despite Jamaat-e-Islami's hostile attitude I have tried to be most reasonable. Daultana is a prominent leader of People's Democratic Movement and he can exercise influence over Jamiat leaders but we are not asking him to do that. We can deal with the Jamiat Secretary. We understand their reasons but we cannot understand reasons of continuous and regular public attacks of Mohammad Rafigue of Awami League. What ideological quarrel has he with us to keep attacking me bitterly? Yesterday he again attacked me (Pakistan Times[96]). If I have worked with the government for eight years and 'my hands are not clean' has not Asghar Khan worked for government for 10 years and Ayub Khan for four years? Rafigue is a stooge of Ghulam Jilani who is the stooge of Daultana.

---

[95]Mumtaz Daultana is one of the prominent leaders of the Council Muslim League (CML), a faction of the Pakistan Muslim League that divided from the Convention Muslim League.

[96]Pakistan Times, 11 January 1969 (Page no. 11).

Surely Rafigue could have been abetted by Jilani, Nasrullah and Daultana. The fact that he has continued to attack me publicly and with increasing intensity shows that he has their consent. In these circumstances they should not expect my cooperation and the fault for it will be theirs and not mine. Be polite but firm. I am not going to tolerate attacks by pimps like Rafigue and it is shameful for Jilani and Daultana to call themselves my friends under these circumstances.'

Anger builds up even as he writes these lines. He begins in soft tones about Daultana, but at the end, he is almost shouting. Mubashir Hasan made these remarks to show how difficult it was for ZAB to take any criticism. 'He had a gargantuan image of himself, which was above all censure. Daultana was big landlord from Southern Punjab whose ancestors had served Brits most loyally. He was a natural leader of Punjab landlords but in his youth he had developed left leanings; he became a follower of Jinnah and opposed Unionist Government. When Pakistan was created, Jinnah's ML split in two factions—one of Daultana, the other of Nawab of Mamdot. The latter had support of Nawa-i-Waqt and was opposed to Liaquat Ali Khan as PM whereas Daultana was supporting Liaquat. Differences within the League itself of supporting and opposing Liaquat brought out basic contradiction between Punjab and the rest of Pakistan. On one side were Punjabi chauvinists on the other was East Wing with huge numbers who were allied with smaller provinces of West Wing like Balochistan, NWFP, Sindh and Karachi, which was then the federal capital. Daultana had a western education and owned a fine library. Mamdot was a huge estate in Ferozpur, which went to India. Rafigue who I. A. Rehman told me, consistently worked for the opposition, was outspoken and crude with right wing ideology. "He was a Punjabi chauvinist. He was hated by most of us. He met a violent death at the hand of an unknown person after PPP came to power."'

Ruminations in Jail

In his cell, ZAB penned thoughts which reflect his philosophy, evolving in tandem with outside events. 'My views on democracy are clearest. We have said, "Let the people decide." We have suffered because systems have been imposed on people. The Chairman is not a dictator to thrust his views. He believes that people are.'

On this philosophical piece, Mubashir Hasan remarked that the entire social system of Pakistan as of South Asia was based on an oppressor-oppressed relationship. To the burning question, 'Mera peer kaun hai' (who is my leader/guide?) ZAB was selling a new answer. 'Mera peer awam hai' (my leader/guide is the people).

'We are with the people. For 20 years people have been ignored. People cannot be ignored that is why PPP cannot be ignored. Politics is not a pious objective and path to hell is paved with good intentions.'

Having shared his thoughts recollected in solitude with his colleagues through Mubashir Hasan, he goes on to practical matters. First is his worry for the party; he does not trust his team to work according to his expectations:

'I am very worried about the future of the party. I sincerely hope that my apprehensions are ill founded and you are in actual fact gaining in strength… Please work day and night and make others do the same.'[97]

'It (Party) should become hundred times stronger than it was on day of my arrest… The opposition should not present us with a fait accompli… If there is any awkward decision to be made just say leader is in prison.'[98]

'Please work out some procedure to avoid clashes in opposition party's demonstration. Talk to Khurshid Qasuri about this. Now that Hayat Mohammad Khan, yourself, Khar, Mumtaz Ali Bhutto,

---

[97]Letter to Mubashir Hasan (date not specified). Copy of the letter is with the author.
[98]Letter to Rao Sattar (date not specified). Copy of the letter is with the author.

Aslam Hayat, Ahmed Raza Kasuri[99] are out, the party work can pick up again.'

'The constitution of PPP is clear and my orders are that there is to be no meeting of a general body on 15 February or on any other day to rescind or change or overrule any decision that has been taken so far. As for future decisions, please seek my prior approval on any important substantive decision before announcing it. This will avoid conflicts and bickering. Your decisions may be right but none of you have the power to prevent mischief of a deliberate nature; neither do I but in my decision, the scope for mischief will be less, because nobody will dare to challenge it without fully exposing himself.'

Second is his impatience to see party literature printed and disseminated.

'What has happened about our literature? I want plenty of literature, pamphlets, posters etc. Amanullah's book should be published very soon if it has not yet come out. The pamphlet "Thus Spake the General" should have been out in Urdu and English long ago. I want a full report from Mubashir on these and other matters, especially our position among students.'[100]

ZAB was adamant; no matter what students should be kept with the party. Even if the student body was politicized by opposition parties, PPP should gain their confidence. In *Pakistan Times,* on 15 December 1968, he saw a statement signed by six student organizations and by Jamiat-ul-Tulaba which acutely disturbed him. The statement deplored that PPP wanted to 'exploit the student community in order to demonstrate their own strength at the cost of the blood of the students and to construct a castle of their power on the dead bodies of the students... They were only keen to see that the student community is protected as stooges

---

[99]Ahmed Raza Kasuri is one of the early activists of the PPP.
[100]Letter to Rao Sattar. Copy of the letter is with the author.

of Mr Z.A. Bhutto by raising pro-Bhutto slogans.'

The clipping was sent by ZAB from his jail to his colleagues. In the accompanying note he lashes out at his colleagues, blaming them for alienating the students: 'In today's *Pakistan Times* there is an item, which has disturbed me much. I am enclosing the cutting. It might be a Government sponsored move but nevertheless it has been signed by a number of student organization heads including the Jamiat-ul-Tulaba. Under no circumstances must we lose guard among the students. They are our most valuable assets. We must convince them that we are their best friends and that whatever concessions the government is now prepared to make to them is on account of our sacrifices. We must never, repeat never, give them the impression that we are exploiting them as the enclosed statement indicates. The student community is our greatest source of strength and under no circumstance should we lose an inch of ground on this front...'

Mubashir Hasan explained that the Punjab University story was about clashes between PPP student supporters and Jamaat-e-Islami's Jamiat-ul-Tulaba, which was financed by JI as well as Pakistan intelligence. His tirade therefore was excessive.

His jail instructions reflect his meticulous memory, recollection of detail, and worry about personal projection. Under the pressures of prison life, he was restless, uncertain about the future of the party in his absence and anxious to push further, anticipating a tempestuous journey ahead.

'For my case on the 8th, I want as soon as possible the following material in Urdu to prepare my defence:

1. Bertrand Russell's letter to *The Economist* (London) written about me in September 1966.
2. My reply to Musa's[101] Hyderabad speech. It is cyclostyled

---

[101]General (retd) Mohammad Musa Khan was a Hazara Shia. He was governor of NWFP who owed a lot to Ayub Khan and was most loyal to him.

and was released on 25 October 1968.

3. President Mikoyan's tribute to me given during President Ayub's visit to U.S.S.R in April 1964.

4. President Soekarno's tribute to me while conferring the decoration of highest Indonesian award in June 1964. I am not sure if it was in June, but the occasion was the 10th anniversary celebrations of the Bandung conference held in Jakarta in 1964—either June or July. Also from these requirements you will see how important it is to publish Amanullah's book.'[102]

Jail Conditions: Letter to Home Secretary

Conditions in the jail were deplorable. ZAB wrote several letters of complaint. 'This is my fourth application. First to Home Secretary, Government of West Pakistan on 23 November and on 5 December 1968, third to Superintendent Jail Sahiwal on 5 December 1968 and now fourth to Superintendent Jail, Lahore on 16 December 1968.'

'By providing barest essentials to sustain life, you are not in the least treating me according to what my status certifies, according to the precedent followed in the detention of others of my position. The provisions for my food are inadequate and of the poorest quality. Not a single periodical is provided to me...'[103]

He then goes on to complain about being denied letters from family and friends. 'To show you how unabashedly you lie, I am attaching to this application the total mail that has been given to me since my detention...'

Then he threatens, 'I will be constrained to take some steps which will have serious political consequences if you continue

---

[102]Letter to Rao Sattar. Copy of the letter is with the author.

[103]Letter to Home Secretary, Govt of West Pakistan dated 4 December 1968 (Copy of the letter is with the author).

to maltreat me and subject me to psychological and mental discomfiture in violation of my rights and against norms of decency.'

'Permission for fortnightly interview has been denied. The list of people to visit was submitted but not allowed to visit. Solitary confinement is also violation of rules. The post is also withheld. (Gives a list of letters received, which contain nothing from friends, family and staff).'

'The *Pakistan Times* is sent late in the afternoons after repeated enquires for it. *Nawa-i-Waqt* is not provided to me and I am not interested in the one controlled Urdu paper which is sent daily. I have, since my detention, received four letters from persons not known to me personally and four telegrams. Not a single letter has been delivered to me from my family or friends. Your statement is incorrect when it says that 35 letters and 11 telegrams have been delivered to me since my detention.'[104]

The letter was signed

'Zulfikar Ali Bhutto

Hilal-e-Pakistan (If your government has any respect for its own highest award)'

---

[104]Letter to Home Secretary, Government of West Pakistan.

Sir Shahnawaz Bhutto's Family Portrait

With fellow students from UCLA

Bhutto at a Lahore public rally raising his hands to the crowd.
Haneef Ramay seen in the background

Zulfikar, the sword of Hazrat Ali hanging in 70 Clifton

Kutcheri being held in Lahore. ZAB listening to an old petitioner with Haneef Ramay and Sadiq Hussain Qureshi, Chief Minister of Punjab

Right to Left: Sheikh Rashid, Ammanullah, Haneef Ramay, ZAB, Mubashir Hasan, Mustafa Khar

Presidential Cabinet Meeting. Left to Right: Mohammad Haneef Khan, Abdul Hafeez Pirzada, Sheikh Rashid, Justice (Retd) Kundi, Mubashir Hasan, Mahmud Ali Qasuri, J.A. Rahim, Vice President Nurul Amin and ZAB

ZAB with H.H. Sheikh Zayed Bin Sultan Al-Ninyan,
President of UAE and ruler of Abu Dhabi

ZAB with his sons Murtaza and Shahnawaz

Haneef Ramay, Mubashir Hasan, ZAB and Mustafa Khar

Islamic Summit 1974 at Badshahi mosque

Ayub Khan with ZAB and his children

Quran presented by ZAB to his son Murtaza Ali Bhutto

Portrait presented to Mubashir Hasan

Nusrat and ZAB on their China visit

ZAB and Indira Gandhi signing 1972 Shimla Agreement

ZAB and Nusrat's visit to Vatican

ZAB looking at Mubashir Hasan's draft statement at 70 Clifton

ZAB with Muammar Qaddafi of Libya

ZAB and Ziaul Haq: Takht ya Takhta

Taking over power from Yahya Khan. Left to right—J.A. Rahim, Ghulam Isak Khan, ZAB, Yahya Khan

Portrait in Lapiz by Ismail Guljee from private collection of Begum
Ghinwa Bhutto at 70 Clifton, Karachi

70 Clifton, Zulfikar Ali Bhutto's residence

6

The Four P's: Popularity at Peak Price to Pay

Lahore, 1967

At Ichchra's Dongi ground, the crowd was so thick that if you threw a discus, it would glide over a canopy of heads. ZAB appeared on the stage, in a shalwar suit with his sleeve cuffs open as usual. The crowds raised slogans to rent skies, no sound system was needed. 'Mere Doston' (My friends),' he began. 'Jeeyo Bhutto', the man on the left of the stage became delirious. Once again Bhutto thundered, 'Mere Doston'. Then again, and again, and again! The man on the left was by now beside himself, 'Jeeyo Jeeyo Jeeyo.' After the fifth interruption, the speaker turned to his left and looked him straight in the eye. Then, straight into the mike, floated the words, 'O Yaar tu te chup kar' (Hey Dude! Shut up!) Two men, one each from either side, jumped up on stage and threw their arms in the air, 'Hai sadqe jawaan! Tuadi enian adaon te usi marte yaan' (May we be sacrificed for you, these gestures of yours are killing).

And the audience shouted, 'Bhutto, you are our leader. We will act on your slightest gesture. You are our choice.' PPP was founded later in the same year.

Lahore, 1970

A massive gathering had been planned for Mochi Gate. The date fixed was 8 March 1970. Mubashir Hasan, Chairman, PPP Lahore, had obtained permission from the deputy commissioner for the meeting as far back as December 1969. At this time of year, Lahore's tradition was to hold the annual Horse and Cattle show along with all its pageantry. This time the Shah of Iran had accepted the invitation and along him, many foreign dignitaries. In addition, the diplomatic and power elite of Islamabad would be there to witness the spectacle. PPP leadership decided that this occasion was perfect to show ZAB's popularity to diplomats, officials and to the world. It was the best time to hold a meeting in full international gaze. Mochi Gate grounds had always been the most authentic and popular spot for political leaders of all types to demonstrate their popularity.

A general invitation was issued by PPP Chairman, Lahore:

4 K, Gulberg II, Lahore,
22 February 1970

Dear friend,

On behalf of the Pakistan People's Party, Lahore, it is my pleasant duty to invite you to the public meeting to be addressed by Chairman Zulfikar Ali Bhutto at Mochi Gate, Lahore on the afternoon of 8th March, 1970. The Chairman will be addressing the citizens of Lahore after a lapse of a long period and the entire city of Lahore is most enthusiastically and eagerly waiting to hear him. The Party is working hard to arrange a meeting worthy of our Chairman.

The programme of the meeting shall be as follows:

2.45 p.m. Poems by Mr Aslam Gurdaspuri

3.00 p.m. Arrival of the Chairman
3.02 p.m. Recitations from the Holy Quran
3.05 p.m. Chairman's address

Seats will be reserved for guests from outside Lahore. The entry will be by passes and all the guests will be requested to be in their seats by 2.30 p.m.
This is to request you to kindly let me know by return of post if it will be possible for you to visit Lahore and attend the meeting and also how many members from your city will accompany you.

With best wishes.
Yours sincerely,
(Mubashir Hasan)
Chairman Pakistan People's Party, Lahore

That year, since the Shah of Iran plus other foreign dignitaries were expected, the security was tight. Some party workers suggested postponement in case people preferred to go to the show. But once Mubashir Hasan had decided, nothing was to be moved. Knowing that administration would not permit this meeting during the grand show, Hasan took the necessary permission far in advance of the date. No one in Deputy Commissioner's office remembered the Horse and Cattle show, so they gave permission. Announcements of the meeting were posted all over the city, in anticipation that international visitors and press would see them. Party workers' expectations were at a pitch. Word got to Hasan that the DC may serve him a notice of cancellation. The tall lanky stalwart of the party jumped the wall of his Gulberg house to avoid the DC's notice.

Then a series of letters were exchanged. The first one was from DC on the expected lines—asking for cancellation.

Phone no. 53231
No. Reader/ML/42/3823.
Deputy Commissioner's Office,
Dated Lahore 2.3.1970

Dr. Mubashir Hasan
Chairman, Pakistan People's Party
4 K, Gulberg 2, Lahore

Subject: Public Meetings.

My dear Dr Mubashir Hasan,

Reference your letter dated February 4, 1970 in which intimation to hold a meeting on March 8, 1970 as required by the provisions of Martial Law Regulation No. 60 to be addressed by Mr Zulfikar Ali Bhutto, was received in this office.

Due to the visit of His Imperial Majesty, the Shah of Iran and the President of Pakistan to Lahore and other important functions connected with the visits of these V.I.Ps, our entire police force would be committed elsewhere and we may not be in a position to ensure law and order if there is any disturbance. The meeting should not, therefore, be held on March 8, 1970 and it may be shifted to March 9, 1970 or to some other date, which suits your convenience.

The other political parties have also been asked to defer their meetings during the above-mentioned period.

Yours sincerely,
(Iqbal Ahmad Khan Lodhi), PCS.
For Deputy Commissioner, ADC (G) Lahore

Promptly, Mubashir Hasan replied:

4 K Gulberg 2, Lahore
March 3, 1970

To, Mr Masud Mufti, C.S.P, Deputy Commissioner, Lahore

My dear Mr Mufti,
Please refer to your letter No. Reader/ML/42/3823 dated March 2, 1970.

The original intimation to hold the meeting on March 8, 1970 was given to you on January 20, 1970. On February 4, 1970 we merely informed you of the change of venue from the University Grounds to the Mochi Gate Gardens. Thus our intimation to hold the meeting stands duly cleared by you for over 40 days.

The dates for the Horse and Cattle Show, as well as for the arrangements for the visits of the President of Pakistan and His Imperial Majesty Shahenshah of Iran to Lahore must have also been known to you well in advance of your intimation delivered to me on the night of March 2, 1970.

All our preparations for the meeting are complete. The meeting has received widest possible publicity. Guests from both the wings of Pakistan have accepted the invitation to attend the meeting, and some of them have already arrived. Others are on their way. With great difficulty we have been able to arrange accommodation for them. Now, at the very last moment you wish to defer the meeting on the grounds that you may not be in a position to enforce law and order as your entire police force would be committed elsewhere.

During the last two months, since the revival of political activities, the Chairman of PPP, Mr Zulfikar Ali Bhutto, has addressed mammoth public meetings all over West Pakistan and at no place a problem of law and order has arisen. Every meeting has been a tremendous success. The problems you fear arise only in the case of those politicians who do not enjoy public support and affection. This is not true in our case. There is no doubt that the people of Pakistan have given their overwhelming support to Mr Zulfikar Ali Bhutto. They repose their trust and confidence in him and hear him with great enthusiasm and reverence. You can rest assured that, like in all other meetings held so far, in this meeting also there will be no difficulty in maintaining law and order. Moreover, in a metropolis like Lahore, there is enough police available to handle the requirements of administration. Should however a necessity arise, it is an established practice to secure additional police help from adjoining districts and this can be done in this case also. We do not see any reason why it should be necessary to ask for deferment of a function on account of lack of police, particularly when the timing of the function does not clash with any other function. The Horse Show ends before noon and the Tattoo Show does not begin till late evening, whereas our meeting is scheduled for the afternoon and is not in conflict with either engagement.

I would once again reiterate that both the dates of the visit of the President and Shah as well as that of our meeting had been known to you for a long time. Had we been informed earlier considerable expenditure would have been saved and inconvenience to the people avoided. In these circumstances we request you to take into account our difficulty in changing the date of the meeting.

This meeting scheduled for March 8, is a part of our election activities for the purpose of mobilizing public support in favour of Pakistan People's Party. It is therefore essential that this meeting be held as announced. From your letter under reference, it appears that you have only advised us to postpone the public meeting. For the reasons

given by me, we intend to hold the meeting as scheduled.
We will however reconsider this decision only if you pass a
clear order prohibiting it from being held. This is necessary
as otherwise the people will be greatly disappointed and it
will cause a setback to our election campaign.

Yours sincerely,
(Mubashir Hasan)
Chairman Pakistan People's Party
Lahore

Deputy Commissioner Mufti was left with no choice but to allow
them to proceed.

D.O. No. Reader/86.
Dated the March 4, 1970.

To,
Mr. Mubashir Hasan, Chairman Lahore,
Pakistan People's Party, 4 K, Gulberg 2, Lahore.

My dear Mubashir Hasan,
Kindly refer to your D.O. dated the 3rd March, 1970.
The postponement was suggested in order that our entire
administrative machinery could attend to the visit of our
distinguished foreign guests. However, since you seem to have
finalised all the arrangements for holding the meeting the
postponement of which would entail additional expenditure
and inconvenience, you may now hold it as originally
scheduled. Although we shall be making arrangements for
additional police force from outside yet I hope that you
will also adopt every possible means for ensuring peace
and order in the meeting.

With regards,
Yours sincerely,
(Masud Mufti) TQA, CSP

As the day grew close, Mubashir Hasan was apprehensive about the government sabotaging the meeting. He feared that to prevent the meeting, the government would flood the Mochi Gate ground. So he called his faithful carpenter, nicknamed 'Behra Badhai' who, like him, had migrated from Panipat and asked him to block the six-inch-diameter pipe, which was used for watering the Mochi Gate ground. Behra did a superb job by pushing a wooden piece in the mouth of the pipe to block the discharge of water. The plan worked beautifully. As a first for Lahore meetings, it was decided to build a platform for the speaker. Four poles were dug into the ground and a platform was made resting on the poles; thus a small stage was built, enough for a small table and a microphone. No proper stage or dais was built. Total cost was less than Rs 4000, which mainly included the cost for sound system. Rafi Raza writes that this was ZAB's first public meeting at Mochi Gate, a test venue for all leaders, and was reasonably well attended despite rain. He was wearing a Western suit, but in a typically dramatic gesture he threw off the jacket, saying that he wanted to get properly wet like the crowd. He had learnt how to rouse the masses and hold them in rapt attention, which would become one of his major political assets. Although his Urdu was not good, the populace loved the mixed Sindhi-Punjabi-Urdu language that he spoke.[105] The crowd sat on durries, no chairs were provided. An unprecedented crowd of approximately forty thousand came to listen. Not only Mochi Gate, but the wide circular road around the inner city was filled with people. ZAB spoke against Pakistan government's obedience to US and aligning with the left alliance led by USSR. He was full of praise for China. He maintained his plank of confrontation with India on the basis of 'No War No Peace' policy. His speech at the meeting was the culmination of similar speeches he had

---

[105]*Zulfikar Ali Bhutto and Pakistan, 1967-1977*, Rafi Raza, Oxford University Press, p 9.

made in Multan and Khanewal, plus roadside meetings in Okara, Sahiwal and Bhai Peru. In his speech, he extensively quoted Liaqat Ali Khan to support his ideas of Islamic socialism. Speaking in his enthralling and halting prose for three and a half hours; he held his audience spellbound.

The rising popularity of ZAB is explained in Mubashir Hasan's incisive words, 'The problems the establishment fears arise in the case of politicians who do not enjoy people's respect and affection.' In every meeting, ZAB was hailed as saviour and hero. He was the first leader who had given dignity and stature to Pakistan. The populace hung on every word he had spoken before the UN because each argument he presented took Pakistan a notch higher in world acclaim. Had that been a world of global media such as now, the story of ZAB may have veered away from the deadly course it was to take within a short span of eight years.

Two months later, another massive rally was planned. On 8 April 1970, J.A. Rahim had written to Mubashir Hasan about his deep commitment to celebrate May Day. 'However it is done, the main objective of demonstrating the solidarity of workers, peasants and all those who desire a just economic and social order should be kept in view. Please also don't forget that May Day has an international significance, it is the day to extol the memory of heroes who have laid down their lives for fighting imperialism. It is our duty to express our support of those who are today actively engaged in fighting imperialism whether in South East Asia, Africa or Latin America. Very close to our heart is the liberation of Palestine from Zionism, which is not only a Jewish but an American colonial adventure.' Rahim's vision as expressed in his letters and articles extended far beyond his immediate space to other oppressed regions of the world.

For the May Day procession, Mubashir Hasan wrote to all trade unions offering PPP's cooperation in the Juloos on Shahrah-e-Quaid-e-Azam. 'On that day from one end to the other the Shahrah should be swathed in red colour,' he wrote. Organizational matters were left to them. He sensed that the rallyists were reluctant to align themselves to any party. They told him, 'Sir, this is our day.' Mubashir Hasan saw the force and fairness of their argument. How was he to convince them?

When he spoke, his words as usual were gentle and firm. 'You are right. You take the lead. All of you do the "qayadat". The Quaid will follow you.' The point made with conviction and humility won over the crowd of 'jiyalas' of Lahore. A truck was swathed in fabric of resplendent red. At its centre was placed an armchair for the leader. From Mubashir Hasan's sprawling Gulberg house its route was chalked out until Golbagh. The chair was placed so its occupant was hidden from view. When it reached its destination, dramatically a figure rose waving both his hands before a cheering crowd. A lehar could be felt and people became delirious with joy. Media reported that this was the most spectacular May Day ever celebrated in Lahore, before or after. Mall Road was a glow with red banners and flags. The Chinese Communist party actively took part. Banners carried the words 'East is Red', 'The sun will rise from East'. The entire route was awash with red colour.

Despite enormous public support, there were enemies on the prowl, hired by the political opposition to stop ZAB's rising popularility. As they watched the adoring crowds, and his rallies covered by the Urdu and English media, their panic rose. Attempts to hurt him and his party workers have been recorded in letters and files to which I had exclusive access.

J.A. Rahim and Mubashir Hasan were always on the alert. His security was a big headache for all his close associates; Mubashir Hasan always dreaded the possibility that he would be attacked while he moved from one venue to another. With his usual precision, he directed that several alternate routes be chalked out. These routes were communicated to the person who was appointed to escort him to his destination. The final decision on which route to take was left to the escort. Not a single party official except Mubashir Hasan knew from which portion of the qana'at ZAB would appear. First, his car would be driven quietly in an unexpected spot near the outer qana'at of the shamiana. Quietly alighting, he would safely and freely walk towards the inner qana'at. Inside the shamiana, Mubashir Hasan would be watching the clock. Then he would casually call two hefty party workers to a side. He would gently draw them to one special predetermined spot, which was only known to him. Then the words would be whispered. 'He will appear from here; you open the qana'at and shut it immediately, understand?' A few words, a few moments, and there he would be, appearing, waving both hands before an astounded, cheering, delirious crowd.

Mubashir Hasan once asked General Atiqur Rahman, the Governor of Punjab why was it that the police was never there to safeguard ZAB's meetings, although it was present to guard the meetings of all other leaders. 'Well Dr Sahib, your own arrangements are so perfect that my police is not needed.' Mubashir Hasan made sure that there was a bunch of well-built youth to protect ZAB. They would hold four long dandas in a square around ZAB; thus the Chief would walk freely from his car to his meeting ground.

Despite all this caution, it was precisely because of his great popularity that great danger was imminent. Many attempts were made on his life. Despite official effort to play down these murderous intents, his core group ensured media coverage so the public was informed of the aborted attempts of state and non-state forces to finish him off. With every attack, however, his popularity grew.

In a press statement dated 1 April 1970, Mubashir Hasan condemned the murderous attempts made on his life. He likened his political opponents to 'grasshoppers trying to stop a locomotive'.

In December 1969, ZAB had gone on tour to Multan and Bahawalpur Divisions. After the return of Maudoodi (Jamaat-e-Islami) from a meeting of Rabta-i-Islam held in Saudi Arabia, a cold-blooded attack was made on him and his party workers at Sadiqabad. While the President Yahya Khan ordered a probe, one of his ministers Nawabzada Sher Ali Khan, known for his contact with American imperialists and Indian expansionists and as defacto lieutenant of Maudoodi, undertook a tour of Bahawalpur Division.

According to the report in weekly *Nusrat* of 7 December, the success of ZAB's tour unnerved Jamaat-e-Islami. When he was returning from Sadiqabad to Multan, the Jamaat goondas attacked his party with stones, lathis and hockey sticks. Timely action by Mustafa Khar saved ZAB but his young companion Amanullah Khan[106] was badly injured. The weekly journal *Nusrat* which carried the story was edited by the man who would become CM of Punjab later, the artist and littérateur, Mohammad Haneef Ramay. Its cover had a banner headline, 'Naked demonstration of violence of Maudoodiyat at Sadiqabad'. A large photograph of an injured Amanullah with his head in bandages and a smaller cartoon of Maulana Maudoodi in his underwear, holding a danda illustrated the headline. The text read, 'Well known worker of PPP and famous student Amanullah Khan gravely hurt and admitted to Rahim Yar Khan hospital.'

In the vehicle which took him to hospital, Amanullah was sitting between ZAB and Mubashir Hasan. He was bleeding from the wounds. Mubashir Hasan recalled his own squeamishness in trying to avoid getting blood on his clothes. For many months,

---

[106] Amanullah was a protégé of Sheikh Rashid, staunch leftist who was close to Indian CPI leader Harkishan Singh Surjeet. In fact it was on his advice that later Rashid would remain close to Benazir despite her insults. Party discipline demanded it.

he would be teased by ZAB by provoking Amanullah to tell the story about Mubashir Hasan's discomfort at the sight of blood.

The Jamaat promptly threw the blame on 'Red Guard', a left formation, which according to the report by eminent journalist Husain Naqi did not even exist in Pakistan. Another statement of condemnation was issued on 13 December 1969 by Mubashir Hasan about the Jamaat's invectives against his party, words such as Kafirs, Murtids, Wajibul, Qatl.

Murderous attempts on ZAB's life continued which justified his colleagues' concern. In another press statement issued from Lahore on 1 April 1970, Mubashir Hasan deplored the dastardly attempt on his life made on 30 March 1970 at Sanghar district of Sindh in which three party workers were killed and as many as sixty were injured.

In the above statement, Mubashir Hasan details previous murder attempts. In June 1967, the first murderous attempt on his life was made when he had just launched a mass movement against the oppressive regime of Ayub Khan. He was attacked by goondas at a public meeting in Gol Bagh[107] in Lahore. There was a rumour that this was masterminded by one of Ayub Khan's provincial ministers. The meeting ground was flooded with water and then electrified by throwing live wires with the intention of electrocution. When that was averted, the Chairman and his workers were attacked by brickbats and the shamiana was pulled down. He received injury in his head and in his back. 'The people of Lahore, however, stood like a steel wall against his attackers and thus saved the life of a leader who had the courage to stand up against the fascist dictatorship.'

Next year, in 1968, another attempt on his life was made in Multan. Hired goondas of Ayub Khan and local feudals, armed with swords and lathis, attacked the dais when he was attending

---

[107]Gol Bagh was later named Nasir Bagh.

a Citizens Reception at Shehzan Hotel. After that, he was to address a mammoth public meeting. During the same tour, another murderous attempt was made at Qadirpur Rawan when his cavalcade was held up and the entire party was ambushed.

On 19 February 1969, J.A. Rahim wrote to Mubashir Hasan, 'I have been reliably informed that arrangements have been made to attack and burn ZAB's house in Karachi on Friday next. The gangsters are men of Gohar Ayub who, I am told, is busy in Karachi organizing a wave of massacre and terror. The regime is playing with fire. It has started to burn down East Pakistan. It will burn down West Pakistan if it allows its gangsters free rein. Let me warn Ayub Khan that if this happens, the whole country will be in flames and with it the men of the regime will perish.'

In September 1967, when ZAB began a mass movement for social and economic revolution in the country, he addressed innumerable meetings including large meeting of workers at Hyderabad. From there he went on the tour of the Frontier region. There, in Dera Ismail Khan on 31 October, a handful of hired goondas with guns attacked him and the party workers. One of the provincial ministers of Ayub Khan was involved in this dastardly attack. The police tear-gassed and lathi-charged the ordinary people. Their plan thus having failed, ZAB was placed behind bars but released immediately due to immense pressure of students, workers, labour, including women. After the release while he was on hunger strike, an armed attacker was caught red-handed in Larkana while he was leading a huge procession. The day after the Larkana incident, while he was leading another procession of half a million citizens of Karachi, another attack was made near Empress market. Bricks and rocks were hurled from rooftops, as a result of which many people received serious injuries.

The following press statement of Mubashir Hasan explains the reasons for the state's unceasing efforts to kill ZAB. 'His growing popularity across the country spells death to the decadent and unpatriotic forces that have been sapping the blood of our people during these 23 years of our existence as an independent nation.' The statement accuses the regime of aiming their guns at Bhutto. 'History tells us that the reactionary forces are always first to resort to acts of violence whenever they are on the verge of extinction... Those who are trying to stop these processes of change are like grasshoppers trying to stop a locomotive. They are flies trying to topple a giant tree. Long live Chairman Zulfikar Ali Bhutto. Long live the Revolutionary Movement Struggle of the People of Pakistan.'

The year 1968 witnessed a whirlwind of tours to establish contact with the public. The party was gaining strength and popularity despite government obstacles and contrary forecasts by political pundits. ZAB's speeches through the year were sparsely reported in the newspapers. Mainly they were tape-recorded and replayed by devoted party workers at various venues.

His speeches were an increasing attack on the military rule of Ayub Khan. They stressed the PPP's programme, particularly how socialism was not in conflict with Islam. ZAB also felt the need to explain why he had left government and his earlier silence on this subject. Towards the end of the year, there is evidence that he began to lay the groundwork for his candidature in the forthcoming presidential elections. As with all his actions, the planning was done with utmost care and caution.

He appealed to the disadvantaged sections of society who, almost for the first time since 1948, had found a spokesman. 'I am the agent of the people, I am the servant of the people', he would proclaim in public meetings, and the masses, from Karachi to Khyber, would raise full-throated slogans of zindabad in his favour.[108]

---

[108] *The Mirage of Power: An Enquiry into the Bhutto years (1971-1977)*, Mubashir Hasan, Oxford University Press, p 29.

On 29 January 1968, he addressed Party women at Lahore where he declared: 'We will offer the women of this country their proper place without prejudice. The place you are given today is by chauvinistic male courtesy.' To the Bar Association at Nawabshah, on 21 February, he said, 'The student community is annoyed and up in arms, because the Government had introduced "oppressive and obnoxious University Ordinances" and even had the "audacity to take away degrees from them". The legal profession was unhappy "because the laws have been tampered with". The labouring classes were being "exploited under the system of plunder and loot which exists nowhere in the world today. It is absolute highway robbery." He stated that state lands should be given to peasants and tenants. He also attacked the Government for throwing people into jails. How long can you fill the jails? Ideas cannot be imprisoned. Principles cannot be imprisoned. The entire population cannot be imprisoned.'[109]

Once ZAB had started his 'meet the people' tours, there was no stopping him. He addressed every gathering which was prepared to listen—the countryside or roadside tea stalls, however small the spaces were. He was a new phenomenon on the Pakistani political scene, young, well-groomed, articulate and charismatic. He directly went to the people. They were impressed and awed by this man who they had seen in a Savile Row suit, Turnbull and Asser shirt and Sulka tie—a style he would soon set aside for Awami Shalwar kameez, open cuffs, and a neck scarf. His great asset, as Rafi Raza describes, was 'his unlimited energy, flair for politics and appetite for work'. His driving force was above all his ambition, supported by his intellectual vigour.[110]

In hundreds of thousands, people from all over Pakistan

---

[109]Collected from Politics of the People, Vol 2—Awakening the People—Nineteen Sixty-Six to Nineteen Sixty-Nine—Statements, Articles, Speeches of ZAB.

[110]*Zulfikar Ali Bhutto and Pakistan, 1967-1977*, Rafi Raza, Oxford University Press, p 7-8.

would attend his rallies, follow him in procession and listen to his rhetoric with rapt attention and believe in it. This adulation predictably also earned him and his party powerful enemies.

7

Governance, Grind, Glory

In 1969, President Ayub Khan's government was seized by his Army Chief General Yahya Khan.

The new president held elections in 1970, the first ever in Pakistan on the basis of adult franchise. To the utter surprise of the U.S. and the feudal landlords of Pakistan, PPP won a landslide victory in the province of West Pakistan, bagging 81 seats against a total of 131 seats. In the other wing of the country, the province of East Pakistan, Sheikh Mujibur Rahman's Awami League swept the polls with a stunning victory of 151 out of 153 contested seats.[111] ZAB himself won the election in five out of six constituencies in which he had contested, but in terms of law, he retained only one of them—his home seat of Larkana constituency. However, the General refused to transfer power to the elected legislature; indeed, he proceeded to crush the elected representatives, one by one, by force of arms. His military action in East Pakistan led to India-Pakistan war of 1971.

The military action by India resulted in a general revolt of people of Pakistan against Yahya Khan's military government. In East Pakistan, the popular revolt against Yahya Khan was assisted

---

[111]*Zulfikar Ali Bhutto and Pakistan 1967-1977*, Rafi Raza, Oxford University Press, p. 38.

by the Indian army; thus was born the state of Bangladesh. In the Paltan Maidan of Dacca, the Indian General Manekshaw accepted the surrender of Pakistani General Niazi, who had neither put up much fight nor had he received orders to confront the Indian army completely. Later, Manekshaw stated that although the Pakistan army was fully capable of fighting the Indians, it held back. It was a case of surrender, much to the disgust of the people of Pakistan given the disgraceful action of the Pakistani General. The province of East Pakistan emerged as the new nation state of Bangladesh. In West Pakistan, General Yahya Khan was forced out by his army commanders and the power was transferred to Zulfikar Ali Bhutto and his PPP in December 1971.

ZAB's PPP with its promise of established Islamic socialism was a setback for the reactionary forces in a country long dominated by force of the Right. The slogan of 'Food, Clothing, and Shelter' (roti, kapra, makaan) shifted the focus of Pakistani politics from theological to economic issues. Bhutto nationalized the commanding heights of the economy which was another blow to the capitalist world. The long-awaited economic reforms in agriculture sector were also undertaken by him. The price of wheat which was Rs 17 per 40 kilograms was raised to Rs 37. Similarly, the price of rice was substantially raised. Money was pushed into agriculture sector, a policy which boosted the popularity of the party. There was a massive transfer of resources into in the dominant rural economy by setting higher prices for agricultural products.

In *The Mirage of Power*, Mubashir Hasan writes, 'Our government began the task of making a defeated country stand on its legs, by implementing the nationalization programme as promised in the party's manifesto. We were extremely fearful of further Indian aggression, this time on our Western border. As Minister of Finance, Planning, Development and Economic Affairs, I gave as much funds as I could for guns, aircrafts and new divisions of the army.'

Within six months of PPP forming the government, Pakistan and India signed at Shimla an agreement on bilateral relations to put 'an end to the conflict and confrontation that had perpetually marred their relations'. Theoretically, Pakistan and India were still at war with each other. Now they resolved to 'work for the promotion of friendly and harmonious relationship and the establishment of durable peace in the subcontinent'. It was a resolute step forward for peace.

The Shimla Pact was a great victory for Pakistan. Pakistan had been a nation defeated by war. 93,000 of its civilian and military personnel were in India's custody and a considerable territory (5,000 square miles of West Pakistan) was also occupied by India. It had no cards in hand for the settlement. And then there was the perpetual Kashmir dispute. Pakistan entered the Shimla meeting as a defeated nation; in palpable economic and military stress. But when ZAB and the Indian Prime Minister Indira Gandhi sat across each other, flanked by their respective advisors, what happened was a miracle. India agreed to withdraw its troops and return Pakistani prisoners. No vital concession was made for the return of territory. Being an astute negotiator, ZAB had said to his group, 'Pakistan is not going to beg their (prisoner) return; prisoners are a commodity of losing value for India.'[112]

'While Shimla negotiations were going on, we in Lahore were ready with our plans, either way, whether success or failure. Pakistanis did not know what would be the result of the negotiations between President Bhutto and Indian Prime Minister Indira Gandhi, who was the victorious party hence in a commanding position. We in Lahore knew the date of Bhutto's return but were not aware which way the dice would roll. Two kinds of receptions and two kinds of slogans were ready. Code

---

[112]Oral history from Mubashir Hasan.

words were already exchanged between us in Lahore and Bhutto in India. We were to receive ZAB at the airport and raise whatever slogans the occasion demanded,' recalled Mubashir Hasan.[113]

At home, on every front, ZAB passionately wanted to transform Pakistan into a modern country. He had little or no patience for listening to or being confronted with details of what was needed to be done to carry out orders, that is, the details of planning, designing or financing. In discussions with Bhutto, Mubashir Hasan tended to go into details, for which ZAB had no time. All he wanted was that the job he assigned be done fast and done as a 'first-class' job. As for the paucity of finances to carry out development works, he wrote to the Deputy Chairman Planning Commission on 13 September 1972:

'We cannot effect any cuts in our defence expenditure for the foreseeable future. At the same time we are pledged to a radical economic programme. In these circumstances we have no alternative but to indulge in deficit financing... I would take the risk of inflation in preference to all other risks. I am afraid, finding ourselves in the circumstances in which we stand, we have no alternative but to go for massive deficit financing. If most of the expenditure is earmarked for public sector, I think we will be able to face the inflation.'

ZAB seemed very unhappy and disturbed those first few months. He wanted all his dreams for Pakistan to become reality at the wave of his hand. He was frustrated because of the non-fulfilment of his dreams of new factories, roads, parks, housing, increased fertilizer production, relief to the farmer, and, above all, by the lack of funds, which the Ministry of Finance was refusing to release except for a certain category of industrial projects. 'Bhutto's frustration,' writes Mubashir Hasan, 'was not quite justified, although there was considerable room for

[113]Narrated by Mubashir Hasan to the author in July 2017.

criticizing the prevailing inefficiency and ineptness. He did not realize that an economy which had been in such dire straits as that of Pakistan would take time to pick up. So much should not have been expected so soon.'

On 19 September 1972, ZAB wrote a letter to all the PPP ministers at the centre as well as in the provinces. He lashed out at the leaders of the party who were holding office: 'Whether young or old, with or without experience, those leaders of the party holding high office have done many unusual things since assuming responsibility of the State machinery.'

He accused the members of the central committee of abusing one another in the central committee meetings and making public statements contradicting each other on sensitive policy decisions, of violating law in talking openly about Cabinet meetings, and of showing files of the government to Members of the National Assembly to prove their petty points. He had thought that the leaders would learn with time but his hopes had been dashed. It was also obvious that the intelligence services were feeding ZAB against his ministers and party men in a massive way. They were hitting him where it would hurt him the most.

ZAB wrote, 'The bureaucrats are laughing at us; all manners of nasty jokes are being cut; the opposition leaders have ridiculed us good and proper and diplomats have been bewildered by our performance.'

'Bhutto was exaggerating,' Mubashir Hasan writes. 'People have made fun of governments probably since the state first came into being. That is how the cartoonists of the world make a living. There seemed more to his series of warnings and rebukes than what his notes indicated.'

ZAB wrote again, 'At first I hoped that, with experience, our new leaders will acquire maturity and settle down but alas, I see no signs of it. In order to put things right I have reprimanded some of my colleagues, I have tried to reason with some others,

I have shown patience, I have tried to guide and instruct. But no appreciable difference is visible.'

The fact that he was blaming his entire team for the lack of diligence shown by a few was the first sign that he was beginning to lose patience with his team of ministers and party office holders.

On 25 September 1972, ZAB fired yet another salvo at all the central ministers—governor of Punjab, chief minister of Sindh and at his special assistants. He complained that the prices of essential commodities were rising and corruption was rampant and that there was a sense of disillusionment amongst the people. In this note, his chief targets were Members of the National Assembly. He observed, 'The Assembly is indulging in monkey tricks. The Assembly of the Frontier Province is at sixes and sevens. Since the inception of Pakistan, today we have the largest Cabinet the country has seen. If we divided the Assembly work properly, every Minister could look after five to six MNAs without difficulty but this is not being done. The MNAs are bitter. There is petty intrigue taking place all the time.'

'His complaint that the National Assembly was indulging in "monkey tricks" was without basis,' Mubashir Hasan writes. 'For example, as Finance Minister, I received a request for an excise inspector's transfer from one post to another. Seventeen Members of National Assembly had signed to stop the transfer. I stopped the transfer for one year. At the end of the year the Excise Department again came to me so I agreed to transfer.'

The position of the Assembly was such that barring a few members, the entire Assembly was with ZAB. True, some of the members were irrepressible. Before an opposition member could finish his speech they would be on their feet. Those who had any parliamentary experience could be counted on the fingers of one hand. Very few of them had studied the rules of business. They could not listen calmly to the Speaker. It is also true that some of them were unhappy at not being able to get a permit or a license, or at not being able to get a relative or friend transferred or promoted but this unhappiness did not mean that they were not loyal to the party. But ZAB came down hard on his ministers: 'With the least provocation some of the ministers flare up and even attack the person of the President. Those stories are carried back to me with a big laugh and all I can do is to lower my eyes in embarrassment. Efficient and effective control is lacking. There is little respect for punctuality. After making strong speeches against the opposition, ministers and the members of the majority party go to the opposition members and fraternize with them. This is supine cowardice and it only confuses and intrigues the people.'

Mubashir Hasan, looking back after 50 years, views this frustration of his leader against the prism of a theory he has developed and propounded all his life. 'These were difficult months for Bhutto and his team,' writes Mubashir Hasan. 'He was not conscious of the fact that the basic obstacle in their lack of achievement was structural in nature. The undemocratic system of governance through a tiny salaried elite over a vast multitude that was created by the British in the last century was no longer workable. This was the British mantra of ruling the colonies. It worked then, it was unviable in the present context.' Ministers and office holders in the Party were dedicated to the service of the masses and were not corrupt. ZAB's exhortations did make them work harder but the month of October 1972 saw three resignations. The first departure from the original political team was that of Law Minister Mahmud Ali Qasuri. 'The reasons for the resignation have remained obscure, for neither side thought it fit to go public about them. ZAB was too astute a politician to give Qasuri a chance to air differences on their approach towards the future constitution. As a minister, Qasuri had remained on the sidelines, for he never became a close associate of Bhutto. Perhaps, he just left in disgust. His departure was a blow to the progressive stance of the party.'[114]

Soon after Qasuri's departure, Mairaj Mohammad Khan resigned; the reasons behind his resignation were mainly political. And the third was Mubashir Hasan who resigned due to his poor health; his was a resignation which ZAB refused to accept. Later, he would relent and Mubashir Hasan on his own expense would proceed for treatment to Switzerland.

In *The Mirage of Power*, Mubashir Hasan writes, 'In September 1972, a request came to the Ministry of Finance under the Exchange Control Act to allow Murtaza Bhutto, the eldest son of President Bhutto, to purchase one hundred dollars through the State Bank. He had been studying in the United States and was in Pakistan to spend his vacation with the family. On his way back to University, he wanted to stop over to see the Olympic games being held in Munich, Germany, hence the request before the ministry. I wrote on the file that a president's son was entitled only to what any other Pakistani student was entitled, and returned the file to the Finance Secretary. This was interpreted as a rejection of the request. Someone must have informed the President's office and, in no time Afzal Saeed, the Secretary to the President, was on the telephone with me. I told him that I had given my decision and there was no question of changing it. He pleaded at length but ultimately made the mistake of informing me that he had spoken to the President before submitting the request to the ministry. I lost my cool and barked into the phone that he did not know what was good for the President and what was good for his son and that I would speak to the President about this myself, and banged the receiver. The occasion arose later in the evening when I told the President of my reasons for rejecting Murtaza's

---

[114]*The Mirage Of Power: An Enquiry into the Bhutto years (1971-1977)*, Mubashir Hasan, p 189, Oxford University Press.

request. He seemed unperturbed.'[115] I confirmed with Mubashir Hasan on 27 July 2017 that Murtaza Bhutto never got $100 in foreign exchange that he had requested. Several facts are revealed in this one incident. Mubashir Hasan knew the repercussions of granting 'special favour' to the president's son. By the same token, the president's personal staff was unable or unwilling to protect him. And most of all is the fact of ZAB's reaction. The word 'unperturbed' says it all.

It was not surprising that when the prime minister was expressing his unhappiness with his ministers, MNAs, and MPAs in such a blatant manner, the civil establishment decided to avail the opportunity of winning over Bhutto to their point of view and to weaken the position of politicians in the government. The other intractable problem was the intelligence services. They were all the time poisoning Bhutto's mind against the members of his team.

Mubashir Hasan writes, 'The major goal of the intelligence community is to wean the Prime Minister away from the principal members of his team, his old political comrades and also his favourites from the services. One cannot find a single chief executive of Pakistan who had ruled for a few years and still maintained a good relationship with his old colleagues. Thanks mainly to the poison served to the ruler by the intelligence services against the strong and the serious; only the weak and pliable ones among his original team manage to evade their poison... It can be safely asserted that the biased and misleading intelligence reports supplied by the secret services have played a significant role in the tragic end of many governments in Pakistan.'[116]

He narrated how the role of the Inter Services Intelligence

---

[115] *The Mirage Of Power: An Enquiry into the Bhutto years (1971-1977)*, Mubashir Hasan, p 199, Oxford University Press.
[116] *The Mirage Of Power: An Enquiry into the Bhutto years (1971-1977)*, Mubashir Hasan, p 208, Oxford University Press.

in advising ZAB increased over the years. The service was headed by Lieutenant-General Ghulam Jilani with whom he had a very revealing encounter. His elderly mother (who was also my grandmother) lived at 11 Temple Road in Lahore, where he visited her often and where ZAB would often call him. On one of those visits, his sister Zehra complained about the persistent faulty working of the telephone. That was not the first time she had complained and he had tried to get it fixed before. So he decided to inform the General Manager, Telephones. Shortly, a linesman of the Telephone Department, a PPP enthusiast, showed up and immediately detected that there was a parallel connection to the line. 'There is no such connection in the house,' he was told and was asked to go and find out where it went. In a short while, he returned with the news that 'a colonel' was the culprit. 'A colonel! How did he know he was a colonel?' Mubashir Hasan asked. He replied that nobody, except the army, had the kind of wire that had been used. He explained that he had followed the wire to the end of the street along Temple Road for a little distance, then across the road into a locked room where he had seen it connected to the telephone apparatus by peeping in through the window. The neighbours told him that a 'colonel' had rented that room. The Subdivisional Engineer Telephone Dept arrived next and said that the parallel connection was illegal; the law had been violated. The General Manager arrived soon after and they decided to register a case with the police. Mubashir Hasan informed the Director General Intelligence Bureau who was a man from Punjab Police. When he learnt that the case was with the Punjab Police, he was delighted and said, 'Leave it to me now, Sir'. A few hours later, a man came and said, 'I am Colonel so and so. I am sorry they connected me to your line, I needed the phone urgently'. Mubashir Hasan replied that it was a matter between the police and his agency, and that he should be talking to the police.

After this brief altercation, Mubashir Hasan wrote a letter to

ISI chief General Jilani asking him for an investigation. He did not inform the prime minister knowing that Intelligence would do so in any case. Two or three days later, when Bhutto did not hear anything about the incident from him, he called him over. After discussing some official business, he kept on inquiring about how things were. He was most friendly and relaxed. At one point, Mubashir Hasan said, 'I know what you want to know' and told him of the phone incident and added that he was waiting for the report from Jilani.

The report marked 'For Eyes Only', which meant that it could not be discussed with anybody, arrived a few days later. It said that ISI had nothing to do with what Mubashir Hasan had reported. About a week later, there was a meeting in Quetta. After the meeting, Bhutto sent for him and pointed to his left. They were standing in the great lounge of the Quetta Government House near the staircase which overlooked the sprawling lawns. He said, 'I have given hell to Jilani. Look at him now. I have made him stand there'. Mubashir Hasan looked outside and in the grounds beyond the verandah, he saw Jilani, standing under a tree. Jilani was called in and Bhutto told him that he took a very serious view of what had happened. There was Jilani, his face bespectacled with rimless glasses and the sharp nose of a spymaster, meekly explaining that the ISI has nothing to do with the matter and hinting at another direction. His needle pointed in the direction of Mahmud Ali (a Minister of State since Ayub Khan's days, trusted and tested by ISI) in the PM's office who had earlier worked for Ayub Khan and Yahya Khan. ZAB looked at the sleuth direct in the eye, 'Don't go by the polite manner in which Dr Sahib puts his case, he was quite harsh in his complaint.' Jilani meekly repeated what he had said earlier. After Jilani had left, Bhutto told Mubashir Hasan, 'They were torturing that "colonel" in the Lahore Fort; I have stopped them.'

Mubashir Hasan writes, 'Right from the beginning, I had

suspected that he was not a colonel of the Pakistan army and that he had been recruited for spying, even he did not know by whom. Once caught on the wrong foot he was dropped by the intelligence people as is customary with their community all over the world.'

Then there was a case of an economist of global fame. ZAB had selected Dr Mahbub ul Haq[117] to be the deputy chairman of Planning Commission. This matter leaked in the press and resulted in usual power games. His big support came from senior civil servants Aziz Ahmad and M.M. Ahmad. ZAB had drawn a proposal to create a Planning Council for Haq. The file was sent to Mubashir Hasan, 'What do you think of this?' Mubashir Hasan's reply was that there were enough councils, therefore, another one would be useless. When Haq learnt of Mubashir Hasan's feedback, he quietly went back to Washington D.C. But ZAB was persistent. On his behalf, another very senior bureaucrat, M.M. Ahmad came to Mubashir Hasan and said,

'I can't find Mahbub ul Haq. Where is he?'

It was September 1974 and Mubashir Hasan was leaving for US. 'I am going to D.C. Shall I bring him back?'

'Yes, bring him back.'

Meeting Mahbub ul Haq in DC, Hasan said, 'Do you want to come and take charge?'

'First you write a letter to McNamara.'

'Draft the letter, I will sign it.'

Next day, Haq came but without a letter.

Mubashir Hasan asked, 'Where is the letter?'

'Let me talk to Aziz Ahmad and M.M. Ahmad.'

'What is the matter Mahbub?'

---

[117]One of the best known economists of South Asia. The series of Human Development reports produced by the United Nations Development Programme was initiated by Haq in 1990. He later served as the thirteenth Finance Minister of Pakistan. At the time he was working with the World Bank.

'How will I get along with a feudal prime minister?'

When he returned, Mubashir Hasan asked ZAB, 'Why did you want Mahbub ul Haq?' And then he told him about Haq's remark. 'Mr Bhutto was angry. He summoned his secretary, who seeing me there, opened his mouth and was probably going to say, "Mahbub ul Haq."'

'Forget him', snapped his boss.

'That ended the matter; some people gave me credit for "getting rid of" Mahbub ul Haq. But I had nothing to do with it except reporting his remark verbatim to Mr Bhutto.'[118]

At home too, the challenges were enormous.

In a file jotting dated 24 January 1973 from Karachi, ZAB wrote his anxiety about the tendency of planners to concentrate on Punjab and Karachi, leaving out the vast undeveloped territories of the country.

'We have a vast desert in Sindh and Punjab and Balochistan. If we give serious attention to the development of the desert with half of the intelligence and enthusiasm that Israel has given to its desert, we would be most flourishing but we regard our desert as a wasteland and a liability. In this defeatist attitude we have virtually written off half of the country and we have brought the other half to the edge of precipice by our misdemeanours.'

Balanced growth and equitable treatment of all the provinces was the promise of PPP to Pakistani awam. The future lay in exploring the vast resources of Sindh and Balochistan with sensitivity for people of those regions; this vision was shared by his core team. To implement it was the biggest challenge.

In the government, there were matters demanding urgent attention which needed statesmanship and sagacity; the trusted comrades were departing one by one. He was getting increasingly lonely. On 11 February 1973, he wrote on a file analyzing the

---

[118]Interview with Mubashir Hasan dated July 2017.

situation on the Western border of the country, 'Events are moving fast. We will be able to anticipate some of them but others we might not be able to foresee. The test of our intelligence lies in our ability to foresee as many future events as possible.'

'In addition to the Soviet Union, we will have to take into account the attitude of India, Iraq and Afghanistan. Judging from the drama of East Pakistan, on this occasion the Soviet Union may direct Afghanistan to do something similar to what India did in East Pakistan. We have to watch every move and every step of Wali Khan, Bizenjo, Mengal and Marri.[119] It is likely that Afghanistan diplomats will try to get in touch with them. They must not move before us. We must ensure that nothing takes place, even remotely, to give the political situation the colour of an armed movement or a resistance movement. Attempts may be made to give the situation the impression of a freedom struggle.'

While he dreamt of a prosperous Pakistan by driving a policy of inclusive growth, traps had been laid by adverse forces and its tentacles were slowly closing around him. Intelligence Agencies were hard at work. Mubashir Hasan's encounter with them was recounted earlier in this chapter. They did not even spare the prime minister.

Once, when he was staying in Intercontinental Hotel in Lahore, Mubashir Hasan came to see him and immediately smelt sleuthing. 'This floor is bugged Sir'. 'Let us shift,' he said without

---

[119]Wali Khan was the son and heir of Khan Abdul Ghaffar Khan who led the Pashtun National Movement in NWFP. His National Awami Party was banned twice during Yahya Khan and ZAB regimes.

Ghaus Bakhsh Bizenjo, Khair Bakhsh Marri, and Ataullah Mengal were Baloch leaders who led the Baloch nationalist movement, as it evolved through the sixties. They would pursue their opposition to the centre through the NAP and would be unwilling to accept any deals from the government that did not come with statutory guarantees of full provincial autonomy and an equal share of state power.

a moment's hesitation. They went down to the lower floor. Just as they reached, Mahmud Ali Qasuri walked in. 'We were looking for your party upstairs. Why did you shift?' ZAB's quick excuse was, 'Masons were working upstairs, they were very noisy.'

'It is a well worn cliche,' said Mubashir Hasan, 'but top is the loneliest place in the world. You can trust no one, I mean no one.'

With the loss of East Pakistan in 1971, questions arose whether Pakistan should remain rooted in the subcontinent, a geographical imperative, or should it seek historical links with Muslim countries to its west. It became clear to Pakistan that they could not count on either the Western countries or the Communist Bloc, apart from China, for support in its dealing with India. The Muslim world was a source of immediate support, more moral and political than material, plus it was emotionally linked to Pakistan. ZAB therefore began looking westward. A testament of this endeavour was the Islamic Summit in Lahore in February 1974. Here the contribution of King Faisal, in arranging the Summit of the Organization of Islamic Cooperation (OIC) in Lahore, was significant[120].

The first World Islamic Summit was held at Rabat, Morocco in September 1969. It was attended by 24 of the 30 invited states, including India, much to Pakistan's frustration and dismay. There it was decided to create the Organization of Islamic Cooperation. A permanent Secretariat was charged inter alia with the responsibility of making contacts with governments represented at the conference, and to coordinate their activities.

The devastating event of 21 August 1969, an act of arson, caused extensive damage to Holy Al-Aqsa Mosque. Middle East was teetering on the edge. The attack destroyed several parts of the historic mosque, including 1,000 year old wood-and-ivory pulpit dating back to the time of Emperor Saladin. It took a

---

[120] *Zulfikar Ali Bhutto and Pakistan, 1967-1977*, Rafi Raza, Oxford University Press, 1997, p 227.

whole month for the UNSC to respond. On 15 September 1969, Resolution 271 was adopted which condemned the destructive attack on the mosque and chastized the Israeli government for failing to respect UN decisions.[121] Moved by this tragedy of Palestine, the heads of state, government and representatives of Islamic nations established the multilateral Organisation of the Islamic Conference, which was later renamed the Organization of Islamic Cooperation (OIC).

The Second Islamic Summit was held in Lahore from February 22–24 in 1974 and came to be known as the Lahore Summit. ZAB launched this historic initiative. The first Islamic summit had been attended by only 24 of the 30 invited states, but the Second Summit was attended by the head of states, ministers and dignitaries from Muslim countries all over the world. Some of the participant countries were Afghanistan, Algeria, Bahrain, Bangladesh, Chad, Egypt, Gabon, Gambia, Guinea, Guinea-Bissau, Indonesia, Iran, Iraq, Jordan, Kuwait, Lebanon, Libya, Malaysia, Mali, Mauritania, Morocco, Niger, Oman, Pakistan, Yemen, Qatar, Saudi Arabia, Senegal, Sierra Leone, Somalia, Sudan, Syria, Tunisia, Turkey, Uganda, United Arab Emirates, Palestine Liberation Organization, Arab League and Delegation of Oriental Christians. Thirty-eight kings, amirs, presidents, and prime ministers participated in it, King Faisal of Saudi Arabia and President Gaddafi of Libya being the star participants. President Idi Amin of Uganda, who came uninvited carrying his little son was also the object of great interest, as were President Sadaat of Egypt, Boumedienne of Algeria, and Hafiz Asad of Syria. The Shah of Iran did not come himself but sent a minister from his government.

Mubashir Hasan recalled some important and unreported facets of the Summit such as ZAB's relationship with Shah of

---

[121]https://www.middleeastmonitor.com/20170821-palestinians-mark-48-years-since-al-aqsa-arson-attack/

Iran. 'One day, *The Wall Street Journal* correspondent came to me and said, "I can't believe it. I was with Shah of Iran the day before and he was passing derogatory remarks about ZAB who visited him the next day. The next day I found out that he gave $450 million to ZAB for Pakistan." I said to the correspondent, "You don't know the power our leader has to convince people. ZAB did what no other leader of Pakistan could do before and after. He made very good friends in the Muslim countries who, in turn, were very generous to him. Why? He spoke the language of their national interest. Libya was against USA; ZAB was not happy with USA. When Libya needed help ZAB sent airforce pilots to Libya. Hafiz Al Assad was almost at war with Israel. So ZAB sent a Pakistani squadron to Syria. He made friends with each and every Muslim ruler of the Gulf countries; Qattar, Abu Dhabi, Doha, Dubai. He was on cordial terms with King Faisal of Saudi Arabia. These countries had problems with each other. Iran and Saudi Arabia were historical rivals but ZAB was friendly with both. The same was for Syria and Libya."

This is why ZAB was able to hold a conference of all heads of Muslim states in Lahore in 1974. He convinced them that interests of Pakistan were the same as theirs. He would come to their help whenever they needed. One contingent of Pakistan army was sent to Saudi Arabia to train their military force. The same was done for Abu Dhabi. He conveyed to them, as only he could, what was in their best interest. They returned with the assurance that they had no better friend than Pakistan.

Prime Minister Bhutto opened the conference. Important decisions were made such as support to Jordon, Syria, Egypt and Palestinian people for their legitimate struggle for recovering their lands. Highlighting that Palestine issue needed to be resolved, all those states having relations with Israel were condemned and it was suggested that steps should be taken to affirm Arab sovereignty over Jerusalem. Finally, for the enhancement of

Islamic culture, solidarity and education, the Islamic Solidarity Fund was established[122].

The Summit adopted resolutions against the occupation of Arab territory by Israel, for the return of Jerusalem, and for the restitution of national rights of the Palestinian people. A decision was taken to set up a group to study the question of eradication of poverty, disease, and ignorance from Islamic countries. The Islamic Summit placed on record that it was essential to end the exploitation of developing countries by the developed nations.[123]

The success of the Summit brought great popular support to ZAB and his government. The strenuous personal effort and singular energy on his part proved to be one of his greatest diplomatic triumphs. It had attracted every major Muslim head of state except the Shah of Iran. He was unhappy about Bhutto's 'unstable' report about him to the US President Nixon. ZAB flew to Tehran in mid-October 1973 to reassure the Shah and mend fences which he had broken in what he thought was an off-the-record remark in the White House. The Shah was cool to his apology and declined his invitation to the summit. ZAB later wrote that the Shah 'had a complex towards me. He was intensely envious. His grandiose designs and fanciful ambitions of being the modern Cyrus the Great if not greater contributed in no small measure to his ruin. He lost touch with reality.'[124]

The visiting delegations were welcomed by the people of Lahore. Elaborate arrangements were made for the security of the distinguished guests. The Summit was held in the Punjab Assembly building. For the first time in Pakistan, arrangements were made for simultaneous translation of the speeches through a network of microphone and speakers available to each participant.

---

[122]http://ww1.oic-oci.org/english/conf/is/2/2nd-is-sum.htm

[123]http://ww1.oic-oci.org/english/conf/is/2/2nd-is-sum.htm

[124]http://historypak.com/lahore-summit-1974/

The proceedings were secret, but since the arrangement was through wireless, anybody sitting in the nearby Falettis Hotel with a high frequency radio receiver could listen to all that was being said in the conference.

Before the conference, fears had been expressed that the irrepressible and emotional people of Lahore might endanger the security of popular leaders like King Faisal of Saudi Arabia and Gaddafi of Libya. ZAB ordered elaborate measures to prevent opposition parties from using the occasion to create propaganda against his government. In a detailed directive, he said: 'It is painfully embarrassing but we have to live with these ignorant and uncouth individuals, untutored in the elementary code of state conduct. Typical of them, they have to brainstorm the foreign Heads of State during their visit to Pakistan for the Islamic Summit Conference. They have decided to seek interviews with them and to fall at their feet and to beg them for their cooperation in overthrowing my tyrannical government... They want to bring down the high pedestal of the conference to the gutter...'[125]

Appeals were made in the media for the people not to break security lines and to maintain discipline. In *The Mirage of Power*, Mubashir Hasan states, 'they responded marvellously.'

Following were the significant outcomes of the Lahore Summit:

- Many Arab and Islamic countries had not yet recognized Bangladesh as a separate country. In the atmosphere of Islamic fraternity generated by the Islamic Summit, Pakistanis forgot the past and embraced Sheikh Mujeeb-ur-Rehman along with the recognition of Bangladesh. After Pakistan's recognition, other Muslim countries also recognized Bangladesh's independent status.

---

[125] *The Mirage of Power: An Inquiry into the Bhutto Years (1971-1977)*, Mubashir Hasan, Oxford University Press. p 237

- At this Summit, the Islamic World accepted the status of Palestine Liberation Organization (PLO) under Yasser Arafat as the sole legitimate representative of Palestinian people. This acceptance strengthened the cause of Palestine in UN and other international bodies and Yasser Arafat said 'Palestine was born in Lahore.'

- It brought up the solidarity and fraternity among the Muslim world and made them aware of the worth of their resources, especially oil.

- The Summit made it clear that Jerusalem was of profound importance for Muslims and was religiously sacred for the entire Muslim Ummah.

- It strengthened the Arabs, particularly Egypt, in the negotiations post Arab-Israel War 1973.

Analyzing the Islamic Summit 40 years later, columnist Khalid Ahmed was to write about the tension between ZAB and Saudi Arabia which started during the Summit. 'Bhutto had built up Libya's President Mummer Qaddafi in opposition to the Saudi King during Islamic Summit in Lahore in 1974; thus taking sides in a polarized Arab world;[126] Khalid contends that the kingdom therefore never took to ZAB and fawned on the right wing Muslim League supported by the Pakistan army. But as events unfolded, it was ZAB who due to plethora of reasons capitulated to Saudi influence and this fatal compromise pushed the country on the Islamization road.

---

[126]*The Indian Express*, 13 April 2015.

8

President's Men: Companions, Contenders, Saboteurs

Companions

Philosopher, Guide and Friend: The story of J.A. Rahim[127]

S. Najmuddin was the modest publisher of a pamphlet[128] written by J.A. Rahim on the philosophy of PPP flag. His preface on J.A. Rahim reflects the common man's understanding of him as well as the political discourse of the time. Rahim was held in awe in the party as the main architect of the party's philosophy. This writing also reflects the common worker's understanding and enthusiasm for what PPP stood for.

'This article comes to you from the scholarly pen of Mr J.A. Rahim who is not only an eminent leader of Pakistan People's

---

[127]Jalaluddin Abdur Rahim was former officer of the Indian Civil Service and senior diplomat who had fallen out with Ayub Khan. His father Abdur Rahim was Speaker of the Central Legislative Assembly of India from 1935 to 1945. Rahim helped ZAB to write *The Myth of Independence*. When ZAB administered the oath of office to his ministers on 24 December 1971, a new portfolio of Presidential Affairs was created for Rahim. Every paper for the President was supposed to pass through him. It showed how completely ZAB trusted Rahim and valued his advice in those crucial days.

[128]The 1970 Election Manifesto of the Pakistan People's Party was drafted mostly by Secretary General J.A. Rahim and printed by Vision Publications Ltd., Karachi.

Party but also a diplomat of international fame. He has won laurels for our country as an unknown and self-effacing soldier at the diplomatic front and international forums. Mr J.A. Rahim was also our acting chairman when our dynamic chairman Mr Zulfikar Ali Bhutto was put behind bars by the anti-people regime of Ayub Khan, the ex-president. According to Mr J.A. Rahim, "Socialism is applied knowledge. The Pakistan People's Party's workers should not only study Socialism but should also merge with the masses of the people in order to educate them politically." Chairman Bhutto has rightly pointed out, "We should always rely on the masses. They make history and can create realities. The masses of Pakistan can move mountains if they are properly mobilised. The party workers should go to the countryside, the factories and all other fronts of the working classes in order to serve them and to educate them on political, economic and other national issues. The masses, are also excellent teachers. They can teach us how to create realities and how to combat challenges confronting the country.'"

ZAB and Rahim were a curious couple, essentially complementary to one another in the early days. Once the party was formed, Rahim provided the ideology and ZAB the pragmatism and popular appeal. Their different approaches were exemplified in the Foundation Meeting Document.[129]

The question arises that given this interdependence and complementing minds of the two, what caused the rift between ZAB and Rahim? What was his 'fault' which finally led to goons breaking into his house and literally beating him up; and at whose behest? Why was he banished from ZAB's presence? The relationship ended with Rahim leaving Rawalpindi for Karachi preferring to spend the rest of his days far from political limelight.

---

[129]The Foundation Meeting documents provide a basis for understanding the motivation of PPP and the forces it unleashed.

Some answers are yet to be found. Facts that gleaned from correspondence are given below; they tell a story that needs to be pieced together.

The fact was that nobody in the Party could level with ZAB except Rahim who, together with him, had drawn the party's blueprint in Europe in the autumn of 1966. He was his mentor and became the guiding spirit of the Party. It was a partnership of equals. The two men, Rahim and Mubashir Hasan, were brains of the party; deeply reflective, most of the writing work fell to their lot. After the Party formation, however, there were times when ZAB-Rahim relationship became very tense.

The set of letters exchanged between them speak volumes. ZAB wrote a letter to Rahim on 28 September 1969, in which he complained about a Press Statement made by him. This letter triggered a host of misgivings which Rahim must have been nurturing for a while. The most important of them was violation of the Party's founding principles, which was being reflected in some of ZAB's recent decisions. He wrote:

> 'You complain about my press statement of 14 February 1968, which you say hurt your feelings. I have carefully read it over again now and fail to spot a single matter therein that might hurt your sensibilities. You say that the inference was obvious. I am too stupid to understand that inference whatever it is. I shall not be so unkind as to attribute the discovery of the said inference to you, but would rather like to think that it was triumphantly brought to your notice by some of your friends nurtured on dissimulation and intrigue. Or is the whole offence simply this that in the eyes of your august self I am too humble a person to presume to have anything to say on my own to the public? What about my feelings which you hurt?
>
> 'It has been accepted by us that the Party should have a

broad appeal, but be in substance socialistic. I have carefully adhered to the policy which was discussed between us when the Party's program was being drawn up. In order not to give any room for misunderstanding I have been deliberately keeping in the background for some time. I feel now that I have carried this self-abnegation to excess at a time when former Convention Muslim Leaguers and supporters of Ayub Khan are immigrating into the Party. When you say that there is in the Party opposition to me at all levels (which you underline) I accept the fact. It is bound to be in a Party so heterogenous as this is becoming. Take any other 'leader' in this Party, take one of our rich landlord friends, there will be in his case also opposition at all levels (and I doubly underline).

'Of the six gentlemen who are to be my advisers, four are rich landowners. This is a Vadera Cabinet. Each one of them may be a worthy man, but it is wrong to compose what is virtually a Party Council in this manner. I will not be instrumental to putting the Party under the tutelage of such a group. I don't accept the position, so the question of my taking their advice does not arise.

'I notice that you have not made public the arrangement of leaving the Party supposedly in my charge. Therefore my refusal to take over the supposed charge will not make any difference.'[130]

Earlier, ZAB had written two letters to Rahim dated 14 August and 17 August 1970. At the back of his mind was Rahim's dislike for bypassing rules, which is anticipated in these two letters in which he tries to rationalize the decision he made without adhering to the established procedure. In the first letter, he says that an important announcement had to be made without consulting the

---

[130]Copy of the letter is with the author.

Secretary General (aka Rahim) because these were 'abnormal times'. He promises to make every effort in the future to follow the correct procedure. The second letter is self-congratulatory about the tremendous impact his tours have made on the country. There is an attempt to elicit sympathy. He writes that his health had been deteriorating since 1958. 'I have to continue to bear the main brunt. I have made this party with my blood and I intend to reach it to its highest destiny.'

He then rationalizes not giving adequate representation to East Pakistan in the Party hierarchy. 'Actually, I am still not in a position to give adequate representation to East Pakistan in the structure of the Party.' He says that tried and tested individuals have to be found first. Later, he adds that the time has come for forming the Party structure. Attached to his letter was the structure of the Party which he devised. This he says supersedes all previous instructions on the subject. He also names persons who he had already appointed, 'This is my prerogative and I am exercising it until general elections are held and the present constitution is replaced by a permanent one.' With characteristically feudal mindset he writes that although this is his 'exclusive prerogative' but he has 'nevertheless' held discussions with the relevant functionaries of the party before making appointments.

Given the fact that the elections were postponed to December, he wrote that the manifesto should come out within a month, by end of September. The rest of the letter is another example of his propensity to micromanage affairs of the party instead of leaving some of the decision-making in the capable hands of Rahim and three or four key founders. Anxious, tense, distrustful of those closest to him were messages the letter emitted; they would have made a man like Rahim wince. His rejoinder was therefore neither excessive nor unfair. The letters were copied to Rasool

Bakhsh Khan Talpur,[131] Sheikh Mohammad Rashid,[132] Hayat Mohammad Khan Sherpao,[133] Mumtaz Ali Bhutto,[134] and Abdul Hafeez Pirzada[135]. The letter was not copied to Mubashir Hasan. On 23 August 1970, Rahim wrote back to ZAB. 'Since your hasty decision is not valid, you can go back on it without difficulty; the party as a whole is uncommitted, although some of your friends may have applauded your ill-advised scheme.' This was Rahim's sharp condemnation of ZAB's Draft Party Structure. He condemned it for its disregard of the party's ideological principles. He was categorical that until the final constitution came into force the interim one could not be abrogated. Later, ZAB, impervious of any view contradictory to his own, decided to abolish the interim constitution. Rahim wrote, 'There is no personal prerogative vested in you to abolish the interim constitution. I would therefore, earnestly request you to reconsider the whole subject...' He then states that the formation of an ideologically sound cadre of Party members was a necessary condition for ensuring the successful implementation of the Party's programme. 'According to the declaration of principles, the PPP is a Socialist Party. If you want to change this conception to satisfy the rush of new members mounting the Party's bandwagon, then please first hold elections

---

[131]Talpur a wealthy zamindar from Sindh, was the President of PPP Sindh.

[132]Sheikh Mohammad Rashid was the Chairman of the PPP Punjab, a veteran of left-wing campaigns for land reforms and peasants' rights. In December 1971, Bhutto assigned him the portfolio of Health and Social Welfare.

[133]A 34 year-old Bhutto fida-ee (ardent devotee) from Sherpao, District Mardan of the NWFP. From the day the party was founded, Hayat was responsible for the organization of the PPP in his province. ZAB appointed Hayat as Governor and Martial Law Administrator of the Frontier.

[134]Mumtaz Ali Bhutto was Governor of Sindh and Martial Law Administrator of that province. Later, he was appointed as Minister for Communications.

[135]Abdul Hafeez Pirzada was a Barrister and Chairman PPP, Karachi. He was made Minister for Information on 24 December 1971. Earlier he was Bhutto's lawyer in the case of detention before the Lahore High Court at the end of 1968 and joined the party soon after.

and thereafter another Convention to amend suitably the Party's principles.' He then makes a scathing comment which only he dared to make. 'In your new scheme the Principles Committee is abolished, which is an indication to my mind of its general purpose. You do not want the Party, you want the personal following.'

Advising ZAB to follow a principled path, he expresses his anguish at the Chairman's contention that he has the exclusive prerogative to change anything and yet 'hold discussion' with relevant party functionaries. 'It follows from what you are saying that I am not a relevant functionary, and I know some other office bearers who are not in this sense relevant functionaries.'

Then he asks, 'When did the functionaries who were consulted become Party members? In my opinion, your scheme is unconstitutional and my earnest advice to you is not to proceed with it.' He then writes of the creation of the Post of Secretary of the National Solidarity for the Liberation of Jammu & Kashmir. 'I must point out to you that the question of National Solidarity is a separate issue from that of Jammu and Kashmir, and to mix them together is a very impolitic step... There are people in East Pakistan who can retort to you that their country has already been conquered, while the conquest of J&K lies in unknowable future. The exercise of the right of self-determination of a people outside the national boundaries is a question entirely different from that of promoting the nation's internal cohesion.'

Dismayed at the leader deviating from the most cherished principles of the party, he warns of consequences which, much later, time would vindicate.

'In the Party's structure, the Secretary of Public Affairs will, I suppose, occupy the key position after you. You have chosen a priest to fill it, please reflect on its consequences. The class composition of the names so far in your list is itself interesting. We know that 85% of the population of Pakistan is rural, but should they be mainly represented by big landowners?...Paragraph 14 of the Constitution says, 'Representation of Workers and Other Groups: Representation shall be ensured in the Organizing Committees and later in the Party Committee, at all levels, for active party members from amongst the workers, the peasants, the youth, the women and the intellectuals'. This original idea, Rahim asserts, was perfect and it should be respected. 'Amongst the relevant functionaries created under your schemes there is no place for the problems of industrial workers, peasants, women and youth, about whom you have been so eloquent in the past, and no place for the problems of the intellectuals. To add to all this, there is no place for Mohajirs to whom you have been recently giving promises. I earnestly request you to drop the scheme you have formulated.' He then proposes the creation of a Central Committee and urges him to consult the class of people mentioned in paragraph 7 of the Interim Constitution.'

This following sentence of the letter predicts the tragic end of this relationship, which the leader perhaps anticipated in his heart but never heeded. 'I never regarded my being a Secretary General as no more than a convenient arrangement for carrying on work. The post is just *dicis causa* (naam ke waste) but so long as I am in the Party I have the responsibility towards it which I will fulfil.'

Every word of Rahim's letter must have been read by the Chairman with rising anger, doubt, regret, and apprehension.

On 30 September 1970, Rahim addressed the press. News that there was disagreement between him and ZAB was doing the rounds. The above letter of 23 August had got into the hands of the media through some official agencies or unofficial source. Rahim avers, 'The incident that has occurred is very interesting evidence in support of Mr Bhutto's contention that the government is not impartial. I can imagine how Nawabzada Sher Ali Khan[136]

---

[136]Nawabzada Sher Ali Khan, a feudal related to Loharu family. He was a minister in Ayub's Government.

must have let out a Napoleonic squeak of delight on receiving from the police my stolen correspondence.' He then goes on in dry clipped prose, 'The leadership of the party doesn't claim infallibility, mundane or divine. Now if my party leader bore such a name as Abul A'la, "Father of the All Highest,"[137] nobody would be entitled to differ with him. After all, one can't contradict God Almighty, and less even the Father of the All Highest. However, Mr Bhutto and myself are both mortals and neither claims to possess the one and only absolute truth.'

Rahim's disdain for Maulana Maudoodi is at times echoed by the leader, and sometimes dismissed and rejected. 'Father of the Highest', he mocks. 'Blasphemy even to deconstruct the meaning of his name!... The campaign of news about disagreement within PPP is selective and accords with the policy of selective arresting of our party leaders. Mairaj Mohammad Khan is under arrest... They have now arrested Maulana Kausar Niazi who has been courageously exposing the imposture of self-styled religious leaders... And as I write I get the news that Mir Ali Ahmed Talpur has also been arrested.'

ZAB's note of 8 January 1973 to Mubashir Hasan regarding the economic crisis and personal comment on Rahim speaks of his growing wariness about J.A. Rahim: 'There are many reasons for the economic crisis. Everyone has his own thesis. I want firm answers. I will support any sensible and unanimous decision of the Ministers, but on important issues, none of the Ministers are of the same view. They differ fundamentally. There is no coordination. Nobody is in overall charge. Mr Rahim has his views, and heavens really fall when anyone, including the President, disagrees with him. Mr Feroze Kaiser has his views, Mr Qamarul Islam[138] his views and you as Finance Minister, your own views. Each and

---

[137]J.A. Rahim's ironic reference to Maulana Maudoodi.
[138]Deputy Chairman, Planning Commission.

every little matter is therefore referred to me. This is not fair. Besides it causes delays.'[139]

Caesar's Antony: Story of Mustafa Khar[140]

There was something very attractive about the man who sat across from me when I went to meet him in the hope that he would speak about his mentor, for whom he was the younger brother he never had. I had accompanied Mubashir Hasan, who had been his comrade in arms and there was still, after 50 years, a strong bond between them. A tray of tea with several choicest snacks was brought on a trolley. I sensed shadows lurking behind half-closed doors, a caution which I learnt is taken by most feudals. Soft spoken, courteous, almost musical was his saraiki speech. Mubashir Hasan had told me the background of this man who I was now seeing for myself. Ghulam Mustafa Khar was the closest associate of ZAB, a man he loved as a brother, friend, confidante and on whom he showered many favours and to whom he meted out the worst punishment.

On 15 June 1968, ZAB wrote a letter to Mustafa Khar from 70 Clifton which reveals his long-term plan to launch him as the star of PPP. 'I am delighted to hear of the great impact your speech made in the National Assembly and outside. I am sure that this will enhance the standing of the party and serve higher national interests. I wonder what action the Government is contemplating? ...[It] can take no action other than to expel you

---

[139]*The Mirage of Power: An Inquiry into the Bhutto Years 1971-1977*, Mubashir Hasan, Oxford University Press, p 193

[140]Khar was elected to the National Assembly in 1962 and again in 1965. He was a member of the central committee of PPP and in 1970 was appointed the Party General Secretary of Punjab. Within hours of taking the oath of office, ZAB appointed him as Governor of Punjab and Deputy Chief Martial Law Administrator of the province. (*The Mirage of Power: An Inquiry into the Bhutto Years 1971-1977*, Mubashir Hasan. Oxford University Press, p 13)

from the discredited Muslim League. Expulsion will do your career immense good… You have put the Government in a dilemma. As time passes you are bound to give a greater measure of your strength and intelligence in the interest of the country and in the service of the people. I am confident of that.'[141]

Mustafa Khar, gazing through time, a hint of poignancy and resignation written all over him began speaking.

'At the start there was great trust between him and me. He always used to say, "Let Mustafa come and then I will decide." Of all members of the core group I was the one who spent maximum time with him. Before leaving for the UN Security Council in New York he said: "Mustafa, I am leaving you in charge of everything," "Mustafa, the way you understand me no one does."

Mustafa was now immersed in the past. Secretly glowing with pride while remembering ZAB's trust in him, he narrated the following incidents: 'ZAB phoned all his colleagues. "While I am gone, whatever Mustafa Khar says consider that to be my word." Understandably, Rahim did not like it. His words to Rahim were to the effect, "You have been out of Pakistan a long time. This boy, he understands it all."'

'His instructions to me were clear. "You are not to leave Islamabad. Don't… for more than 15 minutes… don't leave the phone."

"Sir. May I go home for 2 days? It has been a long time."

He was visibly annoyed. "Is this how I have trained you? Remember, political people have no homes, no families."

'So I sat by the phone. Day one nothing, day two nothing. On the third day, the phone rang and never stopped ringing.'

It was the news of ZAB's electrifying performance at the UN.

ZAB had been sent by Yahya Khan to Security Council as the plenipotentiary representing the government of Pakistan. He

---

[141]The letter is with the author.

was to plead the case of Pakistan before UNSC. While he was there Yahya Khan suffered the worst defeat in Dacca.

On 15 December 1971, in Security Council, ZAB uttered the words that stung the heart of every Pakistani. This magnificent speech, the tearing of the papers, and storming out of the Security Council have been discussed in chapter two.

On his return from the UNSC, he halted at Rome. While he was there, another drama was unfolding in Islamabad and Mustafa Khar's phone was ringing. It was Lt. General Peerzada.[142] 'Go and meet the General today. Just go. No need of taking an appointment.'

Mustafa Khar continued with his narration. Drama was unfolding before our eyes and Mustafa was transported in time. 'It was 1971, the third time India and Pakistan were at war. The city was in total blackout. In pitch dark I drove the car for 90 minutes to reach the President.

'The General was sitting at his desk with a glass of brandy. He was struggling with the desk drawer. He looked up at me and in his rich baritone, he spoke, "Mustafa, I have a great affection for you. When Bhutto was sending you to Dacca to talk to Mujeeb, I asked, 'Why are you sending this boy? He is very precious and the mission is highly risky.' When you left, I asked my commandos to protect you. This is proof of my affection. So I am trusting you with a crucial mission. Call Bhutto back." The words went into a spiralling echo. Call Bhutto back…Call Bhutto back…Call Bhutto back…

'Did I hear him right? I reached for the glass of water that had been placed before me. Stifling my own emotions that threatened to spill over, I heard myself speak in clipped and flat words. "Sir, Mr President. Send a private plane to get him. Let there be a bed

---

[142]Lt. Gen. S.G.M.M. Peerzada was President Yahya Khan's Principal Staff Officer who maintained a low profile but was very influential as the *de facto* chief of staff and virtual prime minister, although not a formal member of any of the governing bodies.

on which he can lie during the journey. He is very tired." He stretched his arm. "Here" he handed me the phone. "Talk to him."

'I did not move. We had agreed never to speak to each other from the President's House. No call from that quarter will be honoured. There was nothing more to say. When I left the room I saw once powerful, now the loneliest man of the country still sitting at his desk as I had found him an hour earlier.

'Pitch dark drive back was the most difficult driving I had ever done in my life. My colleagues were waiting. I dialled his number in Rome. Four pair of eyes looked on. "Please return. This is a turnkey job". At the other end there was no word just a sound, was it a sob or a sigh?

'President Yahya Khan's plan was that he would hand over power to him so long as he could stay on as president... all for the sake of the country! I knew that ZAB would resent this condition especially at the time when army's popularity was at its lowest ebb. But to Yahya Khan, I said what was as far as possible from the truth "Don't worry, Sir I will explain this to him."

'I was staying at the MNA hostel and this was the fourth night in a row when I could not sleep. So I strolled over to Intercontinental Hotel for a glass of lassi. There I saw, Air Marshall Asghar Khan with A.B. Awan[143]. Seeing me there, they looked surprised; then I saw the unmistakable... smirk. I sensed there was something amiss. Later on I found that they had a plan; Asghar Khan would become Prime Minister and Mr Bhutto would somehow be stopped; not allowed to return.

'My next job was to inform key party members that the Chairman was coming back and we had to make sure that nothing went wrong. Khurshid Hasan Mir, President, PPP, Rawalpindi wanted money to ensure his security. I began collecting funds. We got a total of 1.5 lakh.

---

[143]Director General intelligence Pakistan.

'ZAB's plane landed at Chaklala Airport. I drove on the tarmac upto the plane. For a moment he tarried at the doorway, next he was standing next to me. He slid in the front seat and we drove away. The car was owned by PPP Stalwart Nasrullah Khattak[144] who was sitting at the back. I turned to Bhutto Sahib and said, "I told you there this is a turnkey job; within two hours you will be President of Pakistan." At that moment Bhutto realised that someone was sitting at the back seat. He spoke three words, "Throw him out." So I stopped the car and asked Nasrullah to step out. He ran.

'The General was waiting. "I have no regrets, I have exercised absolute power. But before you take oath of office, take one order from me. And the order is Hang Sheikh Mujibur Rahman." Bhutto looked at the General straight in the eye. "This is no longer your job. This is my job. And I will do what is good for my country." Then Yahya spoke again, this time his voice was soft. "Mustafa must have spoken to you. I want to stay on for a while—for the sake of the country. You must help me." Bhutto was quiet. Yahya looked at me, question in his eyes. I looked down to avoid his eye. Then Bhutto spoke, "Mr President you don't understand the hatred against you and the hatred against the armed forces. Sorry, I cannot do this. But be assured; we will look after you." At that moment there were just three of us in the room. Then Bhutto asked if Rahim could be called in. But first Ghulam Ishaq Secretary, General Defence Ministry who later became President of Pakistan, was called in. Next to be called in was Rahim. In the presence of very few people, ZAB was sworn as the president and Chief Martial Law Administrator of Pakistan.

'Rahim came out to where few close friends were waiting and said, "Sab theek hai". In the very same car in which I brought him, I drove him home that night.'

---

[144]Nasrullah Khattak later became Chief Minister of NWFP.

Mustafa Khar sat back after he had spoken for almost an hour. There was silence for a few moments.

In *The Mirage of Power*, Mubashir Hasan wrote that the comradeship between Bhutto and Khar was deep. Khar was devoted to Bhutto who reciprocated in full measure. Just as Rahim was closest to Bhutto in deliberating and deciding questions of policy, Khar was closest to him in assessing and dealing with people. Both were men of courage and integrity. Rahim was Bhutto's political comrade. Khar was his personal comrade. Rahim could be relied upon for his intellectual capability. Khar could be trusted for his personal loyalty and courage. 'They could talk to each other through movements of their eyes or other gestures. Once, at the end of a party committee meeting, I asked Mustafa why he had suddenly decided to speak so harshly against one particular participant. His reply was "Sahib nay ishara kia tha" (Sahib had signalled)... From the day of the founding of the PPP, Khar was rightly considered to be the person nearest to Chairman Bhutto... They understood each other better than any two men in the Cabinet.'

Khar continued his recollections. 'Once, Mubashir and I were together. I had to go to Data Sahib's Dargah. I took his permission and we both went. There was a huge crowd of Zaireen outside. Suddenly the slogans were raised. "Sher-e-Punjab Zindabad," "Mustafa Khar Zindabad."

'Do you remember what you said to me at that time?' The question was directed at Mubashir.

'Yes I told you *apna boriya bistar bandh lein*. The leader cannot bear any one else's popularity.'

This apprehension surfaced in other instances. During the floods in August 1973, Bhutto was addressing a public gathering in Jhang. As soon as he appeared, the crowd shouted Sadda Quaid Zindabad. Suddenly a young man, Khar enthusiast, shouted 'Mustafa Khar Zindabad'. Bhutto ordered the Superintendent of

Police who was standing nearby to restrain the young man. Either the man did not stop or the policeman believed that the only way to stop him was by beating him up mercilessly. The man was a well-meaning worker of the Party and his beating by the police in the presence of the Party leadership was an ugly spectacle. Khar, who was standing next to ZAB, asked the policeman to stop. That infuriated Bhutto who curtly told Khar that the beating had been ordered by him and that if Khar wanted to become prime minster he was free to do so. The episode had taken place in full public glare.[145]

According to Miyan Mohammad Aslam, a friend and confidante, Khar had always wanted to stay near Bhutto and work under him rather than work on an independent charge. It is possible that Bhutto interpreted this desire for proximity as Khar's wish to become prime minister.

Mubashir Hasan writes about ZAB and Khar's complex relationship. They had been close comrades for a decade and were very loyal to one another. 'I cannot forget Bhutto's anguish on 8 November 1970, the day when he made his triumphant train journey from Rawalpindi to Lahore. On that day, since the police was out to get him, Khar was ordered to travel by public transport. When Bhutto reached Lahore he was told that Khar had not yet arrived; he was hugely upset. Again and again, he said "Khar has been nabbed, Khar has been nabbed." Khar arrived late in the evening. We hid him safely at Haneef Ramay's residence'. The first point of difference that emerged between the two friends might have been related to Khar's decision to marry Sheharzade Haq. Bhutto tried to dissuade Khar saying that he would have no time left for his job as governor, but ultimately relented and

---

[145]This was confirmed by Khar to Mubashir Hasan. Taken from *The Mirage of Power*. p.240.

attended the private marriage ceremony at the Governor House.[146]

However, the years 1972–1973 saw the distance between Khar and ZAB grow. Mubashir Hasan said that he was aware of Khar's doubts about the rightness or wisdom of some of the decisions taken by the boss, which Khar had to carry out. But these were not serious differences on questions of policy or programme. They related mostly to Bhutto's choice of people. What ultimately tore them apart was Bhutto's suspicion of Khar's ambition for power. 'The eventual decision to part company must have been difficult for both men, he was Mark Antony to his beloved Caesar.'

Our meeting with Mustafa Khar was approaching its end; I asked him, 'Sir, any last words about your fascinating relationship with your leader?' Mustafa's words were laden with sadness. 'He began listening to others' gossip against me. I was deeply hurt. One evening he came to my house. We sat in the lawn. After a few drinks he got up to leave, I quietly placed an envelope in his hand—my resignation. He said nothing. Three days later I went to receive him at the airport. While I waited for the flight to land I told media about my resignation. When he landed, the media asked him. He was obviously angry. A few days later when I went to see him off for Larkana he asked me not to resign. He said "I am not threatening you but once you leave the Governor House we cannot remain so close..."

It was summer of 1974 when ZAB decided to relieve Khar as the chief minister of Punjab. He was staying at Khar's personal house before making the momentous announcement of dismissing his host and friend as the chief minister of Punjab.[147] 'There are guests in my house. Suddenly I find out that I am dismissed and Haneef Ramey is appointed CM Punjab'. The next morning

---

[146]*The Mirage of Power: An Inquiry into the Bhutto Years 1971-1977*, Mubashir Hasan, p 238-239.
[147]*Ibid.* p 241-242.

Mustafa Khar told Mubashir Hasan that ZAB said to him, 'I had thought that tonight you will kill me.'

Mubashir Hasan added, 'Khar's friends, thirteen good party workers were arrested in Azad Kashmir, an area where the Federal Court could not interfere. I appealed on their behalf but to no avail. Was this his way to punish Khar when he "revolted"? Was it his way—not to touch Mustafa directly but hurt him through his companions?'

Khar continued, 'After resigning I began seeking a ticket. It was Haneef Ramay who said to me "Ticket to mein doonga nahin. Jeetney bhi nahin doonga. Phir aap Punjab se bhi farigh ho jaenge," meaning, I won't give you a ticket, I won't let you win. Then you will be relieved of Punjab.

'After this I left for London. There I got word from him which brought tears to my eyes. "I could not take you in my sailboat. Will you join me in my sinking boat?"'[148] After these lines, Mustafa Khar became silent, as if years of history, its burden and its wrongs had been vented.

Son-rise Sunset: Story of Mairaj Mohammad Khan

Young, loyal, dearly loved; ZAB once mentioned at a Press Conference in 1971 that he nominated Mairaj Mohammad Khan and Mustafa Khar as his two successors. According to him, the PPP had a parliamentary and a revolutionary face, which these two represented.[149] Mairaj had been assigned portfolio of Minister of State for Political Affairs because of the position he enjoyed among students and a large section of organized labour. But he was not satisfied with his portfolio. In July 1972, he told ZAB that prior to 1958, the allowances and privileges of the Ministers of State were almost the same as were admissible to Cabinet

---

[148]Ghulam Mustafa Khar narrated this to Mubashir Hasan and the author in 2015.
[149]*Pakistan Times*, Lahore and Rawalpindi, 20 February 1971.

Ministers. He asked for his discretionary grant as Minister of State to be raised from 2,000 to 10,000 per annum as was allowed to Cabinet Ministers. He also asked for raising the rank of his private secretary to that of Class I Gazetted officer and one of his peons to that of a jamadar. ZAB only granted the last request.

Then, something happened. ZAB's letter of 19 September written to all colleagues was a clear call asking for Mairaj's resignation. The letter was precise, mincing no words:

'So despite the crisis and despite my patience and regard for all my colleagues, there comes a time when human endurance gets exhausted, one sees a line beyond which it is intolerable to tolerate. Yesterday in a speech, a Minister of State made a scathing attack on a colleague in Central Government. I will not be able to run the Government of Pakistan if I permit such flagrant displays of indiscipline. I have seen many shocking things but I was shocked to see the way the Minister of State ventilated his prejudice against a colleague of Government in open air. This unabashed criticism in public of the limbs of the same body will lead to ruination. Immediately I disassociate myself from such foolish mudslinging. I have said a thousand times that there is a place and a time for criticism. I have never discouraged internal; but external criticism of any nature and especially of this kind cannot be condoned. In view of these circumstances I give a final warning to all Governors and Ministers and Special Assistants to desist from such deplorable violations of discipline, to desist from foolish antics, to bring down their own Government to contempt and ridicule. I am giving this final warning as the Minister concerned is a young man whom I have tried to groom and bring up as a leader. I have spent much time and effort in training him. On many occasions, in the past he has taken a different path, even on small matters, but at the time we were not running the country, so I ignored his defiance. I have stood by him when he has been attacked by colleagues and friends before we came into office and after assuming office. On occasions I have been told that he still follows his own line which is not in conformity with the Government line and this has caused us increasing difficulties. I have not taken notice of such criticism. I had hoped that with passage of time better sense would prevail. I am not taking action because at one time I said that this young friend of mine might become my successor. I am sorry to say that he has not measured up to that expectation. On account of his long association with me I am giving this final warning. I hope that in future none of us will have cause to face such an ugly embarrassment. This warning is not a threat. It has been given in good faith and in the higher interest of the Government's proper performance of its functions and, shall we all halt to say, in the supreme interest of Pakistan.'

These scathing words, precisely articulated meant the end of Mairaj Mohammed Khan. Mubashir Hasan said that the fact that ZAB was blaming his entire team for the lack of diligence shown by a few was the first sign that he was beginning to lose patience with the kind of team he had at his disposal. The above note was a virtual parting of the ways with his close associate and Minister of State.[150] But the fact behind the tirade was the growing power over him of the intelligence machine.

Mubashir Hasan writes, 'At last, the intelligence services had succeeded in poisoning Bhutto's mind against the competence of his team of ministers and particularly against the man the Intelligence community had hated since his student days in the

---

[150] As told by Mubashir Hasan to the author in January 2017.

early 1950s—Mairaj Mohammad Khan.'[151]

Events piled up and Mairaj resigned in October 1972. A few months later, he was sent to jail. The next Mubashir Hasan heard was that he was hospitalized. He appealed to ZAB, 'Release him please. His eyes have become very bad.' ZAB did nothing. ZAB had once said that from Mairaj he had learnt more than a thing or two in the art of addressing public meetings. Rafi Raza wrote that it was the group around Mairaj that devised 'Roti, Kapra aur Makaan', the rallying call of the Party. In Pakistan, the slogan electrified the masses. It was a catchy version of a slogan among students in India:

> Roti, Kapra aur Makaan
> Mang raha hai har insaan
> (Bread, clothes and housing is the demand of all human beings).[152]

It was not just Mairaj. Within a few months of becoming head of state, a gulf began to form between Bhutto and most of his colleagues, even his old personal friends. Not one amongst them could address him with his nickname 'Zulfi'!

Bloodline: Story of Mumtaz Ali Bhutto[153]

ZAB's closest cousin was Mumtaz Ali Bhutto, who was educated at Christ Church, Oxford (1954-57), and studied law at Lincoln's

---

[151] *The Mirage of Power : An Inquiry into the Bhutto Years 1971-1977*, Mubashir Hasan, p 187.

[152] *Zulfikar Ali Bhutto and Pakistan, 1967-1977*, Rafi Raza, Oxford University Press, 1997, p 8-9.

[153] Mumtaz Ali Bhutto was a member of the National Assembly of Pakistan from 1965 to 1969. He won the 1970 election against Qazi Fazalullah and became Governor of Sindh and Martial Law Administrator on 24 December 1971. He then became the chief minister of Sindh Province in May 1972, later resigned from this post in December 1973. He was arrested during the struggle against the arrest of ZAB in 1977 and then exiled by General Zia's government. He stayed with ZAB until the end.

Inn in London. He was called to the Bar in London in 1959. He and ZAB called each other 'adha', 'brother' in Sindhi, although Mumtaz's grandfather and ZAB's great-grandfather were brothers.[154]

Of him, ZAB once said in his speech, 'The people of Pakistan are my family. Of course, I have a talented cousin who is outstanding in his own right. He will have a right to serve the people because he has gone to jail. He is intelligent. He has gone to Oxford.' In the feudal set-up of Sindh, Mumtaz's family was considered to be the senior family. His father had served as a member of the State Council of the Governor General of India.[155]

He was an important figure in Sindh's politics when PPP formed government in 1971. He, who had held the banner of the Party and the provincial government of Sindh in the most difficult period of 1972, was sidelined as Minister of Communications.

The paranoia of ZAB became evident one day in 1976 while they were on a tour of Sindh. Night halt for ZAB was arranged in the home of Pir Sahib of Hala, and Mumtaz was to stay at the Resthouse. ZAB summoned Mumtaz to his room that night and showed him an Intelligence report. In utter disbelief, Mumtaz read the words of the report. It stated that he (Mumtaz) has plotted that the PM should be shot at the meeting scheduled the next day. 'Do you believe this nonsense?' ZAB spoke three words, 'I don't know'. He ordered the staff, 'Bring Mumtaz Sahib's luggage from the Rest House. He will stay here.' Staff scurried around to arrange a room and Mumtaz moved in a room next to ZAB's. Next morning, the Hala meeting, which was to be held 30 miles from Hyderabad, was cancelled. It was announced that the Chairman had fever.

---

[154]*Zulfikar Ali Bhutto and Pakistan, 1967-1977*, Rafi Raza, Oxford University Press, 1997, p 22.

[155]*The Mirage of Power: An Inquiry into the Bhutto Years 1971-1977*, Mubashir Hasan, p 13-14.

Contenders

Sheikh Mujibur Rahman[156]

That two leaders rose, one in West Pakistan, Quaid-e-Awam, and the other in East Pakistan, Bangla Bondhu, is fact of history.

In March 1969, Ayub Khan had transferred power to Yahya Khan and martial law was imposed. In 1970, Yahya Khan called elections. There was an overwhelming win for Awami League in East Pakistan (Sheikh Mujibur Rahman) with a stunning victory of 160 out of 162 seats and PPP in West Pakistan (Zulfikar Ali Bhutto) with 81 out of 131 seats.

On 19 November 1969, Mubashir Hasan, on his return from Dacca, issued a press statement in which he described conditions prevailing there. He wrote that there was food crisis, labour unrest, education in disarray, crisis in jute. Flight of capital to West Pakistan was hugely resented. 'It is essential that a full measure of autonomy must be conceded and power transferred unreservedly without delay. It is my firm view that demand of people of East Pakistan for autonomy should be acceded forthwith. Only those bonds are strong bonds that are based on mutual interest, understanding and respect. The rest is a myth.'

It was in 1971 when ZAB wrote a letter which reveals his intense desire to make united front with East Pakistan. He wanted maximum cooperation with Awami League without compromising principles of PPP. Never comfortable with Mujibur Rahman's Six Point Formula,[157] he expressed his hope that they may drop one or two in 'national interest'. National Awami League—NAP

---

[156]Mujibur Rehman was a political figure from 1955 while a student in Calcutta. Fiery speaker and nationalist Bengali. In his youth, he was associated with the great Bengali leader Hussain Shaheed Suhrawardy.

[157]The six point program of the party incorporated a set of demands which would free East Pakistan from the control of the central government and transfer economic and political power in the region to its middle classes.

(Moscow) was receptive and he hoped Mubashir and Khar who were meeting Professor Muzaffar would get NAP (China) in the same mood. He liked to balance the two NAP factions but warned against Maulana Bhashani[158] who he said was very mercurial. 'We have to watch him, not eliminate him, but at the same time be very careful of another betrayal.' He commented on Syed Mahbub Morshed[159] who had said that with a few amendments the constitution would work well.

He wrote to Rao Sattar, 'I was delighted to learn that Awami League of East Pakistan is co-operating with PPP. This is excellent. We should do everything to have maximum co-operation without affecting our principles and positions, without compromising on the six points as they exist. I am glad they are willing to drop some of the points in national interest. In these circumstances our co-operation will be the most formidable in the country. I am also glad to learn that Moscow NAP of East Pakistan is also in a more receptive mood. It is good that Professor Muzzafar met Khar and Mubashir to discuss co-operation. This is a satisfactory trend and should be encouraged.[160]

'It was silly of Morshed to say that with a few amendments this Constitution can work well. This will give a big handle to government if they are wise enough to capitalize on this observation. The whole Constitution is undemocratic. ...'[161]

---

[158]Abdul Hamid Khan Bhashani was the founder and President of the Pakistan Awami Muslim League which later became Awami League (AL). Later, however, owing to differences with the right-leaning leaders in the AML, such as Shaheed Suhrawardy, on the issue of autonomy for East Pakistan, he formed a new progressive party called National Awami Party (NAP). He gained popularity among peasants and helped establish the East Pakistan Peasant Association.

[159]President PPP Dacca and Former Chief Justice Dacca High Court who refused to administer oath to Tikka Khan as Governor and Martial Law Administrator.

[160]Letter sent to Rao Sattar from Sahiwal jail. Undated letter is with the author.

[161]Undated letter to Mubashir Hasan from Sahiwal jail. Copy of the letter is with the author.

On 13 January 1970, Rahim wrote to Nuruzzaman apologizing for ZAB's inability to attend the Kisan Labour Conference convened by Maulana Bhashani in Santosh. 'Struggle for socialism cannot be successful until peasants and workers combine together. Establish active collaboration between trade unions and kisans. I believe in East Pakistan this is happening. But in the West Wing there is a big gap.'

PPP leaders went back and forth to East Pakistan trying to build bridges. Their schedules were punishing. They wanted to cover maximum ground to instil confidence in the people of the region. During my research, I found one handwritten itinerary of Mubashir Hasan's visit to East Pakistan. It was written on the letterhead of Hotel Inter-Continental Dacca:

> First day Dacca to Bogra, Rajshahi—first flight
> Second day, night stay Rajshahi
> Third day, Rajshahi to Dacca—first flight
> Fourth day, Dacca to Mymensingh—by train
> Fifth day, night stay Dacca
> Sixth day, Dacca to Jessore
> Seventh day, Jessore to Dacca
> Eight day, Dacca to Chittagong—by train (day tour)
> Ninth day, Chittagong to Dacca

On the margin in Mubashir Hasan's hand are written names of other districts, probably the ones he wanted to visit. Khulna, Bogra, Faridpur, Barasol, Dinajpur, Comilla.

One small handwritten note of Mubashir Hasan to ZAB, summarizing East Pakistan's resentment and demand has survived in his papers. It reveals the root cause of the final breakaway:

> 'East Pakistan had been exploited for 24 years. Was not given share. Deep resentment against West Pakistan.
> Suggested by Mujibur Rahman:

Two separate economies
Two separate State Banks.'

On 22 March 1970, ZAB, Mustafa Khar, Mubashir Hasan and Rahim, reached Dacca. All day long, ZAB phoned Mujibur Rahman but the phone just rang and rang. ZAB wanted to make common cause with Mujibur Rahman but he had other plans in mind. While arms were being sent and forces gathering at Dacca, Yahya arrived ostensibly to sign a deal with Mujibur Rahman, nominating him PM and transferring power.

What happened then became the last blow to a United Pakistan. But what actually transpired behind the scene remained a mystery to me until July 2017 when Mubashir Hasan recalled the events:

'Years had passed when Dr Kamal Hussain (who later served as foreign minister of Bangladesh) and I were at the Bombay airport waiting lounge. I asked Kamal, "What went wrong? Why didn't MR and ZAB not devise a common strategy? Why did they break the pact? "Kamal Hussain revealed that Mujibur Rehman had come to an agreement with Yahya Khan about transfer of power. It was agreed between them that on 23 March 1971 Yahya Khan will transfer power to Mujibur Rahman as Prime Minister of Pakistan. An agreement with the i's dotted and t's crossed was to be signed by Yahya Khan and Mujibur Rahman that very day. All day on 23 March Kamal kept phoning Yahya Khan who was staying at government house Dacca to ask the time Mujibur Rahman should come to sign the agreement. The phone was never received. Then came the bombshell; we learnt Yahya Khan and his men suddenly left Dacca. That night, by order of the President the brutal military action to crush Awami League was started."

'It is recorded that Mujib spoke words which marked

the end of the story of East Pakistan, "Woh haramzada chala gaya" (The bastard left).

'In the military code, moral values do not exist when you are negotiating with the enemy or potential enemy. False promises are very easily made. It was the biggest fraud on Mujib and people of East Pakistan.' Mubashir Hasan said with a sigh![162]

Wali Khan[163]

Mubashir Hasan recounted this brutal story to me.

Wali Khan held a big rally in Pindi. There was propaganda that thousands of his supporters would come there with guns. When he learnt of this, ZAB with the head of his security force made a plan to disrupt the meeting and turn it into a failure. As it turned out, Wali Khan's supporters did not possess as many weapons as the government had suspected. In midst of meeting, forces in plain clothes started firing. The meeting was disrupted and there was crossfire. Fourteen workers of PPP who had come from Mandi Bahauddin were killed. Several rallyists of ANP were shot. Wali Khan returned to Peshawar with intense hatred for ZAB. It was the case of miscalculation and knee-jerk ruthlessness.

On 2 October 1974, ZAB wrote a file note about Wali Khan:

'We can knock the hell out of what he said in Karachi. But unfortunately we are more busy with internal strife and routine quarrels. We like to sit and grumble. Very few of us go out to do the job. Wali Khan is an agent of India and Afghanistan. His background and political career is summed

---

[162]As told by Mubashir Hasan to the author in July 2017.
[163]Khan Abdul Wali Khan was President of National Awami Party. In the 1970s, he also served as the leader of opposition in Pakistan's first directly elected parliament. During the freedom movement while he was a teenager he was active in the Indian National Congress.

up in his hatred for Pakistan. He and his father have been stalwarts of the Congress yet he has the audacity to speak to the students of Karachi and others in this cavalier fashion.'

Maulana Abdul Hameed Khan Bhashani

Maulana Bhashani was a mullah turned leftist from East Pakistan. He was the head of National Awami Party (Socialist). Bhashani was more akin to PPP ideology. On 1 March 1969, a Joint Statement was issued by him as president National Awami Party and ZAB as president PPP.

In supreme national interest:

We pledge to work together in cooperation on the basis of the following points:

1. For the establishment of democracy of the people on the basis of the recognized demands of the people of East and West Pakistan.

2. For the establishment of socialism in conformity with the ideology of Pakistan.

3. For the elimination of foreign interference, opposition to all kinds of colonialism, Neocolonialism, imperialism, including withdrawal from CENTO, SEATO, and all military commitments as well as for the liquidation of governments's Bada Bear Base. (American airbase at Rahim Yar Khan used for launching spy planes.)

In a letter dated 13 January 1970 to PPP's Maulana Nuruzzaman, Chair Dacca, J.A. Rahim wrote that neither he nor the Chairman will be able to come to East Pakistan for Bhashani's Conference. Directing him to attend on their behalf, he says there was little difference in kisan and labour questions between the two parties. He urges him to ask for closer cooperation of socialist parties. Also, he was instructed to bring to notice of the Conference the necessity of closer cooperation between labour and peasantry.

'Build up constant living contact between city workers and peasantry and establish active collaboration between trade unions and kisans. (I believe in East Pakistan it is happening but in West Wing there is a big gap).'

Saboteurs

Maulana Maudoodi[164]

In a press statement issued on 8 June 1970 by Mubashir Hasan, Chairman PPP Lahore, the differences between the party and Maulana Maudoodi are spelt out. Maudoodi was referred as the agent in chief of US Imperialism, monopoly capitalism and feudalism. His calls for violence are on the Indonesian pattern which means massacre of all those who disagree with him. In a press report, he was reported to have said that time had come once again to perpetrate Indonesia type violence in Pakistan.

Both Rahim and Mubashir Hasan had natural aversion to Maudoodi. When ZAB asked Mubashir Hasan to meet Maudoodi, he ignored the leader's command. This is discussed in detail in chapter five.

Mubashir Hasan's press statement condemns Maudoodi in the harshest of words:

'Such sinister and evil calls are not altogether unexpected. I had drawn the attention of the nation several times in 1969 to his nefarious designs. I had also pointed out the threats of violence and murder that his front organisations had sent to pro-people elements in the country, including many workers of the PPP. But this time there is a difference. More fascist groups have come into being. They are giving open calls for

---

[164]He was the founder of the Jamaat-e-Islami. He and his party are thought to have been the pioneer in politicizing Islam and generating support for an Islamic state in Pakistan. They inspired General Muhammad Ziaul Haq to introduce 'Sharitization' to Pakistan.

liquidation (see issues of their weekly rags). This time the call is accompanied by action. His henchmen have begun to harangue the public on an unprecedented scale. The first victim of violence has been a shop on the Mall which they suspected was selling pro-people and un-Islamic literature. Copies of Holy Quran, books of Hadith and Fiqah have been burnt down. Conscience of the Pakistani nation has been stirred to its depths.'

Dozens of books and pamphlets were written by left thinkers against Maudoodi whose own writings were full of ignorant and ludicrous paragraphs about politics and history. He and other Islamic parties had been against the very foundation of Pakistan. He had even declared that fighting for Kashmir by Pakistanis will not bring them martyrdom but they will die like dogs. In another press statement dated 30 September 1970, Rahim describes Maudoodi as a self-styled righteous leader who had done enough and said enough to be condemned as an enemy of Pakistan.

Maulana Kausar Niazi[165]

Many aspects of Maulana Kausar Niazi vis-a-vis ZAB were revealed as oral history in the course of my research, which I decided to focus on rather than relying on secondary sources. Explaining his background, Mubashir Hasan said Kausar Niazi became an intelligence agent from his youth. He was recruited

---

[165]Kausar Niazi was a religious scholar and orator. In the 1950s and 60s, Niazi was a prominent member of the Jamaat-e-Islami (JI). The JI denounced Bhutto and the PPP of being a party of communists who were being backed by the Soviet Union to 'destroy faith in Pakistan'. After disagreeing with JI's line of attack against Bhutto, Niazi broke away from the party. Niazi's entry into the PPP was not welcomed by the party's leftist ideologues. But Bhutto overruled their concerns. He served as the minister of Religious & Minorities Affairs till 1976 and was later appointed the Federal Information Minister.

by them when he used to serve tea at a shop in Mianwali.

Mubashir Hasan explained his reluctance to accept him in the party, 'We suspected he was asked by Intelligence to join PPP. We refused to accept him in the party. He came to Lahore and held a meeting which PPP workers disrupted. I as Chairman Lahore refused him membership. A while later, ZAB was holding a public meeting in Karachi. From the platform of that meeting he invited Kausar Niazi to speak. We were shocked at this gesture. Most of us considered this as dilution of principles. In his speech Kausar Niazi condemned Yahya Khan. Later, Kausar Niazi called a conference of Mullahs. He took it upon himself to bribe all the Mullahs of Pakistan. He was well-suited for this work.

'I.A. Rehman was told by Aftab Ahmed Khan, Secretary Finance, about this incident. At ZAB's house, Kausar Niazi was running along the border of the lawn, huffing and puffing. He came to Mr Bhutto and said, "Is that enough?" Bhutto cooly said, "No, two more rounds." When asked the reason, Aftab was told that he was being punished for embezzling funds which were meant for hiring women escorts for entertaining a royal visitor from Saudi Arabia.

'Yahya Khan sent him to jail. Then 1970 elections took place and Kausar Niazi contested from Sialkot Jail and won. Anyone with a PPP ticket would have won. So no special praise was due for Niazi.

'ZAB had a love-hate relation with Kausar Niazi. The first time ZAB called for him it was evening. Drinks had been served. When Kausar Niazi arrived ZAB hid his drink. People in the room were amazed. "You never know," said the boss, "Niazi may write an article titled 'Jo mene dekha against me just as he had written 'Jo mene dekha against Maudoodi.

'In Pakistan, his nickname was Maulana Whiskey! At the second meeting with ZAB when Kausar Niazi stepped out of his room, Bhutto asked that whiskey be poured in his drink. He did not seem to notice and enjoyed the drink.[166]

'ZAB made him Minister of Religious Affairs. Over the years, he became ZAB's close advisor. The saddest part was that he and Hafeez Pirzada gave him wrong advice. They were the ones who persuaded ZAB to compromise with opposing political parties in March and April 1977.'

An interesting aspect is seen in Mubashir Hasan's own equation with Kausar Niazi. He disliked him but came to his help to maintain image of the party. On 16 May 1970, a press release was issued by Mubashir Hasan and Mustafa Khar which condemned attack on Maulana Kausar by Shorish Kashmiri. 'A wave of resentment has spread among the masses and poor people at the news of the dastardly attack on Niazi by Shorish Kashmiri, (editor Chattan) the leader of the fascist organization known as Sarfarosh Tanzeem and his henchmen. ... The attack can only be understood if viewed against the background of the atmosphere of hate and violence which has been created in the last few months by the rightist press and organisations against the people's forces. Deliberate attempts are being made to perpetrate violence to create another Indonesia.'[167]

On 27 November 1970, Niazi wrote to Mubashir Hasan. First he stated his loyalty to his leader and pledged his life for Islamic socialism. Then, he bitterly complained against Mahmud Ali Qasuri. ZAB had given him ticket for Pasur constituency but MAQ made one Khizr Ali (advocate) file papers for the same halqa. He then asked Election Commission to invite fresh nomination papers. In his letter, he accused Qasuri of being close associate of Maudoodi and Shorish on whose behest he was creating trouble.

Zuhoor Alam Shaheed, a columnist of *Nawa-i-Waqt*, writes 'After Supreme Court judgement of 1979, Kausar Niazi did not

---

[166] As told by Mubashir Hasan to the author.
[167] Press statement is with the author.

have the courage to utter a single word. But after the execution he said, "Bhutto's real murderers were his party leaders. If only they had let him (Niazi) meet him in the prison, the hanging could have been called off."'

As they say, 'When a ship is sinking, rats are the first to jump off.'

9

There Was a Man

'Who was the man, ZAB, as you knew him from the day you met him in 1967 when on the spur of the moment your group of men and women decided to join hands with him? Who was the person who you saw walk into Yahya Khan's office with Mustafa Khar where behind closed doors he took office as the president of Pakistan? Then who was the man you knew over those years when he held the highest office?' These were questions which I asked Mubashir Hasan over the years to help me get into the head and heart of a man I had never met.

A portrait began to emerge through Mubashir Hasan's words:

'Try to understand the mind of a sovereign, a man in whose name the state acts. Don't judge his actions as ethical or unethical. When you act for the state—you are the Sovereign. There are no ethics. State is accountable to no one. Interest of the state is paramount, it often clashes with the whims of the individual. State is ruthless, compassionate, criminal, builder, destroyer—all at one and the same time. "Badshahat qaim rakhne ke liye" sovereign has to resort to ruthless measures—measures which public forgets easily. Aurangzeb dethroned his father and blinded him, killed eight brothers, won battles, yet was known as a great ruler. History is replete with such examples.'

Machiavelli laid the rule about what a prince should do. There is a story from Herodotus[168] which I heard from Mubashir Hasan during our sessions. When I read my notes several years later it was my epiphany to understanding ZAB.

'There was a prince who went for shikar near the border of his father's kingdom. There he was accosted by the neighbouring prince. A battle ensued, the prince defeated his opponents and occupied the territory. Then the question arose, how to govern? It was a new territory with a new conqueror So, he sent his emissary to his father. "Go ask my father what shall I do with the new conquered land?" The man appeared before the king and gave the son's message. The King listened carefully and asked the emissary to wait. The man was escorted to guest quarters and very well looked after. Days passed. There was no word from the king. One day he received orders to accompany the king on his royal hunt. The man was relieved, now the king will talk to him. During the entire hunt the king did not speak. After the game was hunted the shikar party started the return journey. When they reached a field with standing crop, the king ordered to stop. He got down from his horse walked into the field and began brandishing his sword over his head. The taller of the crops were slashed. He then mounted his horse and resumed the journey. The next day the emissary received word that he was to return. There was no option but to obey. He returned to the prince and narrated the story of his failed mission. "I only met him once when he asked me to accompany him for shikar." The Prince thought for a while. "Did he do any thing unusual?" "Nothing except..." He narrated the incident of the standing crop in the field. The Prince looked happy. "I have my answer".'

'Cut off the heads of the most prominent ones, only then

---

[168]Herodotus (ca. 484 B.C.–ca. 425 B.C. was the first Greek writer who succeeded in writing a large-scale historical narrative that has survived the passage of time.

would you gain complete control.'

Was this the modus operandi of ZAB? Then why did he make some fatal mistakes, the most lethal being the appointment and elevation of Ziaul Haq?

A few lines that he wrote from his death cell reveal an aspect of the man which has few parallels in history except perhaps his ideal, Napoleon. It is the clinching fact, which turned him to politics and ultimately into the tallest political figure of Pakistan, perhaps of South Asia and Islamic world. 'On my 21st birthday on 5 January 1948, I received in Los Angeles two birthday gifts from Larkana. One was an expensive set of five volumes of Sloane's biography of Napoleon Bonaparte. The other was an inexpensive locally printed pamphlet. From Napoleon I imbibed the politics of power. From the pamphlet I absorbed the politics of poverty. The pamphlet ended with the words of Karl Marx, "Workers of the world unite. You have nothing to lose but your chains. You have a world to win."[169] He recalled the advice about politics given by his father, 'Politics is like building a temple, a house. It is like writing poetry, music...' In an interview, he told the Italian journalist Oriana Fallaci, 'There are many conflicts in me. I am aware of that. I try to reconcile them but I don't succeed and I remain this strange mixture of Asia and Europe. My mind is Western and my soul is Eastern.' Then becoming deeply thoughtful, he spoke his views of politics and power. 'You don't go into politics just for the fun of it. You go into it to take power in your hands and keep it. Anyone who says the opposite is a liar. Politicians are always trying to make you believe that they are good, moral, and consistent. Don't ever fall into their trap. There is no such thing as a good, moral, consistent politician. The rest is Boy Scout stuff. And I have forgotten the Boy Scout virtues ever since I went to school.'

---

[169] *If I am Assassinated.* Zulfikar Ali Bhutto, 1979. Vikas Publishing House. p 224

There is frame after frame of TV grabs and file pictures testifying that he was adored by the people, a love he reciprocated to an extent. One incredible image that rises to the mind is of a shepherd of the flock of poor illiterate people of Pakistan leading them to claim a life of dignity! One late afternoon as he and Mubashir Hasan were driving from Kharian to Rawalpindi, after offering condolences at the death of President Fazal Elahi Chaudhry's mother, he saw labour engaged in breaking large pieces of stone into smaller bits. Tears came to his eyes when he said, 'Dr Sahib, when will my countrymen not have to break stone with their hands?' Later, speaking at a massive rally, he said, 'From this day onwards no hari will touch the knees of a Vadera'.

Street gossip swirled about him as Ayub's Minister, 'Known for womanizing,' 'Playboy,' 'He drinks, womanizes,' 'Not worth being PM,' 'He is not a socialist,' 'He has become a Mulla,' 'He was Ayub's Foreign Minister, then made a party against him. Betrayed his own Mohsin'. Mubashir Hasan for his own reasons did not give much information about the sexual innuendos. 'At least he was not a "ghatiya" (degraded) playboy. His women friends included people like the elegant Tahira Mazhar Ali and her sister who was married to Bashir Qureshi CSP plus an elite clutch of women in East Pakistan. After he entered politics he became somewhat careful.' He drank every evening but Mubashir Hasan vows that he never saw him drunk. 'When I used to visit his home, which was at least three or four nights a week, drinks were the norm. But the incontrovertible rule was, no decisions only discussion in the evening over drinks.'

'He was either intensely loved or hated,' said Mubashir Hasan while he recalled some of ZAB's contradictions and anomalies. Whatever he said should be viewed as a promise of a political leader and not a promise of a gentleman. 'When I say something as head of the state, my topmost priority is the good of my state. If I put someone in jail it is because that is for the good of the state.'

In his letter to Mohammad Haneef Ramay, editor of *Nusrat*, ZAB wrote about Fazlul Qadir Chaudhry, calling him a 'madman' who was being influenced by the Haroons. He hated the Haroons. Once General Musa Khan, Governor of Punjab and former Commander-in-Chief of Pakistan Army under Ayub Khan, viciously attacked him in his Hyderabad speech by saying 'What does he think of himself! We will take off his trousers.' When this was reported to him, ZAB calmly replied that if he did that he would see what the entire army lacked.

Dost Mohammad Khoso, Member National Assembly from Sukhkar, was in tears. ZAB had asked Mumtaz to 'fix' him for daring to lift his plate before ZAB had lifted his at the buffet dinner. The man was pleading, 'I was not holding a plate in my hand'.

Then there were other stories. Jamaat-e-Islami's VP Miyan Mohammad Tufail was buggered in jail. At whose instance?

Mahmud Ali Qasuri's son Umar Qasuri was in jail. The boy was alleged to have been assaulted. Was it done at Bhutto's instance? To teach him a lesson? On the subject of Qasuri, Hasan continued, 'Once I said to ZAB that Qasuri's National Awami Party (NAP) was speaking against our party. ZAB asked me to issue a statement. I called a press conference and issued a statement; from there I went to see him in Sahiwal jail. As I entered, Qasuri was there complaining against my statement. ZAB looked at me with questioning eyes. It was as if saying what I did was wrong. He thereby exonerated himself before Qasuri, giving himself full flexibility to change the decision.

'He had great power to convince people. I resigned so many times; he would always ask me to stay on, giving me any number of good reasons. "Abhi na jaao." "Constitution ban jaaney do," "abhi election ho jane do," "Budget bana do," "Tum kaise chhor kar jaa saktey ho. Tumhi tau mere ek sathi ho."

In September 1975, Mubashir Hasan left the country with the firm idea of not returning for a while. Illness that suddenly afflicted him was not the only reason why he wanted to quit. Ministership did not seem to be his 'cup of tea'. For personal reasons, he was never attracted to a job involving the use of authority. While he was away, ZAB decided to reconstitute Cabinet. He phoned Mubashir Hasan a few times asking him to return and pick his preferred portfolio. Politely, but firmly, he begged ZAB to excuse him.

It was 1977. Mubashir Hasan recalls the long meetings in those troubled times and the pressure on him to become Secretary General (SG) of the party. ZAB had said it was not his fault that things were bad; there was no SG of the party. Haneef Ramay stood up and proposed Mubashir Hasan. 'I was asked for my opinion. I said that things are very bad and I am unsuitable for this work. No one agrees with me.' ZAB asked them to break for tea; forty of us left the room. During the break, Mubashir's friends were able to persuade him. So he said yes, but placed a condition that the office should move to Lahore. In Islamabad, the office was located Rafigue Saigol's office complex. Saigol told Mubashir Hasan, 'Take the files but not the air conditioner.' Even as he moved to Lahore, he doubted if this would work but he still collected a band of committed leftist party workers for running the office. A Vadera was made his deputy (DSG) in Islamabad. Literature printed by him in Lahore stated that anyone who had any record of oppressing agriculture labour or farmers would be ineligible. This directive was instantly rejected by ZAB.

Sitting in his cousin Salim Jilani's house in Islamabad, Mubashir Hasan waited for long but no candidate's application came to him. So he asked the Chairman. 'I can't send them,' he replied. 'We have already decided'. Instead of taking umbrage, Mubashir Hasan decided to put up a fight for his hand-picked candidates. A slate of eight people for Lahore was presented by him. The first, second and third went to his candidates. When the fourth name came up, ZAB said, 'I won't hear anything. I will give it to Miyan Salahuddin.' Nothing could have been more violative of party principles. But this man also won because of the trend; everyone from PPP won.

Just before the election, ZAB had called a meeting with the District Commissioners, who bitterly criticized his ministers. As a fall out, that very day Jatoi resigned. In the evening, ZAB came to the party meeting and asked Jatoi, 'Why do you trouble me so much; you are my saathi.' Both ZAB and Jatoi cried on the stage. ZAB had a feudal concept of loyalty, said Hasan. He thought he would recruit feudals and they would remain loyal to him. But they all turned out to be 'Kausar Niazis'. Mubashir Hasan's firm assessment was that the election would go in his favour for a variety of reasons; in 1973, the trade balance had been favourable, in 1974, the wage increase was greater than inflation. Regardless, ZAB was full of doubt.

Mubashir Hasan told him, 'You have alienated all your good workers, only the landlords are left. There is not a single landowning family to whom you did not give a ticket. We gave tickets to Vaderas but why are we giving them to their goondas?' The truth was that ZAB had become prisoner of state apparatus. For assessing the forthcoming election, he had called a meeting of Collectors, District Commissioners and Inspector Generals who told him, 'You will get 33 per cent seats'. But Mubashir Hasan had a different take, 'In Lahore you will win eight out of eight. Tell me one seat, one single seat where you don't have a majority?' Late during the polling night, Mubashir Hasan sat in the office of the man he suspected would stuff the ballot box. ZAB called at midnight. 'What is happening?' Mubashir Hasan spoke four measured words. 'You are getting votes.'

As a journalist, I.A. Rehman was touring Punjab covering elections. He reached Okara where Rao Sattar was running. Before the polling started, the local maulvi announced on the loudspeaker, 'Rao Sattar is badmash (bad character)'. The next day, after the vote had been cast, the same maulvi announced,

'Rao Sattar is the best candidate'. I.A. Rehman's comment on this to the writer was, 'Maulvi ko safey ke liye paisa chahiye' (Maulvi needs money for his turban). Rehman then went to Chichavatni where the DC told him, 'Sir, I have cleared two seats for you.' He was trying to convey, 'It is we who are making you win.' In Gujar Khan, the local officer said to I.A. Rehman, 'Sir, these lines are for PPP.' When there was still so much popular support for PPP, where was the need for rigging?

All through, Mubashir Hasan had been watching the downward slide. The man he had admired and loved was hurtling towards disaster. He could not keep himself detached regardless of having been rebuffed in the past. So he sought an appointment. He was meeting him in his private capacity. No longer was he Minister or held any office. The words he spoke were precise and sincere. 'Sir you know that for myself I have no political plans. But I want to say about you. You are on the verge of disaster. If you keep yourself surrounded with the kind of people you are with now and have been with for many months, it is recipe for disaster. Maybe one year, may be two years is all you have. When the time comes they will nudge you overboard'.

'What do you want me to do?' ZAB's words were softly spoken.

'I want you to gather your power from the people, not civil and military officers.'

This is when he heard the saddest sentence ever spoken by a world-renowned leader. 'What you want me to do, I don't have the power to do'.

At that moment, Mubashir Hasan, six-feet tall, went on his toes, stretched his hand and removed the bugging device from his sitting room ceiling. He had been noticing this device from the moment he had entered. ZAB called his wife. 'Nusrat see what Mubashir has found.' Begum Nusrat took the device, a small bug, and turned it around with her fingers. 'Yes. This is exactly like the other one which Mir had shown me saying, "Look Mother, what I found stuck at the bottom of my bedroom phone."'

At the end of March 1977, Mubashir Hasan wrote a 17-page letter which gave the most frank and unequivocal message to ZAB. Only a true friend could have said what he did without fear of displeasing the boss. Appraising the crisis, he wrote that the protest waged by the opposition and the procession being taken out by them was a battle between the rising industrial and commercial interests and the feudal government. In this battle, the feudals were sure to lose unless drastic measures such as introducing land reforms were adopted. 'It was evident that ZAB did not like this letter and we did not converse with each other for over one week. Before this incident, Bhutto Sahib used to speak to me on the phone every day. On 12 or 13 April, two of his ministers, Meiraj Khalid[170] and Sheikh Rashid asked why I was angry with ZAB. I said, "I am not angry." They said, "Then phone him and tell him that you want to see him." So I phoned him. He said, "Come along to see me. I am in the Governor House in Lahore." I went there at 10:30 a.m. and stayed all day until past 9 p.m. I told him that we were in great difficulties and no measures such as banning alcohol and narcotics, stopping gambling and imposing other shariat measures, as advocated by the right wing opponents, will help the party. We were sitting, just the two of us in a room in the Governor House. Then he said, "We sit here lonely, closing one window and opening another according to the movement of the sun." I became emotional and said to Bhutto, "What a great folly is this! What about our political popularity and power?" Then I added, "These Islamic measures being suggested by the Mullahs will not help us." Bhutto did not let me go until the evening. I found hours later he was scheduled to attend a meeting of his

---

[170]Meiraj Khalid had a humble beginning from a village Dehrachal, he used to bring milk from his village to Lahore. He had socialist leanings. He rose to become a member of Local Advisory Body and finally became a minister.

advisers later that day. He said to me that he agreed with all I had suggested but his advisers were telling him something else. In a word, I urged him to dissolve the Assembly, call elections. In response, ZAB spoke the saddest words I have heard in my life. He said, "I do not have the vitality to fight an election from Peshawar to Karachi." Years later, I was discussing this moment with Dr Zaki Hasan, Karachi psychiatrist and a long-time supporter of ZAB. He said, "How surprising was his choice of words. He used the word 'vitality' and not 'energy.'" (Later, Hasan learnt that his advisers who arrived in the night advocated Islamic measures, alcohol ban, narcotics ban, and Friday as declared holiday.) As I was leaving, he asked me, "You are leaving, going abroad?" I said, "I know you want me to go out of Pakistan... I am ready, and I am only waiting for your signal." He stopped and there was dead silence for one minute. Then he spoke. "You can go.' I left for Egypt two days later.'

In 1977, Lahore was abuzz with the syllogism 'Ek qabr do aadmi hain. Kaun jayega andar?' (There's one grave two bodies; which one will go inside?) ZAB or Ziaul Haq. They were to each other Master and his Minion before the Minion became Master. Mubashir Hasan recounted anecdotes about their interpersonal relations. At the Murree meeting, ZAB had called Ziaul Haq a 'dog'. In Multan, Zia ran to bring a chair for him, ZAB was pleased. Then he turned around and asked Rao Rashid, 'How did we select Ziaul Haq?' He replied that a team had come from USA. From the military list, they discarded Zia with the remark, 'Useless fellow.' That is why ZAB chose him, as in the story where the Prince was instructed to choose his new wazirs after slashing the capable ones. Mubashir Hasan said that Zia used to claim, 'I am from St Stephens College'. He never was. His father was a mulla, an imam in the army.

ZAB made Ziaul Haq Chair of a tribunal which would ultimately try cases of conspiracy against his own government.

Mubashir Hasan recalled Ziaul Haq speaking about the 23 June 1977 meeting of ZAB with Core Commanders. 'At its conclusion, I told Bhutto Sahib, "If you don't settle with the opposition parties we will have to step in." When the army went to arrest him, he called me and said, "Zia is that you?" I said, "Yes Sir." Then he said, "Zia, together we will make government." I exclaimed, "Sir what are you saying?"'

'The moment he spoke these words, I knew he (Ziaul Haq) had lied. My Bhutto could not have said that,' said Hasan.

For all his bluster, Ziaul Haq was afraid of ZAB. One PPP worker said to Mubashir Hasan. 'Ziaul Haq ne Bhutto Sahib ke jootey saaf kiye hain. A few drops of tea had fallen on his shoe. Zia took out his handkerchief, bent down and carefully dabbed the shoe.' Mubashir Hasan said, 'I don't believe it.' But the worker insisted, 'I saw it with my own eyes.' Mubashir Hasan asked, 'What did Sahib do?' 'He placed his foot on a chair, as if telling Zia to do a good job.' Mubashir Hasan relented, 'Now I believe you; that was my Bhutto!'

There is not a day when ZAB is not remembered in Pakistan today. While one by one all leaders are forgotten, Bhutto is recalled in all forums. Why? The day after the hanging, Peter Niesewand, Asia Correspondent for the *Guardian,* originally from Rhodesia, wrote what could be one answer to this conundrum.

'Millions of Pakistanis mourn the fate of Zulfikar Ali Bhutto. Widely revered by the mass of ordinary people, Bhutto was, to them, a world statesman who gave Pakistan confidence and respectability, a man who ensured, when he spoke, other statesmen listened. He was a politician who broke away from the gentlemanly cabals of wealthy landowners and bureaucrats who had previously ruled Pakistan between military dictatorships. Bhutto brought power to the people, campaigning in a western style. He promised food, clothing and shelter. He exchanged his Savile Row suits and silk handkerchiefs for baggy trousers and long Pakistani shirts, and he went electioneering in the bazaars and in remote areas previously shunned by his rivals. The people loved him.'

There was unspoken fear in the minds of the rulers who would pull the plank under his feet. Pran Chopra in his introduction to *Zulfikar Ali Bhutto: If I am Assassinated,* wrote: 'Bhutto would be ten times more potent against President Zia than the Ayatollah has been against the Shah, who at least had glamour if not charisma, at least had a vision to his credit if not wisdom, and a record of some performance in pursuit of the vision.'

Free one day, he may return to power the next day. First thing he would do in the position was settle scores with a man called Ziaul Haq. So if it is to be either his neck or ZAB's, the best line would be to break his neck via the hangman's rope.

In 2015 while I was browsing in his library, I came across a small selection of poems written by several Urdu poets, during the few weeks following his hanging—few weeks when the collective shock and grief had gripped the common people. The title of this small poem is 'Rassi' (Rope).

Ek rassi Allah ki
Aur ek rassi tumhari

Allah ki rassi ko mazbooti se thamna
Rahmaton aur barkaton ka inam hai

Aur–tumhari rassi
Zabaan aur ankhen bahaar nikal deti hai
Lekkin qad lamba ho jaata hai

(One rope of Allah
One rope of yours
Hold firmly Allah's rope
It is a reward of compassion and benediction
And your rope—tongue and eyes—it thrusts out
But, it increases the height.)

10

Judicial Murder

On 5 July 1977, General Ziaul Haq imposed martial law, which completely extinguished all vestiges of a democratic system in Pakistan. ZAB was overthrown and the Army Chief of Staff appointed himself the Chief Martial Law Administrator. In March 1977 election, ZAB's party had won by an overwhelming majority (136 for the PPP against 38 for the PNA[171]) but there were allegations that the elections were rigged and a lot of unrest was created in the country, ultimately resulting in General Zia seizing power. Pakistan National Alliance, coalition of rightist parties helped by ISI, held several agitations.

The events thereafter with the promulgation of martial law led to Bhutto's trial on a charge of conspiracy to murder his political opponent Ahmed Raza Kasuri who was an active member of the Opposition in Parliament and a virulent critic of ZAB and his government. The shooting had resulted in the death of Ahmed Raza Kasuri's father Nawab Muhammad Khan in November 1974.

Bhutto was confined in a Mess at Rawalpindi and later taken to Abbottabad where he was kept till mid-August 1977.

---

[171]Nine opposition parties formed the Pakistan National Alliance (PNA) on 11 January 1976 soon after ZAB announced the date for the elections on 7 January 1977.

In *The Mirage of Power,* Mubashir Hasan describes the mahaul of the day. 'Military courts were set up everywhere and a reign of terror was let loose on Bhutto's party. Hundreds and thousands of party workers and sympathizers were arrested. Thirteen protestors died of self-immolation, fourteen were sentenced to death, and according to one estimate, the number of lashes awarded to our workers totalled 45,000.'

General Zia arrested ZAB on 3 September, accusing him of entering into a conspiracy with Masood Mahmud and some other officers from Federal Security Force (FSF) for the murder of Ahmed Raza Kasuri's father. He was arrested from his home, 70 Clifton at 5:20 a.m. from where he was brought to Lahore and sent to Kot Lakhpat Prison. On 11 September, the police filed an incomplete challan before a magistrate at Lahore. On the same day, the magistrate sent the challan to the Sessions Court and the State moved an application for the transfer of the case to the High Court. Next day, the Acting Chief Justice, Maulvi Mushtaq Hussain, passed the order transferring the case to the High Court and constituted a bench of five judges headed by himself. 'Justice Mushtaq Hussain was in Europe when Zia declared martial law. He was called back and took upon himself to preside over the bench to try the prime minister.'[172]

On 14 September 1977, Justice M.A. Samdani ordered his release for a bail of Rs 50,000. On release, he immediately held a press conference in Lahore. He then left for Karachi and onwards to Larkana. It was from Al Mutuza that he was arrested for the last time. No one could have ever imagined that he would never see his ancestral home again.

From his personal lens, Dr Mubashir Hasan spoke about the events. 'Ziaul Haq had carefully framed the murder case; the trial

---

[172]*A Judiciary in Crisis? The Trial of Zulfikar Ali Bhutto.* T.W. Rajaratnam, 1988. Kaanthalakam. p 9.

began in the lower court as usual and quickly moved to High Court. The trying judge at High Court was Maulvi Mushtaq. He was a friend of my friend Zahid Chaudhry. I knew that this judge held an old grudge against him; at one time ZAB had stymied his chance to become Chief Justice of Lahore High Court. Mushtaq had been requesting transfer from Lahore to Karachi. He approached a number of people to intervene. But Bhutto refused. On my request, Zahid, who wanted ZAB's life spared at any cost, went to plead the case before his friend. But the friend had made up his mind. Maulvi Mushtaq's words were, "Zahid, if I don't hang him, there is no other judge in Pakistan who will dare do that." Zahid was stunned. He did not expect this cold-blooded rejection.'

A Judiciary in Crisis? The Trial of Zulfikar Ali Bhutto[173] is a book by T. W. Rajaratnam, former Judge of the Supreme Appellate Court of Sri Lanka. 'Although the Bhutto trial is the most notable trial of the century, it is a trial about which the least is known,' he writes in the Introduction, 'There are some who even say that whether Bhutto was guilty or not, he should never have been hanged... Never during the appeal or thereafter did Bhutto ask for mercy. In fact, he had strictly instructed his lawyers and the members of his family that no such application should be made.'[174]

Mubashir Hasan continues. 'We knew he would not be spared. So we decided to abduct him. We were convinced he would not get justice from the Lahore High Court. Therefore a plan was made to snatch him by force; a spot was selected on Zafar Ali Road where we would ambush the police jeep that was transporting him. Our plan was to transport him to Turkey or Greece—both had offered hospitality. My man met him in the High Court premises. But he turned down our plan. There could be any or all of the following reasons for his refusal:

---

[173]Published by Classic Press, Lahore 1988.
[174]Ibid. p 8.

1. We would be unable to carry out the plan and he would be killed in the encounter.
2. We would take him somewhere remote and what would then become of his political plan for Pakistan?
3. He did not for a moment believe that they could pronounce the death sentence and hang him.

'The entire government machinery was on the prowl using every means to block any attempt to abduct him. Massive force was deployed; helicopters were circling in case of an airlift, his cell was held within a clutch of security personnel who were armed to the teeth.

'Sitting in the jail he did not know that the market was abuzz with the slogan "Takht ya takhta" (throne or gallows). The public knew by now that in Pakistan there was only one noose and two necks—Ziaul Haq and Zulfikar Ali Bhutto.' These were Mubashir Hasan's words, a man who had been described in 1972 by *New York Times* journalist James Reston as 'a tall, lean, highly intelligent, almost beautiful man.'

Forty years after the event, Mubashir Hasan would speak between tears and smiles when he recalled a small instance which spoke volumes about the man. 'When ZAB was moved from the Lahore Jail to Rawalpindi prison, we were standing in the courtyard to see him off. To our horror, a trash truck was brought inside the compound. Standing still, he looked at his mode of transport without wincing. All eyes turned to superintendent jail, who stood by to hand him in. He motioned to the orderly. A chair was brought from inside. From the high perch on the lowly truck, ZAB, true to character made a speech.' Mubashir Hasan recalled the crux of his speech. 'The nation which does not give due respect to its leaders is bound to be doomed.'

Dr Zeenat Hussain is Lahore's leading pathologist. Thirty-five years later in 2015, she recounted her visit to the jail, the day before he was hanged. 'I met Mr Bhutto in the prison. He had very bad teeth. His dentist, Dr Niazi, was permitted to visit him in the cell. Niazi wanted certain tests done before he could treat him so he asked me to take blood samples. They let me go in, provided a doctor from government would also be present. I asked for an army doctor, Azhar, who had once worked in my lab. They refused. When I went in, there were five of us in that tiny room. My eyes looked into the entire cell. It was painted black. Stretched across its roof was a twisted mesh of wires. If anyone dared to attempt escape it would result in instant death by electrocution. The roof had another use; the jailor used it as an instrument to prevent the prisoner from sleeping. It was beaten with iron rods from time to time. I greeted him as usual, silently took samples of his blood and urine and left.

'He was a brave man. He did not complain. They would have drugged him. At night they must have woken him up from the drugged stupor and hanged him. And then…they gave his shalwar kameez and ring to his daughter, Benazir.'

Zulfikar Ali Bhutto, after his arrest, while in detention, during his trial, during the hearing of his appeal and thereafter, never gave the impression that he was dispirited. He showed no signs of distress or despair. To quote his Court Submission:

'Since the 18th of March 1978 (the day he was sentenced to death by the High Court) I have spent twenty-two to twenty-three hours out of the twenty four in a congested and suffocating death cell. I have been hemmed in by its sordidness and stink throughout the heat and rain of the long hot summer. The light is poor. My eye sight has worsened. My health has been shattered. I have been in solitary confinement for almost a year but my morale is high because I am not made of the wood which burns easily. Through sheer will power, in conditions that are adverse in the extreme, I have written this rejoinder. Let all the White Papers come. I do not have to defend myself at the bar of public opinion. My services to the cause of our people are a mirror in front of them....'[175]

On 20 September, Begum Nusrat Bhutto presented Habeas Corpus application in the Supreme Court challenging the orders of arrest of her husband as unconstitutional and illegal.

On 22 September 1977, General Zia announced that the office of the Chief Justice had fallen vacant. C.J. Yakub Ali Khan would be replaced by Anwar ul Haq as Chief Justice. ZAB objected to Anwar ul Haq's hearing his appeal for the following reasons[176]:

1. That he had publicly criticized Bhutto's government and party and declared General Zia 'a national saviour';
2. That he was closely associated with the Chief Justice of the Lahore High Court which had pronounced him guilty;
3. That he had acted as Head of State during President Chaudhury's absence abroad during the martial law regime and he had temporarily merged the military executive with the judiciary.

On 22 October 1977, ZAB made a three-hour speech in the Supreme Court in support of his petition for his release.

On 10 November 1977, the Supreme Court dismissed the application for ZAB's release and rejected the submission about the unconstitutionality of the processes of the law. It held that the imposition of martial law, although an extraconstitutional step, was validated by the 'doctrine of necessity', as the constitutional and moral authority of Bhutto's government had completely broken down.

While ZAB was in prison, the Party was led by Begum Nusrat assisted by Benazir Bhutto. I was able to access news

---

[175] *If I am Assassinated*. Zulfikar Ali Bhutto, 1979. Vikas Publishing House , p 193.
[176] *A Judiciary in Crisis? The Trial of Zulfikar Ali Bhutto*. T.W. Rajaratnam, 1988. Kaanthalakam. p 7.

reports from contemporary journals. *Al-Fatah*[177] reports how Begum Nusrat Bhutto was attacked at the Ghaddafi Stadium. While wielding dandas on the PPP supporters, a Superindentent Police shouted to a policeman pointing at Begum Nusrat. 'Attack this woman.' He lifted up his lathi and brought it down on her head. Blood gushed out and she fell to the ground. The SP was seen smiling.

On 24 January 1978, the statement of ZAB was recorded in open court. He said he was not presenting his defence but had confined himself to two issues (1) Reason for this trial and the fabricated case against him? (2) No confidence in getting a fair trial and justice.

On 22 March 1978, the edition of *Musawat* was sealed and its distribution stopped after publication of a letter of ZAB to Yahya Bakhtiar,[178] describing the military authorities as 'dirty, miserable and stinking men'. A few days later, on 27 March 1978, police raided *Musawat's* Karachi office and seized all copies containing reports of ZAB's appeal to the Supreme Court. Abbas Athar, popular freelance journalist, was arrested for trying to publish ZAB's speech in the court. The press was seized while the statement was being printed. On 12 April 1978, editor of newspaper *Sadaqat* was arrested. Zia observed at a press conference, 'One or two public hangings will bring saboteurs to their senses.'

Report in weekly journal *Meyaar*[179] on the arrests of PPP workers is titled 'Movement for Restoration of Democracy and Arrests are Happening Simultaneously'. It lists 2,700 lashes given to 240 political workers. In different jails, there were leaders like Mumtaz Bhutto, Hafeez Pirzada, Sheikh Rashid and others.

---

[177] *Al-Fatah*, Weekly (23-30 December 1977), editor, Wahaab Siddiqui, Karachi. Copy is with the author.

[178] Yahya Bakhtiar was Bhutto's principal legal counsel.

[179] *Meyaar*, weekly (7 to 14 January 1978); Editor, Mahmood Shaam, Karachi. Copy of the weekly is with the author.

Names, period of incarceration, volume of cash penalty and number of whiplashes are all listed for each of the 240 political prisoners.

On 10 February 1979, President Zia announced that Pakistan's legal system will be replaced by the traditional Islamic code. Punishment included lashes, stoning to death, amputation of right hand, amputation of left foot for first and second offence and life sentence for third offence.

On 24 February 1979, Bhutto's counsel presented a petition to the Supreme Court to review its judgment with the request that the two judges who dropped off be recalled. SC refused.

Five judges of the High Court who presided over the trial of ZAB had given unanimous decision—'guilty'. It was in appeal that the Supreme Court bench gave a four to three judgement. While all nine judges of the Supreme Court commenced hearing the appeal, one of the judges, Qaisar Khan, retired from the court after superannuation and another Justice, Waheeduddin Ahmad, suffered a stroke at the tail end of the hearing. The court waited three weeks for his recovery, then resumed the hearing without him. The hearing concluded on 23 December 1978 and the judgement was delivered on 6 February 1979. Chief Justice Anwar ul Haq faithfully carried out the orders he had received from his superiors. He convicted ZAB and awarded him death penalty for the crime he deemed was the rarest of rare. I.A. Rehman[180] spoke about the faultlines in the judgment. 'In the case of death penalty, the Court has to give unanimous decision; it has to be resolved beyond the slightest pale of doubt. But in this case at least 3 judges acquitted him, which means the doubt remained palpably unresolved.'

Outside, his popularity was gaining ground. People were secretly praying for him, wishing him back but no one dared

---

[180]Pakistan's most eminent and senior journalist.

raise a cry; terrifying reprisals were feared from the Military Law regime.

But what was this case? On 11 November 1974, Ahmed Raza Kasuri, an active member of the Opposition in Parliament and a nasty critic of ZAB and his government, was returning home in his car after attending a marriage ceremony in Shadman Chowk[181] in Lahore. There were a number of shots fired at the car using automatic weapons. Nawab Muhammad Ahmad Khan (Kasuri's father) was hit on the head and died on the spot. Kasuri, his mother and sister escaped unhurt. The huge irony which can only be termed 'destiny' was that in 1931, this man, Nawab Muhammad Ahmad Khan was Honorary Magistrate of Kasur. It was in this exact spot that he had supervised the hanging of Bhagat Singh. Shadman Chowk was also where Bhagat Singh's central jail was located. The roundabout in Shadman Colony, Lahore—where the execution chambers of the Lahore Central jail used to be—is where the former magistrate was shot in 1974.

The assailants were unidentified and unknown. Within minutes of the death of his father, Kasuri lodged an FIR and asserted that the firing was really directed at him. He was then a member of the opposition and Information Secretary of the Tehrik-e-Istaqlal which was strongly critical of government policies. He stated that in June 1974, he had criticized Bhutto in the House. Bhutto had retorted, 'You keep quiet. I have had enough of you; absolute poison. I will not tolerate your nuisance any more.' Kasuri had snapped back, 'I cannot tolerate your style also.' ZAB then said, 'I have had enough of this man. What does he think of himself.'[182] Kasuri claimed that later, he received threatening calls to face the consequences of his altercation with Bhutto on the floor of the House.

---

[181] A move has been made to name Shadman Chowk, 'Bhagat Singh Chowk'.

[182] *A Judiciary in Crisis? The Trial of Zulfikar Ali Bhutto.* T.W.Rajaratnam, 1988. Kaanthalakam. p 40.

In pursuit of the assailants, the police took some top-ranking officers of the Federal Security Force into custody. Among them were (1) Masood Mahmood, the Director General (2) Miyan Abbas, the Director, Operations and Intelligence (3) Ghulam Mustafa, Inspector (4) Arshad Iqbal, Sub-Inspector (5) Rana Iftikhar, Assistant Sub-Inspector and (6) Ghulam Hussain, Inspector. The first accused, of course, was ZAB, the Prime Minister.

Later, Masood Mahmood and Ghulam Hussain earned their pardon and became approvers and the chief witnesses for the prosecution. Both of them had made their respective confessions. Miyan Abbas, Ghulam Mustafa, Arshad Iqbal and Rana Iftikhar also made confessions before magistrates. ZAB's name was not directly mentioned or implicated in any of these confessions except in the confession made by Masood Mahmood. He had been taken into custody on 5 July 1977 and his confessional statement implicating Bhutto was made 50 days later. He implicated ZAB in the killing of Kasuri's father, nearly three years after the event. ZAB had created a special force called Federal Security Force (FSF) which was headed by Masood Mahmood. The army was resentful since it considered FSF to be ZAB's instrument to control and monitor its operation, hence a grudge against the FSF, and saw it as a rival. On 5 July 1977, the day Masood was taken in custody, a rumour was floated that ZAB was going to arm FSF with automatic weapons and tanks. Was it a coincidence?

Much later, Masood Mahmood was given a new name, new identity and was rehabilitated somewhere in USA.

Kasuri had very often attacked the FSF. One year before the Shadman shooting, he had said, 'This Force has been created to check the processes of democracy in Pakistan. This Force has been created to dislodge the opponents of the Government'. A month or two before the incident, Kasuri bitterly criticized the government and said it was oppressing the people and using the FSF for killing people.

Rajaratnam writes in his book a revealing note about one category of witnesses known as 'pressurized witnesses'. What is important to remember is that when considering the case of pressurized accomplices or participants in crime, we must also consider the case of pressurized witnesses who make confessional statements implicating the man whom the authorities want to nail. It cannot be ruled out that ZAB was the much-wanted person pursued by the martial law regime. Here was a man who would ultimately lead the PPP through promised General Election. 'Could they have risked his coming back to power after all that happened since the promulgation of martial law?' This last sentence in Rajaratnam reveals more than all the volumes on ZAB written over the years.

While his appeal was being heard, White Papers were being published and distributed internally and externally about all the alleged misdeeds and corruption during Bhutto's regime with special reference to how he used the FSF as his 'personal gestapo' and how he interfered with the freedom of the press and the independence of the judiciary. In a statement of 80,000 words, ZAB denied every allegation against him in the said White Papers: 'We did not flog journalists nor did we steal the printing presses of newspapers'.

The Supreme Court meanwhile allowed ZAB to let off his steam. He applied to be allowed to say his piece after his Counsel had concluded submissions on his behalf. The SC allowed this application. He was allowed his say and he spoke for 12 hours during which he referred to the political motivation for the case fabricated against him and a lot more. In hindsight, it was the kind of concession afforded in some legal systems to an accused before he is sentenced to death.

Commenting on the case, I.A. Rehman spoke of the defence lawyer Yahya Bakhtiar who spoke endlessly. This prolonged the case which instead of helping, worked against it. To give him benefit of doubt, he may have prolonged his speech in the hope that given the time, world powers may effectively intervene. But the longer the hearing continued, the judges, those who wanted to acquit him, retired one by one, leaving behind the ones 'baying for his blood' .

The court gave him the last say. His submission, he was told, will be communicated to all the authorities concerned. The question he was asked was why sentence of death should not be carried out. The opportunity he was given to speak out in open court was as though what he said would be considered by the judges in pronouncing their sentence. He used this opportunity to attack his political enemies and their political motivations. One way of looking at this 'permitted' speech is that it totally ruined any chance of the death sentence being commuted. ZAB wanted to speak out his mind and heart and expected the judges to view the prosecution case in the light of his statement. He could not be cross-examined; his speech was an 'extra' to the submissions made by his Counsel. ZAB wanted this opportunity to be given to him u/s 342 of the Criminal Procedure Code as such an opportunity was in effect denied to him in the trial court. But this is a question which begs an answer. When the opportunity was given to him by the SC, did they accept the position that a mandatory provision to provide him with this opportunity was denied to him earlier? Rajaratnam writes, 'One is reminded of doctors, when they find they have done their best and the patient has no chance, telling the patient, "You can eat and drink whatever you like". Was it a matter of judicial diplomacy to have allowed him to say whatever he liked? Did it gain any publicity?' But the fact is that there was no publicity given to his speech. Later, it was smuggled out and surreptitiously published. *If I am Assassinated* is ZAB's own account with an introduction by eminent journalist, Pran Chopra.

In thanking the court, ZAB was misreading the situation if he thought the Court was going to consider and take into account anything of what he said in his long speech. It was only the swan song of Zulfikar Ali Bhutto which was 'so graciously' allowed to him by the single-minded court. In no way was it ever relevant to his case. Commenting on this, I.A. Rehman recalled the leaked news that Ziaul Haq threatened the Chief Justice Anwar ul Haq when it was reported that he had told his bench that ZAB will receive a mitigated sentence.

Attacking the Martial Law Regime most forcefully, ZAB stated that it was not mercy but justice that he wanted. 'I do not want pity from anyone and as I said earlier I do not want mercy. I want justice. I am not pleading for my life as such, not as a way of flesh, because everyone has to go. There have been so many attacks on my life. I was attacked at Sanghar. I escaped miraculously in Sadiqabad. Then in the Frontier tribal territories, a bomb exploded just before I was to speak. There were at least four to five attempts in Balochistan once by a Langah, who threw a hand grenade at me. So it is not life as life that I plead for. I want justice. This is a forged case. It is a completely fabricated case... I want my innocence to be established. Not for the person of ZAB. I want it established on higher considerations for there has been grotesque injustice. All the crimp and colour of political persecution cannot be found in a more classical case than this...'[183]

Another matter to bear in mind, even if it did not disturb the minds of the convicting judges of the High Court and Supreme Court, was the fact that Masood Mahmood was given a pardon on condition that he will adhere to his confessional statement. In other words, the star witness for the prosecution could not afford to even 'deviate into some truth'. He made a confessional statement to save his skin and thereby obtained a pardon.

In dealing with the main appeal, two differing judgments

---

[183] *A Judiciary in Crisis? The Trial of Zulfikar Ali Bhutto.* T.W. Rajaratnam, 1988. Kaanthalakam. p 179.

were delivered. SC agreed that there was no ground for regular hearing. That means judicial process had virtually ended and the matter of appeal remained the judgement of SC and the HC verdict of guilty as charged retained the force of law.

However, on the question of sentence, SC took cognizance of the arguments put forward by the defence counsel. It was argued that the SC was divided in its judgement because three of the seven judges who were on the bench at the conclusion of the hearing had held that the charges against ZAB and other accused had not been proved beyond reasonable doubt, and the extreme penalty should not be imposed on him. It was also said that mitigation of the sentence was the preferred course. This was in view of the fact that the appellant had acceptedly not participated in the actual act, and even if he was considered guilty on other counts, the murderous act on Ahmed Raza Kasuri had not succeeded and the consequential death of his father Muhammad Ahmad Khan had not been intended. Therefore, even if the prosecution's case was accepted, it did not call for capital punishment.

These arguments were given due weight by SC judges, but it was felt that at this late stage the court could not on juridical grounds review its judgment in respect of the sentence. Dealing with this important question in the majority judgment, Justice Akram, with the concurrence of Chief Justice and two other judges emphasized, 'Although we have not found it possible in law to review the sentence of death on the grounds urged by Yahya Bakhtiar, yet these are relevant for consideration by executive authorities in the exercise of their prerogative of mercy.'

On 6 February 1979, ZAB's appeal was rejected. Four judges of the SC convicted him while three judges acquitted him. The SC confirmed the conviction and the death sentence of ZAB by a majority judgement of four to three. There were two separate judgments—first was by Chief Justice Anwar ul Haq, Justice Mohammad Akram, Justice Naseem Hasan Shah and Justice

Karam Ilahi Chohan. The second judgment was by Justice Dorab Patel, Justice Ghulam Safdar Shah and Justice Mohammad Abdul Haleem. The popular contention was that the convicting four judges were Punjabis, the acquitting were non-Punjabis. Justice Dorab Patel (Parsi), Justice Safdar Shah (Baloch), Mohammad Abdul Haleem (Urdu-speaking Mohajir).

It was Justice Mohammad Muneer[184] who told Justice Nasim Hasan Shah,[185] one of the convicting judges, 'You have committed judicial murder'.

Rajaratnam writes of two petitions which could have changed the course of events. The first was by Malik Ghulam Jilani on a very relevant constitutional point which was ably argued by a young Barrister Aitzaz Ahsan before Justice Shafi-ur-Rahman in the High Court of Lahore. It was a writ petition which stated that General Ziaul Haq as the Chief Martial Law Administrator could not deal with any mercy petition as he was only a de facto and not a de jure president. In this state of affairs, the execution of the sentence of death could not be carried out by the jail authorities. The High Court, however, held that what the petitioner was intending to achieve was questioning the authority of the present incumbent of the office of president which he must have first done by a writ of quo warranto, and he could not achieve this by collaterally challenging the authority. The petition was dismissed on 17 March 1979.

There was another inter-court appeal No. 76 of 1979 decided

---

[184]Justice Mohammad Muneer was the second Chief Justice of Pakistan serving from 1954 to 1960. He also wrote a book *From Jinnah to Zia*, arguing that Jinnah stood for a secular state.

[185]Justice Nasim Hasan Shah, one of the senior judges of the four Supreme Court judges who upheld death sentence to ZAB in March 1978. Later, he made a confession—that in a startling press interview to the Daily Jang that the verdict to hang Bhutto was not right—it shall remain inerasable black spot on the face of the highest judiciary.

on 3 April 1979. In this petition, the point was made that the Chief Martial Law Administrator could not deal with a mercy petition as he was not a de jure president. Aitzaz Ahsan again ably argued the matter challenging the validity of the president's order No 13 of 1978 where General Ziaul Haq was holding the office of president. He argued that this constitutional question could be argued collaterally. The court held that the Supreme Court had validated the Martial Law Regime on the doctrine of necessity and also the authority of the Chief Martial Law Administrator in the Begum Nusrat Bhutto case in 1977. This decision was made for the good of the people 'so as to achieve one of the objects of the martial law, i.e. holding General Election as early as possible'. Flowing from the decision of the Supreme Court, the president's order No 13 of 1978 was valid. It was their view that on account of state necessity, the president of Pakistan and the superior courts continued to function under the Constitution subject to the condition that certain parts thereof had been held 'in abeyance'. It must be kept in mind however, that the judges of the Supreme Court had taken a new oath on 23 September 1977 which omitted the paragraph with the words that they once swore earlier to 'preserve, protect and defend the Constitution'. This appeal petition was also dismissed on 3 April 1979. Aitzaz Ahsan requested grant of a certificate to file an appeal before the Supreme Court.

Before an application could be made to the Supreme Court, ZAB was hanged at 2 a.m. in the early hours before dawn of the following day, 4 April 1979, at the Rawalpindi prison.

After the case was complete, Chief Justice Maulvi Mushtaq was made the Chief Election Commissioner by Gen Ziaul Haq.

I.A. Rehman's friend, member of the judicial fraternity, told him later that ZAB was careless in his comments on government files. He would often make marginal notes such as 'arrest him', 'hang him', etc. Ziaul Haq collected all the files with their notes and scribbles and sent them to Maulvi Mushtaq with a directive, 'select the best'. The judge picked up the Kasuri's case, 'I will hang him on this one.'

Justice Ghulam Safdar Shah was one of the three judges of the Supreme Court who acquitted ZAB.

On 1 March 2015, *Dawn* correspondent Sheikh Aziz reported a statement of Justice Safdar Shah that returned to haunt him with a vengeance. Talking to a BBC correspondent, Justice Shah pointed to an SC observation. He said that while rejecting the review petition, the arguments of the defence counsel, Yahya Bakhtiar, could not be disregarded by the executive while it made a decision on the question of implementing the death sentence or not. This interview was held on 26 March 1979. That was two days after the SC had rejected ZAB's review petition and upheld the Lahore High Court verdict. The observation was also mentioned by the Secretary Interior in his summary sent to General Ziaul Haq on 1 April 1979. 'Although we have not found it possible in law to review the sentence of death on the grounds urged by Yahya Bakhtiar, yet these grounds are relevant for consideration by the executive authorities in exercise of their prerogative of mercy.' The summary added that while such court recommendations were not binding on the executive, in the past, such advice had always been honoured. In his above quoted statement, Justice Shah gave the impressions that he would have accepted the argument of ZAB's defence team, and hinted that other judges on the bench felt the same.

General Zia's team of advisers panicked; Federal Investigation Agency (FIA) began an inquiry against Justice Shah. The aim was to malign and discredit the man.

He was framed in a frivolous case of fraud regarding his BA degree. According to an official handout issued by the government on 10 November 1980, it was claimed that during the case trial of Nawab Mohammad Ahmad Kasuri's murder in the LHC, Justice

Shah had tried to influence one of the judges to favour an accused Miyan Mohammad Abbas and to treat him lightly.

Shah saw the writing on the wall; he resigned as a judge of the SC, rendering the proceedings against him as redundant and he escaped from Pakistan to Afghanistan crossing the border on a donkey. From there, he went to London and never returned. His persecution, however, did not end here. His son-in-law Nasr Minullah, Chief Secretary Balochistan was the only Chief Secretary charged with rigging the election. The other three Chief Secretaries were not even touched!

Miyan Abbas and the other three accused, who had turned approvers in the case, were all hanged. They had been promised that they would be set free, the same as Masud Mahmood. An attorney was sent to their cell to assure them that they would be out in a few days; regardless, they were all hanged.

Another SC judge, Justice Naseem Hassan Shah, who had supported Chief Justice Anwar ul Haq in upholding the LHC verdict, was later promoted as Chief Justice of Pakistan. After his retirement, he spoke to a journalist from an Urdu newspaper about the ZAB case, in which he conceded that ZAB could have escaped the gallows and his death sentence could have been reduced easily. The interview appeared on 23 August 1996.

He further commented on the constitution of the trial bench of the LHC, and said that Maulvi Mushtaq Hussain should have avoided naming himself as a member of the trial bench to maintain the dignity of the court. Maulvi Mushtaq Hussain, it was alleged, held a grudge against Bhutto, since the deposed prime minister had superseded his seniority while appointing the chief justice of the LHC.

Later he also said that Bhutto's trial was nothing but a sham intended to physically eliminate him. He also said that there was immense pressure from the military dictator on the SC to uphold the LHC verdict. He also said that General Zia and Maulvi

Mushtaq Hussain both feared that Bhutto's survival could be risky for them, and wanted him eliminated.

Never during the appeal or thereafter did ZAB ask for mercy. In fact, he had strictly instructed his lawyers and the members of his family that no such application should be made. Hafeez Pirzada[186] (finance minister after Mubashir Hasan in ZAB's government) and two sisters of ZAB, were the ones who presented the mercy petition to President Zia on 31 March 1979.

In the meantime, from the time sentence of death was passed by the court on the 18 March 1978, appeals for clemency were pouring in from all over the world. Even before his appeal was heard by the SC; appeals had been sent to General Zia by the governments of many Muslim countries including Egypt, Libya, Tunisia, Algeria, Turkey, Iran, Yemen, U.A.E., Oman and Qatar. Col. Gadaffi told Zia that he was prepared to go personally to Pakistan to rescue 'his friend and brother in Islam'. Turkish Premier offered asylum. There were appeals from Rumania, Greece and Australia. British government and USA were silent. The Chinese Ambassador was reported, on 6 April 1978, to have had two meetings with General Zia and one with former President Chaudhury at which he had pleaded for Mr Bhutto's life. Clemency appeals also came from many international personalities including Pope John Paul II, the UN Secretary-General, Kurt Waldheim, and President Carter. Pakistan diaspora, led by ZAB's two sons, staged a protest in London and so did the Pakistan students in Moscow. General Ziaul Haq had one answer—'Let the law take its course; all must be treated equally before the law'.

After the rejection of the appeal in the SC, there were many more clemency appeals and demonstrations. Keesing's Contemporary Archives record that 'following the rejection of appeal, former President Fazle Elahi Chaudhury visited Rawalpindi

---

[186] Also Mr Bhutto's lawyer

on 11 February to plead with President Zia for his life, he was refused an interview.'

In his written statement, ZAB had described the conditions of his death cell.

'There were six cells—the death cell, a bathroom and four other cells. The other four cells were fly proof and the death cell was completely exposed... It was summer. It was hot. My whole face was full of flies and mosquitos... Then the bathroom was completely open and I was expected to go there with people marching up and down all the time... I refused to eat not that it was hunger strike as such, it was just that in those circumstances I simply could not eat... In June 1978, I fell ill and General Shaukat, an army General, not a PPP man, was sent to see me. He had tears in his eyes when he saw me. The room was full of dust. The springs of the bed were jutting out. My back was examined. It was in a terrible state. There were scars on it.'

It was mid-March 1979 when Mubashir Hasan finally got the appointment with Ziaul Haq that he had been seeking. He got a call that the president would receive him in the Core Commander Lahore's office. The meeting began at 1 p.m. While they were talking, the president got up. 'Maaf karna zara namaz padh lein.' He got up and walked to the prayer mat where he and two attending generals offered prayers. Mubashir sat quietly, watching. When namaz was over, the conversation resumed. 'I gave him many compelling arguments why it was in his interest that he should spare ZAB's life—"Bhutto Sahib alive will be much more useful for you than Bhutto dead. You would have a bargaining counter with the opposition parties. We will take him out of Pakistan and ensure he does not return."' They had been thinking of asylum in Turkey or Greece. Turkey had made fervent clemency appeals to General Zia. The Prime Minister of Greece Kermanalist was ZAB's dear friend and was keen to receive him in Athens.

'The president bent over towards me. I was seated on the

chair next to the sofa. For one hour he had been talking to me and occasionally to the two attending generals. Juice had been served after namaz. He tapped his glass with his fingers, took it to his lips and gulped it down before addressing me. "Mein Bhutto Sahib ko kaisey maar sakta hoon? Woh to merey mohsin hain." (How can I kill Bhutto Sahib? He is my benefactor.)

'As I walked out into the sunlight from the Core Commander's office, I knew the man had lied.'

Then it was the night before the end.

The place reeked of old dampness. A single bulb showed the rope that hung still in the dead night. The hangman stood at the side of the platform with his eyes on the two men walking carefully on either side of the prisoner, carefully, not touching him. The prisoner's cap covered only his forehead throwing in relief the nose and chin. He wore canvas shoes which made no sound. The two men turned back and left him alone on the platform with Tara Masih, the hangman. Both men stood face-to-face. A few shadows shuffled awkwardly near the walls. Silence. There was no sound except the rustle of the rope being twisted by the calloused hands of the hangman. He held the noose near the prisoner's neck who made no effort to veer away. More rustling. One second, two, three... time ticked on. Suddenly, a voice at once familiar and unfamiliar tore through the dark silence 'Oey choodhey jaldi kar' (O scum, hurry). The next moment the earth moved with a shudder and shattered under the ground. The wooden plank opened its trap and the newly twisted rope wrenched out the last breath of the man who once walked tall in the politics of Pakistan. Zulfikar Ali Bhutto was hanged on 4 April 1979.

At the hanging, those present included the magistrate, hangman, jail superintendent and two intelligence persons.

His body was flown to Larkana in Sindh, and there it was buried. The sentence was carried out two hours before the time provided by the prison regulations. The customary 48 hours between the rejection of the mercy petition and the execution was not allowed. His wife and daughter were not allowed to attend the funeral. The public announcement about the execution was made nine hours later on 4 April 1979.[187] The people of Pakistan learnt about the hanging through a broadcast on Radio Australia, followed by Mark Tully on BBC.

In his book *A Judiciary in Crisis*, T. W. Rajaratnam wrote, 'It was altogether unfortunate. It cannot be denied that the circumstances were heavily loaded against Bhutto. There were so many demonstrations and protests in different parts of the country and in Lahore where the trial was held. There had been flogging and arrests of these demonstrators by the Military Authorities. The atmosphere was certainly not congenial and conducive to a fair trial. We must also take note that at a time such as this, how few were in a position to help Bhutto in the preparation of his defense and could have given assistance or moral support? Certainly his enemies would have been active. These human realities cannot be disregarded.'

Almost half a century later, in 2017, I.A. Rehman wrote these lines in my notebook in his beautiful handwriting:

'Bhutto's conviction violates the principle that nobody can be convicted on the basis of uncorroborated evidence of a co-accused. The sole evidence linking Bhutto with the murder of Mohammad Ahmed Khan was Masood's testimony but he was a co-accused who became an approver against promise of discharge from the case.'

ZAB is the tragedy of leader who could never imagine that he would be sentenced to death, despite...despite...despite.

In his poem *Zindagi* (Life), Allama Iqbal wrote a verse which

---

[187]*A Judiciary in Crisis? The Trial of Zulfikar Ali Bhutto.* T.W. Rajaratnam, 1988. Kaanthalakam, p 141-142

I offer as the summary of my assessment of an extraordinary man, who I never met but with whom I have lived for almost 20 years:

Bartar az andesha e sood-o-ziyan hai zindagi
Hai kabhi jaan aur kabhi tasleem-e-jaan hai zindagi
Tu ise paimana-e-imroz o farda se na naap
Javedan paiham dawan hardam jawan hai zindagi'

(Life is higher than calculation of profit and loss
Life is sometimes living, sometimes forfeiting life
Do not measure life by scale of today, tomorrow
Life is eternal, constantly moving, at every moment youthful.)

11

The Quintessence

The nation that hangs its father is forever cursed.
In the Greek Tragedy, Oedipus committed patricide,
unknowingly killing his own father. For this heinous act, he atoned
by plunging spikes in his eyes, thereby condemning himself to
eternal darkness. His final self-banishment to a life of oblivion
was the most chilling admonition for the audience who were
watching the play, as it was for the generations to come. They
watched with mounting grief until the tragic finale in Act V. The
chorus commented about life and death. Thebans who had been
sitting in the Greek amphitheatre returned home to their mundane
routines, having witnessed a play, much larger than their lives.

ZAB was sent to the gallows by connivance of the state while
a helpless nation held its breath, never believing it would happen.
Quelling their emotions, they prayed for the miracle. Pleas from
all civilized countries of the world poured on dead ears. One or
two devoted lawyers found loopholes which they used as desperate
last minute interventions. Friends and comrades knocked at palace
gates hoping to invoke the 'quality of mercy'.

Scenes from his life reeled before the eyes of masses of
people who had been witnesses to the rise of the star called
ZAB. They were not just witnesses, they were delirious fans
of the phenomenon that rose from the badlands of Sindh; of

the phenomenon who was nurtured with a silver spoon—the ground kissed beneath his small feet—who was provided nothing but the best, and whose destiny was to rise and rise. They had watched open-mouthed, rather listened open-mouthed in a trance (it was a time where media meant newspapers and the lowly radio) when he spoke in the UN, a man in a Savile row suit and silk tie, who lambasted the developed nations for their callous treatment and trampling over smaller, poorer, struggling nations of the world.

In thousands they came to his public meetings and jalsas when he explained the meaning of democracy. His essential creed was that you, the people, are the masters, we are your servants; you select us so we are privileged to serve you; people are supreme. The feudal prince once said, 'Never again will a hari touch the knees of wadera'. With tears in his eyes, he watched wayside labour break stones and resolved to end drudgery. He scolded them, he reprimanded, chastised, laughed, cried and admonished. And they hung on his each word and loved him during those tumultuous days when a principled, disciplined party was coming into existence in a country that had known nothing but political instability and military rule.

Very quickly, he set aside his Oxford English and began to speak the most endearing language; halting Urdu mixed with Sindhi and Punjabi. They hung on his each word and swayed to the roughness of his delivery. It was as stunning in its own way as the flawless articulation which the world witnessed on a dozen occasions at the UN.

It was an electoral tsunami, the wave on which he took his party to victory in the first democratic election ever held in Pakistan on the basis of 'one person one vote'.

On all sides, he was flanked by the best men of the country; young professionals, lawyers, engineers, student leaders, trade unionists, and also some land-owners. These were the people who formed Team Zulfikar. Most subscribed, though in varying degrees, to left ideology. All shared his passion to transform Pakistan into a modern nation. From a nation caught in a feudal and military stranglehold, it was a quantum leap to modernity. There was very little time; the man was in a hurry, he did not have time and patience for detail.

Work had to pick up pace. He wanted the country to have international stature, inclusive development, lead the Islamic world. Within the country the issues were overwhelming. There were vast undeveloped areas in Sindh, Balochistan and NWFP. They need special nurture and to be pulled into the mainstream. Punjab's tendency for hegemony had to be tempered. Karachi's direction needed to be firmly steered towards commerce. There were strong provincial leaders who needed to be given assurance, confidence and pride in being part of a vibrant Pakistan. Then there was the huge external challenge in the form of the Indian subcontinent, bordering on the east and west. Kashmir remained the hot spot, achilles heel, *atoot ang* and *shehrug* (jugular vein). Neither country wanted to blink on Kashmir. ZAB vowed to fight a 1000-year war for the liberation of the valley. He saw himself as leader of the Islamic world for which he built an alliance of Islamic nations which culminated in the Islamic Summit held in Lahore in 1974, in which 35 heads of Muslim countries took part.

Then there was the geographical absurdity—East Pakistan. Separated from the West by a vast hostile territory, its reconciliation with the West was a major challenge. There was an added feature of its numerical superiority relative to the rest of Pakistan. Numbers demanded that an East Pakistani should become president. ZAB spoke about the possibility a few times at public meetings. For maintaining integrity of the nation, he was ready to embrace Sheikh Mujeeb. He was in Dacca when Yahya Khan came there, ostensibly to strike a deal with Bonga

Bondhu. ZAB always said that any deal with East Pakistan could be to the country's advantage if it was brokered through him. But Yahya Khan's strategic blunders dealt the final blow to the integrity of Pakistan. Military action caused a bloodbath in East Pakistan, the worst atrocities were inflicted on workers of Mukti Bahini and civilian youth. From across the border, India helped with arms and men, who were smarter by far than the Pakistan battalions. From this bloody haze was born the state of Bangladesh.

ZAB was left with the difficult task of raising the morale of a deeply demoralized and hurt nation. Yahya handed over the power, pleading to be allowed to retain the presidentship. ZAB set him aside and with a competent team of trusted comrades began the task of healing the nation. The final moment of statesmanship came in 1974 when he embraced Sheikh Mujeeb before a cheering nation at the Islamic Summit.

The fault lines began to appear not long after PPP had formed the government. The basic feudal character of the country had not changed. Master and slave mentality was ingrained very deep into the nation's entrails. Religion ruled supreme, as it did all over South Asia. People were ready to die and kill in the name of Islam without really understanding why they were killing and dying. The country was not ready for the roadmap which had been given to it by leaders like J.A. Rahim and Mubashir Hasan. Power to the people was the penultimate slogan of PPP; but it was mere fluff to all the vested interests.

World Bank economist Mahbub ul Haq identified the 22 families which 'ruled' Pakistan. These men and women had momentarily receded. Very soon, they started emerging from hibernation. The very feudals who had been swept away by PPP tsunami found their way back through chor darwazas (secret doors) to corridors of power. The army began to recover from the shame it had heaped on the nation under General Niazi's abject surrender and began to be spotted in the power corridors. Intelligence agencies began their old game of worming their way into favour, slowly establishing themselves as the ruler's well-wishers and confidantes. Islamic parties which had hidden themselves behind their elaborate headgear, when the young professionals loved by populace broke electoral records, began their termite journey into the arteries of power.

As the stalwarts dropped off, one by one, the Captain was left with second rung leadership; what was a ZAB without Rahim, without Mubashir, without Mumtaz and Mustafa Khar? The flotsam and jetsam rose while the best were skimmed off to take different directions across the globe. Recall Mubashir Hasan asking ZAB, 'I know you want me to go, do I have your permission?' ZAB's one word answer was 'Yes'.

The story of decline of PPP is the saddest chapter in the history of Pakistan. The man who could send masses to delirium or reduce them to tears with a single sentence or gesture was beginning to lose confidence. Its starkest example is his last meeting with Mubashir Hasan. Mubashir asked him to call a snap election to once and for all damn the false charge of large-scale rigging. His answer was the saddest admission of defeat. 'What you are asking me to do, I don't have the power to do'.

The rest was downhill all the way. Worst of all was his compromising with the line of Islamic parties suggested by those who were his sworn enemies. If anything could be worse than worst, it was placing trust in a man for whom he had shown utter disdain. The man who would hang him to make sure that his neck was protected from the noose. The bazaars of Lahore were secretly whispering slogans such as:

'Amrika ne kutta pala
Vardi wala vardi wala'

Declaring Friday as holiday, closing down 'dens of vice' like bars and cabarets, stopping short of ordering chopping of hands and feet for theft (it would happen later) was how Islamization played out on the ground. All this, he did against his grain, against his better judgment.

At this point, to quote Mubashir Hasan, they 'tipped him overboard'.

There was one thing Ziaul Haq was determined to do; foolproof, stone cast, death sentence for ZAB carried out soonest. Two necks, one noose, two bodies, one grave. If one was not eliminated, the other was dead certain of a heinous death.

On all counts, the charges were false, witnesses were purchased, judges were hand-picked to obey from start to finish, the case was dragged to ensure retirement of sympathetic judges, on every count, it was a sham. The state apparatus flaunted every rule of law, but who was to raise a voice? A few brave exceptions rose here and there whose pleas fell into ears of lead. Inside, the country watched, and outside, watched the world while Act V, the last act of the Greek Tragedy, was played in a certain prison in Islamabad. Where a 'convict' stood on a plank, face-to-face with his nameless, faceless hangman.

The wood crashed into the pit. Six pairs of eyes watched the motion, six pairs of ears heard the horrible cracking of bones. Did his closed eyes bulge beneath the eyelids? No one knew because the form disappeared in the pit of darkness. The hour was 2:30 a.m. when the devout wake up for tahajjud prayers. Someone may have been offering prayers in the barracks. Close by in the presidential palace, a man in uniform, his eyes lined with kohl, waited for the phone to ring. At last, the faithful servant had killed his mohsin through a web of lies and deceit.

A woman and a girl sat still in a room nearby, dreading the ring of the phone. Old friends were now scattered all over the country and the world had not slept a wink. Some were silently praying. For what? A miracle, a divine intervention? The first public announcement was made by Radio Australia. Mark Tully was the first journalist to break the news.

Col. Rafiuddin, military intelligence on ZAB's duty during 323 days, wrote a book; the original Urdu was translated, *Last 323 Days of Bhutto*, which was published in November 1991, 14 years after the hanging. There is no means of determining its veracity since I found no contemporary comment or review. The colonel revealed the minutest details of the last few hours, minute by second; details of his conversation with ZAB hours before they came for him. The details included position of his hands when the handcuffs were clamped, sound of his shirt tearing from becoming entangled in the orderly's shoes when they lifted his body. What he provides are graphic details. True or false, no one can prove. But the mind refuses to accept the man's account. It does not match the life of a man whose hero was Napolean and who gifted his two sons with two copies of Quran when they were leaving home for the first time. The account seems the work of a small man giving himself importance at the cost of someone who will never refute what he has written.

I found these lines from Ariel Dorfman's poem, 'Last Will and Testament' which were written on a card with a smiling photo of Murtaza Bhutto commemorating his tenth death anniversary. The lines were for the son but they epitomize, for me, the father as well. I read in them ZAB's message for the people of a country for which he gave his all:

> *And finally*
> *When the day comes*
> *When they ask you to identify the body*
> *And you see me*
> *And a voice says*
> *'We killed him*
> *He is dead'*

When they tell you
That I am
Completely absolutely definitely
Dead
Don't believe them
Don't believe them
Don't believe them

Appendices

LIFE AT A GLANCE

Personal Details

Name: Zulfikar Ali Bhutto
Date of Birth: 5 January 1928
Father: Sir Shahnawaz Khan Bhutto
Place of Birth: Larkana, Sindh
Mother: Begum Khursheed
Marriage: Shireen Amir Begum (m.1943)
                      Nusrat Ispahani (m.1951)
Children: Benazir (1953–2008)
                      Murtaza (1954–1996)
                      Sanam (1957)
                      Shahnawaz (1958–1985)

Education:

1937–1947:   Cathedral Boys School, Bombay.
1947–1949:   Bachelor's degree at University of Southern California.
1949:   Transferred to Berkeley Campus of USC.
1949:   First Asian to be elected to the Students Union Council, which governed the Association of Students of the University of California.
1950:   Graduated from Berkeley with Honours in Political Science.

1950:	Studied Jurisprudence at Christ Church College, Oxford.
1952:	Graduated with Honours from Oxford University. (Completed a three-year course in two years).
1952:	Called to the Bar at Lincoln's Inn.
1952-53:	Professor of International Law at the University of Southampton.
1953:	Returned to Pakistan in November 1953 on news of father's illness.
1954:	Set up a law office in Karachi.
1956:	Taught Constitutional Law at Sindh Muslim Law College.
September 1957:	Member of Pakistan Delegation to the UN General Assembly.
25 October 1957:	Addressed United Nations Sixth Committee on Aggression.
February 1958:	Addressed the UN Conference on the Law of the Seas.
1958:	Appointed Minister of Commerce.
1959:	Appointed Minister for Information.
1959:	Led Pakistan Delegation to the UN.
1960:	Appointed Minister of Water, Power, Communications and Industry.
1960:	Led Pakistan Delegation to Moscow to negotiate an oil-exploration agreement with the Soviet Union.
1960:	Led Pakistan Delegation to UN and voted against China's Membership.
1963-1965:	Appointed Foreign Minister.
2 March 1963:	Signed Sino-Pakistan Boundary Agreement about the transfer of 750 square kilometers of territory
August 1964:	Awarded Hilal-e-Pakistan.
22 & 28 September 1965:	Speech at UN General Assembly and Security Council on Kashmir.
June 1966:	Resigned from the Federal Cabinet.

21 June 1966:   Historic welcome in Lahore after resignation as
                     Foreign Minister.

October 1966:   Manifesto of Pakistan People's Party prepared.

30 November–
1 December 1967:   Pakistan Peoples Party launched at Lahore.

13 November 1968:   Arrested for creating disaffection against
                     Government.

February 1969:   Released.

7 December 1970:   First General Election held in Pakistan on basis
                     of 'one man one vote'.

20 December 1971:   Yahya Khan resigns and hands over to ZAB as
                     President and Chief Martial Law Administrator.

21 April 1972:   Adoption of interim Constitution by the National
                     Assembly, ZAB sworn in at the first ever
                     Presidential oath-taking ceremony held in public
                     in Pakistan's history.

2 July 1972:   The Simla Agreement signed.

14 August 1973:   Elected Prime Minister of Pakistan.

28 August 1973:   Agreement for repatriation of 93,000 POWs.

1 January 1974:   Nationalization of Banks.

22 February 1974:   Islamic Summit at Lahore.

7 March 1977:   General Elections. PPP emerges as the victorious
                     Party.

5 July 1977:   Arrested. Zia's Military Junta establishes a dummy
                     government of PNA with CMLA as President.
                     General Ziaul Haq imposes Martial Law.

28 July 1977:   Released.

3 September 1977:   Re-arrested from Clifton, Karachi charged with
                     murder.

13 September 1977:   Released.

17 September 1977:   Re-arrested from Larkana.

22 September 1977:   Chief Justice of Pakistan, Justice Yakub Ali Khan,
                     who had accepted Begum Nusrat Bhutto's Petition
                     challenging imposition of martial law, was forced
                     to retire.

9 October 1977:	Maulvi Mushtaq, Chief Justice, Lahore High Court, cancels the bail granted to ZAB by LHC.
4 April 1979:	Hanged.

CHRONOLOGY OF EVENTS

August 1965:	Indo-Pakistan War.
September 1965:	ZAB at UN. Ceasefire at the demand of UN Security Council. China delivers an ultimatum that it would go to war unless India dismantled its fortifications on the Sikkim-Tibet border. Pakistan's threat to leave the UN unless there is a settlement of the Kashmir question.
12 February 1966:	Sheikh Mujibur Rahman, President of the Awami League, launches his six-point program.
4 August 1967:	Problem of Nationality. Urdu pamphlet asserting ZAB's nationality.
1 December 1967:	Creation of the PPP.
November 1968:	Agitation by students for educational reforms.
11 November 1968:	ZAB arrives in Lahore and addresses the district bar association.
13 November 1968:	ZAB arrested under the emergency regulations on charges of anti-national activities.
28 December 1968:	Statement of J.A. Rahim to Lahore Bar Association proposing ZAB for President.
23 January 1969:	ZAB submits a Writ Petition in which he denies charges of inciting violence, asserting that government is trying to intimidate him so that he quits politics.
2 October 1969:	Withdrawal of Writ Petition and announcement of fast unto death. The court orders release from prison and places him under house arrest.
17 February 1969:	Ayub Khan announces that he will end the state of emergency and will release ZAB plus all persons detained under the Defence of Pakistan rules.
18 February 1969:	ZAB along with some other opposition leaders

	rejects negotiation with Ayub Khan.
25 March 1969:	Ayub Khan resigns. Yahya Khan takes over.
31 March 1969:	General Yahya Khan becomes CMLA.
1 May–6 June 1969	Talks between Yahya Khan and ZAB.
28 August 1969:	President Yahya Khan announces appointment of a Chief Election Commissioner to prepare for General Elections which would be held within 12 to 18 months and decides to appoint a number of civilian ministers.
	Full-scale political activity in Pakistan, including the lifting of all restrictions on public meetings and processions in preparation for general elections originally scheduled to take place in October 1970 but postponed to December due to heavy floods in East Pakistan.
7 December 1970:	First general elections held in Pakistan on the basis of 'one man, one vote'. Overwhelming victory for the Awami League in East Pakistan and a large majority for the Pakistan People's Party in West Pakistan (especially Punjab and Sindh).
17 December 1970:	President Yahya Khan grants Amnesty for all persons imprisoned for 'offences relating to agitational activity'; over 1000 prisoners released.
20 December 1970:	Mujibur Rahman asks that the Constitution be based on the six-point formula, and no compromise on this issue.
1 March 1971:	Yahya Khan postpones the opening of the National Assembly.
2 March 1971:	Decision to postpone the National Assembly evokes angry protests in Dacca.
6 March 1971:	ZAB says that his party is ready to reopen a dialogue with the Awami League on the question of the Constitution.
21 March 1971:	ZAB arrives in Dacca to participate in the talks between the President Yahya Khan and Sheikh

	Mujibur Rahman. No talks. No agreement.
26 March 1971:	Clandestine radio announces the Sovereign Independent People's Republic of Bangladesh. Violent clashes occur. President Yahya Khan announces outlawing the Awami League. Sheikh Mujibur Rahman arrested at his residence.
18–19 April 1971:	Civil War between the two wings of the country.
23 November 1971:	State of Emergency declared by Yahya Khan due to 'external aggression'.
16 December 1971:	Unconditional surrender of the Pakistan army in East Pakistan; next day acceptance of Indian ceasefire.
18 December 1971:	Demonstrations against the military regime begin in the main towns.
20 December 1971:	President Yahya Khan resigns. ZAB sworn as President and CMLA, who would form his civilian Cabinet on 24 December.
21 December 1971:	President ZAB issues decrees commuting all death sentences to life imprisonment; abolishing whipping as a punishment; withdrawing all cases pending in military courts against students, workers and peasants; and remitting sentences passed by military courts. Announces he would not draw any salary and governors, ministers and officials would travel economy class on official business.
22 December 1971:	Appoints new civilian governors to the four provinces to replace the military ones.
23 December 1971:	Abolishes the privy purses and privileges of the former rulers of about 70 princely states, including civil and military titles, right to duty-free imports and special tax concessions.
2 January 1972:	Announces government control (though not financial ownership), of 10 groups of basic

	industries: Iron and steel, basic metals, heavy engineering, heavy electrical industries, manufacture and assembly of vehicles and tractors, heavy and basic chemicals, petrochemicals, cement and public utilities, including electricity, gas and oil refineries.
8 January 1972:	Releases Mujibur Rahman from prison who goes back to Bangladesh via England.
24 January 1972:	States that he would not restore full democracy immediately, as he needed time and the power of martial law to introduce agrarian and industrial reforms. Refusal to end martial law and convene the Assemblies criticized by opposition parties. January and February numerous strikes organized by workers and students lead to rioting on 24 February.
24 January 1972:	President Bhutto begins a five-day tour of Muslim countries (Iran, Turkey, Morocco, Algeria, Tunisia, Libya, Egypt and Syria) to gain international support in his negotiations with India. Announces another tour of Muslim and African countries in May and June.
30 January 1972:	Pakistan withdraws from the Commonwealth in protest against recognition of Bangladesh by British, Australian and New Zealand governments.
31 January 1972:	Official visit to China.
10 February 1972:	Introduces social reforms including changes in laws relating to workers' welfare, social security and trade unionism.
1 March 1972:	Announces a program of land reforms whereby the maximum amount of land that may be held by one family is reduced from 500 irrigated or 1000 unirrigated acres to 150 irrigated or 300 unirrigated acres.
3 March 1972:	Dismisses Lieutenant General Gul Hasan and Air

Marshal Abdul Rahim Khan (Commanders in Chief of the Army and Air Force respectively) and appoints General Tikka Khan and Air Marshal Zafar Chaudhry with the title Chief of Staff. Vice Admiral H.H. Ahmed, the Navy Commander in Chief is also given title of Chief of Staff. Five senior Air Force officers are retired.

15 March 1972: Announces sweeping program of educational reforms, including the introduction of universal free education, nationalization of private schools and colleges and by 1980 doubling of the number of universities.

19 March 1972: Nationalization of all life insurance companies, although the companies concerned would continue to transact general insurance business.

13 April 1972: Promulgates an ordinance for the separation of the Judiciary from the Executive and other far-reaching legal reforms.

14 April 1972: National Assembly meets for the first time and gives to ZAB a unanimous Vote of Confidence.

17 April 1972: New interim Constitution comes into force.

21 April 1972: Martial law is lifted. ZAB is sworn in as President under the new constitution. Massive devaluation of the rupee.

29 June 1972 : Summit meeting between President ZAB and Prime Minister Indira Gandhi began at Simla.

2 July 1972: The Simla Agreement signed.

6 August 1972: The Simla Agreement comes into effect.

8 November 1972: Announces that Pakistan has withdrawn from SEATO and reactivated membership of CENTO.

13 February 1973: Resignation of the Governor of Sindh, Rasul Bakhsh Talpur, replaced by Rana Liaquat Ali Khan.

15 February 1973: Dismissal of the Governors: NWFP (Arbab Sikander Khan Khalil) Balochistan (Mir Ghaus Bizenjo) due to differences with the NAP. They

were be replaced respectively by Aslam Khattak and Nawab Akbar Bugti. ZAB also dismisses the Provincial government of Ataullah Mengal in Balochistan.

16 February 1973: The NWFP government resigns in protest against the dismissal of Khalil. Resignation accepted on 21 February.

10 April 1973: Adoption of the new Constitution ratified by the President on 12 April.

4 July 1973: Senate Elections from 4–10 July. PPP wins 33 of 45 seats.

9 July 1973: National Assembly accords recognition to Bangladesh.

10 August 1973: Chaudhry Fazal Elahi, Speaker of the Assembly, elected President of Pakistan.

12 August 1973: ZAB elected Prime Minister. Formal induction on August 14 of President and Prime Minister.

28 August 1973: Agreement signed between India and Pakistan for the exchange of Pakistani prisoners.

5 September 1973: Government's emergency powers extended until March 1974.

11 November 1973: ZAB accepts the resignation of Akbar Bugti, the Governor of Balochistan, but asks him to remain in power until his successor is found. The Khan of Kalat, Mir Ahmad Yar Khan, sworn in as Governor of Balochistan on 3 January 1974.

18 December 1973: Accepts the resignation of the Chief Minister of Sindh, Mumtaz Bhutto and appoints Ghulam Mustafa Jatoi to succeed him.

21 February 1974: Islamic Countries' Foreign Ministers to fly from Lahore to Dhaka for 'a mission of reconciliation' to ensure the attendance of Sheikh Mujibur Rahman, Prime Minister of Bangladesh, at the Lahore summit. The mission is successful, Bangladesh agrees.

22 February 1974:	Three-Day Islamic Summit Conference in Lahore attended by more than 30 delegations from Muslim countries. Delegations comprise Heads of State and Government or other official representatives. ZAB announces officially the recognition of Bangladesh.
24 February 1974:	Adoption of the 'Declaration of Lahore', the greater part of which was devoted to the Middle East situation.
27 February 1974:	In a press interview, Sheikh Mujib declares being impressed by ZAB's sincerity and the affection shown by thousands of Pakistanis who cheered him. He calls ZAB 'an old friend'.
4 March 1974:	State of emergency is extended by Parliament for six months, which is again extended on 26 August.
7 March 1974:	The Chief Minister of Punjab, Ghulam Mustafa Khar resigns and is replaced on 15 March by Mohammad Haneef Ramay.
23 May 1974:	The Governor of the NWFP, Aslam Khattak resigns and is succeeded by Major General Syed Ghawas.
27 June 1974 :	Arrives in Dhaka for the first official visit to Bangladesh since the country became independent.
22 October 1974:	Major Cabinet reshuffle that marks exit of most leftist members of the Bhutto Cabinet except Sheikh Rashid.
18 December 1974:	Resignation of Khurshid Hassan Meer, Minister of Labour, Health, Social Welfare, and Population Planning. Other Cabinet changes also take place.
8 February 1975:	Hayat Mohammad Khan Sherpao (Provincial Home Minister) killed in a bomb explosion. As a result, NAP is banned and hundreds of its leading members arrested.
17 February 1975:	Governor's Rule imposed in NWFP.

24 February 1975:	End of American embargo on the supply of military equipment to India and Pakistan.
13 March 1975:	Ghulam Mustafa Khar again appointed Governor of Punjab. Chief Minister Haneef Ramay, resigns on July 12 and is succeeded by Sadiq Husain Qureshi.
3 May 1975:	Nasrullah Khan Khattak sworn Chief Minister of NWFP.
24 July 1975:	Mustafa Khar resigns from governorship; Mohammad Abbas Abbasi appointed his successor.
26 November 1975:	Opposition parties resume their boycott and withdraw further negotiations with ZAB.
31 December 1975:	Government suspends Balochistan Assembly and places the province under Governor's rule (Khan of Kalat).
5 February 1976:	Major Cabinet reshuffle. Number of members dropped and replaced by political and military nominations. Lieutenant General Ziaul Haq appointed the new Army Chief of Staff.
8 April 1976:	The Sardari system abolished with immediate effect.
15 April 1976:	Opening of a trial in Hyderabad of 44 leading NAP members on charges of conspiracy, attempting to wage war on Pakistan, and high treason.
17 July 1976:	Announces that flour-milling, rice-husking and cotton-ginning are nationalized under a new Ministry of Agrarian Management.
6 December 1976 :	Sardar Mohammad Khan Barozai is elected Chief Minister of Balochistan and forms a PPP cabinet.
5 January 1977:	New Land Reforms reducing the maximum land held by one family to 100 irrigated or 200 unirrigated acres.
11 January 1977:	Nine parties form an alliance, the PNA, to contest the elections against the PPP. Jamaat-e-Islami,

Jamiat-Ulema-e-Islam, Jamiat Ulema e Pakistan, National Democratic Party, Balochistan National Party, Muslim League (Qayyum), Muslim League (Functional), Democratic Party, Communist Party.

17 January 1977: PNA declares it will not contest elections in Balochistan as the presence of troops there make free and fair elections impossible.

24 January 1977: PPP manifesto for the elections is published calling again for Islamic Socialism but the PPP parliamentary board issues tickets to feudals in a massive number.

7 March 1977: General Elections: Overwhelming victory of the Pakistan Peoples Party, winning 155 of the 200 general seats in the National Assembly. The opposition charges that elections were rigged.

9 March 1977: The PNA leadership announces that its successful candidates will refuse to take their seats in National Assembly, calls for a peaceful general strike on 11 March and states it would organize a series of protest demonstrations in defiance of emergency regulations.

10 March 1977: Provincial elections take place without incident. PPP wins 3 out of the 4 provinces of the country.

23 March 1977 ZAB appeals to PNA leaders to cooperate. He offers to withdraw the Army from Balochistan and drop treason charges against the National Awami Party leaders.

25 March 1977: 24 leaders of the PNA are arrested or placed under house arrest in the early morning including Mufti Mahmud Chaudhri, Professor Ghafoor Ahmad and Begum Nasim Wali Khan.

26 March 1977: General strike is called by the PNA, at least seven people are killed in scattered outbreaks of violence.

28 March 1977:	Sworn as PM. Forms a new Cabinet two days later. Admits in his address to the National Assembly that there have been 'excesses and malpractices' during the voting, but maintains that it is not government policy to manipulate the poll. States that he is prepared to end the state of emergency, release political prisoners and relax restrictions on the press, on condition that the opposition ends its agitation and returns to the Assembly.
31 March 1977:	Election Commission declares void the National Assembly elections in six Punjab constituencies because of grave irregularities and orders fresh elections.
13 April 1977:	Several leading members of the PPP resign either from the party or from official posts. Resignations or expulsions happen throughout April.
17 April 1977:	Repeats the proposition made earlier by Attorney General Yahya Bakhtiar to hold new Provincial Elections saying that if the PNA gets a majority in all the four provinces he would be prepared to hold new elections to the National Assembly. Announces prohibition; alcohol, gambling, bars.
21 April 1977:	Martial law imposed on Karachi, Hyderabad and Lahore and armed forces are empowered to set up courts for the speedy trial and punishment of offenders in those cities.
24 April 1977:	After the general strike of 22 April, many leading PNA members arrested. Among the arrested leaders PNA chairman, Nawabzada Nasrullah Khan, secretary general, Wazir Ali, and vice-president Mohammad Jan Abbasi, who had been named the head of the mission to meet the armed forces chief of staff, Ziaul Haq.
28 April 1977:	Accuses US of organizing and financing the agitation against him.

14 May 1977:	Joint sitting of the Parliament (boycotted by the opposition) unanimously adopts a resolution expressing full confidence in ZAB.
20 May 1977:	About 350 people killed since the beginning of the rioting that followed the elections.
3 June 1977:	Talks between representatives of the Government and the PNA. Agreement on 2 July that the National Assembly be dissolved and new elections held in October, this is rejected by the PNA general council, which demands further concessions from the Government.
5 July 1977:	Army carries out a coup: leading members of the Government and the PNA arrested, National and Provincial Assemblies dissolved and Martial Law regime established, headed by the Army Chief of Staff, General Ziaul Haq.
28 July 1977:	PNA leaders released after each gives General Zia personal assurance to adhere to laws restricting political activities. ZAB continues to hold public meetings.
8 August 1977:	100,000 people gather to meet ZAB when he comes to Lahore.
3 September 1977:	Arrested in Karachi on a charge of conspiracy of murder and is flown to Lahore.
12 September 1977:	Pleads not guilty. He is released on bail the following day.
20 September 1977:	Supreme Court considers a *habeas corpus* petition brought by Begum Nusrat Bhutto contending that his arrest was illegal.
23 September 1977:	Benazir Bhutto is placed under house arrest until 3 October.
5 October 1977:	Victimization of PPP supporters. Country-wide demonstrations.
11 October 1977:	The trial of ZAB for conspiracy to murder Muhammad Ahmad Khan begins in the Lahore High Court.

10 November 1977:	SC dismisses Begum Nusrat's *habeas corpus* petition and takes note of General Zia's pledge that election would be held as soon as possible after ZAB's trial.
9 January 1978:	Tells the court that he would take no part in its proceedings, as he was not getting the justice.
2 February 1978:	Ordered to appear before one of the special court to face charges of misuse of government funds and rigging the 1977 elections.
18 March 1978:	All accused in the murder case of Nawab Muhammad Ahmad Khan found guilty and sentenced to death, plus seven years imprisonment for conspiracy. ZAB is ordered to pay 25,000 as compensation to the murdered man's family. Demonstrations in Rawalpindi, Lahore and Karachi in the next days followed by numerous strikes and arrests of PPP loyalists.
25 March 1978:	Submits his appeal to the SC against his conviction and sentence.
27 March 1978:	Appeals from world over to commute the death sentence sent to General Zia.
1 April 1978:	SC rejects an application for relief by ZAB's family and friends.

Annexures

Excerpt from an affidavit filed by Zulfikar Ali Bhutto with reference to Begum Nusrat Bhutto's Writ Petition (WP No. 1794 of 1968) in the High Court of West Pakistan, Lahore.

Begum Nusrat Bhutto...   —Petitioner,

Versus

The Government of West Pakistan...   —Respondents

Affidavit of the Detenu Mr Zulfikar Ali Bhutto in Support of the Petition

I, Zulfikar Ali s/o Late Sir Shah Nawaz Khan Bhutto, Muslim, adult, resident of Larkana, at present in detention at the Borstal Jail, Lahore, West Pakistan, on solemn affirmation state as hereinafter:

1. That I am the detenu in the above writ petition filed by my wife Begum Nusrat Bhutto the petitioner challenging the order of my detention dated 12-11-1968 passed by the Governor of West Pakistan under rule 32 of the Defence of Pakistan Rules.

7. Nothing that I might say or do can possibly stir the masses in any way unless the objective situation was there. The objective situation is that the masses have been aroused and are protesting on their own initiative. There has been no conspiracy or plot whatever—unless on the government's side affecting the economic and social well-being of the nation. The sugar scarcity, for example, was not caused by any plot of my party, but had the definite effect of enraging the people. It was

the government itself which was responsible for this, amongst other examples of gross economic mismanagement and corruption. Economic mismanagement is a most potent factor of political discontent.

8. The phenomenon of change is the law of nature. It lies in the conditions of society and not in imaginary plans. There must be something brittle about this system if Government feels its edifice crumbled by a week's tour of mine. The people acclaimed me not because I was putting a plan of violence into action but because I represented their feelings when I declared that corruption had reached a nadir, that the students were in chains, that the people were in agony and that the conditions had become intolerable. My Lords, unlike the President who threatened to use the language of weapons in a speech he delivered in Dacca in April 1966, I employed the weapon of language, a democratic means to reach the people and to join them in the common search for a better future founded on egalitarian concepts bound together by the rule of law.

To go to the heart of the problem I submit that I have been arbitrarily thrown into jail not for expressing these views but for the differences I developed with the regime over the cease-fire and the Tashkent Declaration. If the veil is lifted, this question will solve the enigma which hung over my sudden departure from government, and explain my persecution and detention. Stripped of the maze of prejudice and fabrication, the truth, radiant in its clarity, stands as my witness when I say that neither I preached violence nor hatched a plan to instigate the students. Signs of decomposition are writ large on the fatigue face of the regime. But sick or rejuvenated, I did not plan its violent overthrow. On the contrary, the government has employed force capriciously. Everywhere the blood of innocents has watered the land, sometimes in Balochistan and sometimes in East Pakistan. On occasion it is in the Punjab and Sind; on others, in the ramparts of our northern regions. In the melee of elections, the men of the regime hold victory parades in the streets of Karachi in caesarian splendor.

The regime born of force holds its much trumpeted stability on the muscle of force. It justified the use of force in October 1958 to save the country from disintegration. And where, pray may I ask, does the country stand today? By coercion and corruption, the government has brought the country to the verge of collapse. This regime which has slandered the word 'revolution' in describing its coup d'etat, celebrates a revolution day each year, but has the temerity to punish people for uttering the word.

9. Not long ago, while defending the 'democratic' nature of the system, the Governor of West Pakistan gave vent to his wisdom by observing that democracy was not an elephant which could be produced before the people for them to touch it. Yes, my Lords, democracy is certainly not an elephant, but it exists nevertheless like a breath of fresh air, like the fragrance of a spring flower. It is a melody of liberty, richer in sensation than tangible to touch. But more than a feeling, democracy is fundamental rights, it is adult franchise, the secrecy of ballot, free press, free association, independence of the judiciary, supremacy of the legislature, controls on the executive and other related conditions which are conspicuously absent in the regime's system. Under the canons of this regime, the printed word is in disgrace, the franchise limited to individuals subject either to intimidation or allurement, the body of law contaminated by arbitrary edicts, the legislature on sufferance, fundamental rights held in animated suspense and the right of assembly in the furnace of Section 144. By any objective criterion this monument that the regime has built cannot be called democracy.

21. Incompetent rulers do not understand how the mainsprings of history move and therefore attribute their difficulties to the machinations of the person they least like. If the students give trouble, they imagine there must be somebody inciting them. Young people and students in particular, seem to have, in a given situation, the historic function of expressing the desire for radical change; but the reaction of the rulers is to repress the students in the hope of suppressing the possibility of change. The Government wants people to believe that all is well, and that it is a wonderful state of affairs except for a few 'agitators' and 'rabble rousers' who are leading 'the ignorant and illiterate people astray'.

22. The true reasons why I have been pursued by the Government with grotesque harassment and finally arrested and thrown into prison are two:

(i) the fear that I might take the Tashkent affair to the people of Pakistan for their verdict; and

(ii) the fact that President Ayub Khan believes that I am his not powerful rival for the Presidentship, because I enjoy the confidence of the people whereas he does not.'

I have been arbitrarily thrown into jail on account of the differences I developed with the regime over the cease-fire and the Tashkent Declaration. My speeches and the circumstances attending them are not the causes for my detention in jail. My detention is to prevent my bringing to public knowledge how and why the Tashkent Declaration came about. The government cannot afford to let the truth be known, because if it were, the President would certainly not be elected for a third term no matter what devices he employed. By confining me in jail and so removing me from the political arena, he believes he is ensuring his own continuance in the Presidential office. That is the true reason for my detention and not the trumped up charges in the memorandum of grounds of detention. It is in bad faith that the charges have been made against me.

30) d & f (vi) Since my departure from government over a hundred persons connected with us have been troubled, detained and beaten in jails.

(d) It is not possible to recount each and every detail of the way in which my political supporters and friends have been harassed and victimized. The general attitude of the government in this regard has become a matter of public knowledge. To give only an idea to this Hon'ble Court a few instances are narrated.

When the Pakistan Peoples Party was being formed an attempted was made to set fire to the site where the stage was constructed for the Conference. This was at 4 k Gulberg, Lahore.

(ii) I have separately submitted the attempts made by Government to disrupt my meetings at Lahore and Multan. Indeed, wherever I have spoken impediments have been placed by Government. Permission for loudspeakers has been refused, prohibitory orders under Section 144 Cr. P.C. have been indiscriminately applied and provisions of Section 144 Cr. P.C. misused. The whole administration has been geered to prevent me from reaching the people.

(iv) On my arrival in Rawalpindi by car from Sher Pao on the 7th November 1968, I was greeted on the road by a large crowd of students of the Polytechnic, a couple of miles ahead of their institution because the police had closed the highway leading to it. When I arrived at the Hotel Intercontinental, I found the whole Mall area thick with teargas smoke. I was told that a number of students who, having come out of the Gordon College in a procession to protest against the seizure of their purchases at Landi Kotal, had gathered in the lawns of the Hotel Continental, from where, without any provocation they were suddenly and mercilessly beaten up and chased away. About one and a half hours after my arrival in the hotel, I received a telephone call from the Polytechnic informing me that the police had opened fire there resulting in the death of a student Abdul Hamid. I was told that the students were insisting on taking the body in a procession to the President's House and that they wanted me to lead the procession. I advised the students to do nothing that might aggravate the situation. I fervently appealed to them to restrain their feelings and not to exacerbate the tension. I tried to send some of my partymen to the Polytechnic Institute to explain to them the need for discipline in a crisis created by the Government. They were unable to meet the students because the Institution was sealed off by the police. On 8th November I left Rawalpindi by car at about 3:00 P.M. for Pindi Gheb to offer condolences to the family of Abdul Hamid. Mr Khurshid Hassan Meer, Advocate, the Chairman of People Party of Rawalpindi District accompanied me. The following morning he was arrested in an arson case alleged to have occurred at Rawalpindi after 3:00 P.M. on 8th November 1968. When he was granted bail by the Session Judge which order was confirmed by the High Court later, he was again detained on the 10th of November under an order rescinded during the hearing of his writ petition. This briefly indicates the Government's attitude towards my party and my party-men. A member of the Principles Committee of my party, Dr. Mubashir Hasan was arrested on the ground that he was 'creating disaffection against the Government'. Two influential members of the National Assembly one of whom is a relative and the other a friend, were arrested merely because they were seen in the Gordon College, Rawalpindi. In this fashion, a sweep of arbitrary arrests was made on 13th of November and subsequently.

g (i) I was arrested in the early hours of November 13th at Lahore from the house of Dr. Mubashir Hasan a member of the Principle Committee of Pakistan People's Party with whom I and Mr Mumtaz Ali Bhutto were staying. A few minutes after my arrest Mr Mumtaz Ali Bhutto and Dr. Mubashir Hasan were arrested and Begum Mubashir was put under house arrest. I was taken to Mianwali Jail where I arrived at about 7 A.M. After a thorough search of my person and belongings, my papers and books were confiscated although by law I was entitled to keep them.

I was confined in an old call full of rats and mosquitoes, the charpoy was tied to a chain. There was an adjoining little room meant for toilet purposes. But it was so dirty that it was repulsive to enter it. The food consisted of two chappaties made of red wheat with dal which had stones in it or two tiny pieces of meat. A strong light shone for 24 hours through my stay there making sleep at night extremely difficult. I was kept in solitary confinement. When I learnt that the High Court had granted my lawyers permission to meet me I immediately asked for some paper to enable me to make notes for my meeting with them. Despite my repeated requests writing paper was not given to me until the afternoon of the 18th November. My letters and telegrams were not delivered to me. Except for 'Pakistan Times' and 'Mashriq' I was not provided with any other newspapers. As the Hon'ble High Court ordered that all detenus should be kept in one jail, on the evening of 18th November I was taken to Sahiwal where I arrived in the early hours of 19th November.

(ii) Makeshift arrangements were made at Sahiwal for my detention where I continued to be kept in solitary confinement. Here, instead of the rats the room was full of bats and, to avoid them, I had to sleep with a towel over my face. The mosquitoes and flies were in legion. The bathroom was separate from the cell and was shared with others. The practice in jail is to provide Class I and II detenus with a convict for personal service. The convict provided to me was told that he would be skinned alive if he spoke to me. Unlike at Mianwali, this man was not even provided with a kitchen knife to prepare my meals. Again unlike Mianwali, where my cell was locked about 8:00 in the evening, the warden came to lock me in at 5:00 in the evening. The food was as inedible and insufficient as at Mianwali. I showed the 2 tiny pieces of meat constituting my meals to Sheikh Rashid, Advocate, when under orders of the High Court he interviewed me. Contrary to law, I was not permitted the use of a radio or to make private arrangements for my meals. I addressed about 5 or 6 applications to the authorities protesting against the illegal conditions of my detention which were neither controverted nor was any action taken on them.

31. This is the manner in which I have been pursued by the Government. I was a Minister of the Central Government for eight years and the Foreign Minister of Pakistan during time of war. My services to the country won the appreciation of friends and envy of our opponents. The distinguished Bertrand Russell, whose whole life has been a glorious struggle against oppression said in a letter to the 'Economist' of 3rd September 1966 under the caption 'Ayub's Rival' :

Your attack on Mr Bhutto (August 20, 1966) should be placed in context, Mr Bhutto's sin in Western eyes is that he was an important figure in conceiving an independent policy for Pakistan, placing it in the context of Afro-Asia and outside the rank of countries which are dominated by the United States.

'The fate of national leaders who respond to the needs of their people is increasingly clear unless they find the means to resist the pressures applied to them, in which case journals such as the Economist attach unpleasant labels to them. Mr Bhutto is a national leader of his country in the tradition of Jinnah, and the storm of pro-longed applause which he receives is not restricted to London. There are many who wish him well and who admire his role in working for an independent policy for his country consonant with the social aspirations of the peoples of Africa, Asia and Latin America.'

President Ahmad Soakarno who rendered unparalleled assistance to Pakistan, while conferring the Order of the Republic of Indonesia at a ceremony in the Mardeka Palace in Jakarta on the 20th of April 1966 said that it was an honour for him to confer the Order on me in recognition of my 'great services to the friendship of Indonesia and Pakistan'. He concluded by saying that I was 'a great freedom-fighter and great worker for Afro-Asian solidarity'.

In April 1965 President Mikoyan of the Soviet Union, a great Power that was hostile to Pakistan until I went to Moscow in 1960 to conclude an agreement with that country, praised my services to Pakistan at a meeting in the Kremlin, in the presence of the Soviet and Pakistan delegations. He told President Ayub Khan that 'Mr Bhutto is a remarkably intelligent person' and that my 'youth and energy were a tremendous source of strength to President Ayub Khan and to Pakistan'. President Mikoyan congratulated President Ayub Khan for inclusion in his Cabinet a Minister of my 'calibre'.

At the age of 34 in August 1964 the high order of Hilal-e-Pakistan was conferred upon me. While conferring the award in the presence of Muslim League leaders assembled at the President's guest-house at Rawalpindi, President Ayub Khan advised the youth of Pakistan to emulate me.

35. ...The government has put me in jail on the anvil of the elections after it was convinced that it could not succeed in making me relent on my political obligations.

39. How can this regime be allergic to the word 'revolution' when its whole structure is based on force? On several occasions the opposition has been threatened with bloodshed. Recently in Rawalpindi a Vice President of Muslim League of Islamabad after wounding a journalist with pistol shots in the presence of the police struts about fearlessly in the streets of the Capital of Pakistan. A student leader of Rawalpindi was beaten up by thugs. A banner bearing the 'Kalma' was torn to shreds as if Pakistan was a Jan Sangh state.

40. ...In the fullness of time, the wheel of fortune will turn and in the revolution of this turn a better tomorrow will dawn.

The issues that confront Pakistan reach beyond the limitations of time and space. They come once in an epoch to make or mar, they wade across the horizons of the ugly moment and give the future a beautiful image a future in which Pakistan is formidable fortress of the millat of Islam, serving oppressed mankind everywhere, never-relenting until it has liquidated the last vestige of aggression in Kashmir and liberated Baitul Muqaddas.

Excerpts from Dr Zeenat Hussain's Writ Petition submitted on 14 November 1968 submitted in the High Court of West Pakistan, Lahore.

Dr. Zeenat Hussain, wife of Dr. Mubashir Hasan,
resident of 4K, Gulberg, Lahore,   —Petitioner

Versus

The Government of West Pakistan through
the Home Secretary, Lahore; and another   —Respondents

Dr. Zeenat Hussain wife of Dr. Mubashir Hasan,
resident of 4 K Gulberg, Lahore   —Petitioner

Versus

1. The Government of West Pakistan through the Home Secretary, Lahore; and
2. The Deputy Secretary to Government, West Pakistan, Home Department, Lahore —Respondents

Petition

Under Article 98 of the Constitution of the Islamic Republic of Pakistan seeking a declaration that the detention of Dr. Mubashir Hasan is illegal and praying for his immediate release.

Respectfully Showeth:

1. That the petitioner is the wife of Dr. Mubashir Hasan, M.S.C. (Columbia); Ph.D., (Iowa) a consulting Engineer. The Petitioner's husband is the Managing Director of Consulting Associates Ltd., Lahore.

2. That the petitioner's husband hereinafter called the detenu is a friend of Mr Z.A. Bhutto and a member of the Pakistan Peoples Party of which Mr Z.A. Bhutto is the Chairman. During his recent visit to Lahore commencing on the evening of 9.11.1968 Mr Z.A. Bhutto came to live with the petitioner's husband at Gulberg. In the early hours of 13.11.1968 a large force of police came to the petitioner's house to arrest Mr Z.A. Bhutto. Mr Bhutto was arrested and taken away at about 2.30 A.M. After Mr Bhutto was taken away the police

decided to arrest all the male residents of the house (excluding the servants) and in this process arrested (i) Dr Mubashir Hasan the petitioner's husband, (ii) Mr Mumtaz Ali Bhutto M.N.A. (A cousin of Mr Z.A. Bhutto) and (iii) Mr Pir Bakhsh Khan Bhutto (Another cousin of Mr Z.A. Bhutto). This was done at about 3.45 A.M. The police produced the orders for the arrest and detention of Mr Mumtaz Ali Bhutto and the petitioners husband but they did not have even the orders for arresting and detaining Mr Pir Bakhsh Khan Bhutto who was nevertheless arrested and detained. He has since been released. The order of arrest and detention of the petitioners husband is Annexure 'A'. It purports to be under clause (b) of Sub Rule (1) of Rule 32 of the Defense of Pakistan Rules. According to the order the petitioners husband is committed to the custody of Superintendent, District Jail, Gujrat and is to be treated as a Class II detenu. This has since been done.

3. That the order of arrest and detention has been duly executed. It does not specify the period for which the petitioner's husband is to be detained. The petitioner's husband having been arrested and detained and taken to Gujrat Jail, the order has exhausted itself. The continued detention of Dr Mubashir Hasan is illegal and unwarranted by any law or lawful order. He is entitled to be released forthwith.

4. That so far as the petitioner is aware the petitioner's husband delivered no speech and never did anything which could justify his arrest and detention. He is a member of the Pakistan Peoples Party and is its organizer for the city of Lahore. The Party is a legal organisation and is one of the major political parties of Pakistan.

5. That while in the case Mr Z.A. Bhutto grounds of detention were served, no grounds of detention have been served or provided in the case of the detenu which strongly indicates that there are no legal reasons for arresting and detaining the petitioners husband.

6. That the order of detention of the detenu is illegal and malafide. The main reason appears to be to strike terror in the mind of the people of Pakistan and of members of various political parties which do not agree with the practices and policies of the party in power.

7. That those in authority had according to the information given to the petitioner by her husband recently conveyed threats of violence to Mr Z.A. Bhutto. One of the reasons why Mr Z.A. Bhutto was staying with the petitioners husband was to ensure his physical safety. The arrest also appears to be motivated by a desire to frighten the friends of Mr Bhutto from protecting him.

8. That the Defence of Pakistan Ordinance 1965 was promulgated on 6.9.1965 at time when Pakistan was at war with India consequent upon the villainous attack by India upon Pakistan. The President, in view of the grave emergency issued on 6.9.1965 a Proclamation of Emergency.

9. That on 23.9.1965 hostilities between India and Pakistan ceased and the Tashkent Declaration made on 10.1.1966 affectively terminated hostilities and emergency.

10. That in any event the declaration of Emergency made on 6.9.1965 is no longer in force. Under the Constitution it stands revoked. The Defence of Pakistan Ordinance, 1965 and the Rules made thereunder are no longer law of Pakistan and no orders including orders of detention can be made thereunder.

11. That the order of detention is patently illegal. Its recitals are a mere copy of the statutory provision and prove that no case has been given to the decision of such vital matters.

12. That in any event in the performance of its obligations under and in respect of the Constitution and as the Protector of the rights and liberties of the people of Pakistan, this Honorable Court has the authority and duty to determine the validity of the continuance of the State of Emergency. It is solicited that this Honourable Court may be pleased to declare that the proclamation of Emergency is no longer is force.

13. That the order directing the arrest and detention of the petitioners husband is illegal and malafide. Amongst other factors which prove this to be so is the fact the despite the high academic qualifications, financial and social status and mode of living of the Detenu be has been classified as a Class II detenu. This is a part of the Scheme to oppress and frighten the detainee and others who do not agree

with the Government in power.

14. That the Schedule of the new elections has been announced. Constituencies have been delimited and the electoral process is in progress. To continue the state of Emergency at such a period is to negate the very fundamentals of the Constitution and of Democracy.

15. That the petitioner has no other remedy available to her.

For the reasons stated above, it is respectfully prayed that the Court may be pleased to declare that the order of detention passed by respondent No. 2 on 12.11.68 having exhausted itself is no longer in force and the detainee is entitled to his liberty forthwith.

Alternatively and upon failure of the above prayer, the petitioner begs that her husband Dr Mubashir Hasan should be ordered to be brought before the court so that the court may satisfy itself that Dr Mubashir Hasan is not being held in custody without lawful authority.

It is further prayed that as an interim relief the operation of the order of detention should be suspended and Dr Mubashir Hasan may be ordered to be released on bail.

N.B. In view of the special circumstances, the petitioner reserves the right to pray for adding other grounds of fact and law to this petition.

Dr Zeenat Hussain
Petitioner,

Through
(Mahmud Ali Qasuri)
(Dr Javaid Iqbal)
(Sheikh Muhammad Rashid)
(Zaki-Ud-Din Pal)
(Manzar Bashir)

Advocates

N.B. No other writ petition on the same subject has been filed.

GOVERNMENT OF WEST PAKISTAN
HOME DEPARTMENT
Dated Lahore, the 12th November 1968

DETENTION ORDER

No. 2 - 125 - H, Spl. I/68. WHEREAS the Governor of West Pakistan is satisfied that Dr Mubashir Hasan son of Munawar Hassan, resident of 4 K Gulberg, District Lahore, Lahore Division, has been acting in a manner prejudicial to the security, the public safety and interest of Pakistan, the maintenance of public order and the maintenance of peaceful conditions in West Pakistan;

AND WHEREAS with a view to preventing the said Dr Mubashir Hasan from acting in a manner as aforesaid it is necessary to make the following order;

Now, Therefore, in exercise of the powers conferred upon the Government of West Pakistan by clause (b) of sub-rule (1) of rule 32 of the Defence of Pakistan Rules, 1965, read with Government of Pakistan Cabinet Secretariat Order No. SRO-III (R)/65, dated the 6th September, 1965, the Governor of West Pakistan is pleased to order that the said Dr Mubashir Hasan be arrested and detained and committed to the custody of Superintendent, District Jail, Gujrat.

BY ORDER OF THE GOVERNOR OF WEST PAKISTAN
(M.M. USMANI) CSP.,
Deputy Secretary to Government,
West Pakistan, Home Department.

Dr. Mubashir Hasan is to be treated as Class II detenu.
(M.M. USMANI) CSP.,
Deputy Secretary to Government,
West Pakistan, Home Department.

Bibliography

1. *The Mirage Of Power: An Enquiry into the Bhutto years (1971-1977).* Mubashir Hasan, 2000. Karachi: Oxford University Press
2. *If I am Assassinated.* Zulfikar Ali Bhutto, 1979. New Delhi: Vikas Publishing House
3. *Zulfi Bhutto of Pakistan: His Life and Times.* Stanley Wolpert, 1993. Delhi: Oxford University Press
4. *Z.A. Bhutto: Glimpses From the Jail File.* Fakhar Zaman, 1995. Lahore: Agha Amir Hussain Classic
5. *The Discourse and Politics of Zulfikar Ali Bhutto.* Anwar H. Syed, 1992. London: Macmillan Press Limited
6. *A Judiciary in Crisis? The Trial of Zulfiqar Ali Bhutto.* T.W. Rajaratnam, 1988. Kaanthalakam
7. *A Treasury of The Theatre (Vol. 1).* Edited by John Gassner, 1958. New York: Simon and Schuster, INC
8. *Songs of Blood and Sword.* Fatima Bhutto, 2010. New Delhi: Penguin Books
9. *Bhutto ke Aakhari 323 Din.* Colonel Rafeeuddin, 2009. Lahore: Nazaria-e-Pakistan Academy
10. *Pakistan Toofan ki Zad Mein.* Benazir Bhutto, 1983. New Delhi: Vikas Publishing House
11. *Pakistan Peoples' Party: Ek Taarikhi Jaayeza 1968 ta Haal.* Khalid Kashmiri, 1996. Islamabad: Qaumi Commission Baraa-e-Taarikh-o-Saquafat, Pakistan.
12. *Awami Leader.* Dr. Mubashir Hasan, 2014. Lahore.
13. *Zulfikar Ali Bhutto and Pakistan (1967-1977).* Rafi Raza, 1997.

Karachi: Oxford University Press.

14. *Zulfikar Ali Bhutto Sayasi Sawaneh Hayat (Volume-I).* Rasheed Akhtar Nadvi, 1974. Islamabad: Idaara Ma'araf-e-Milli.

15. *Politics of the People: Reshaping Foreign Policy, 1948–1966* Vol. I (A Collection of statements, articles and speeches by Zulfikar Ali Bhutto). Edited by Hamid Jalal and Khalid Hasan: Pakistan Publications, Rawalpindi

16. *Politics of the People: Awakening the people (1966–1969)* Vol. 2 (A Collection of statements, articles and speeches by Zulfikar Ali Bhutto). Edited by Hamid Jalal and Khalid Hasan, Rawalpindi: Pakistan Publications

17. *Politics of the People: Marching Towards Democracy (1970–1971)* Vol. 3 (A Collection of statement, articles and speeches of Zulfikar Ali Bhutto). Edited by Hamid Jalal and Khalid Hasan Rawalpindi: Pakistan Publications

18. *Nusrat*, Weekly, Lahore, editor: Mohammad Haneef Ramay

19. *Meyaar*, weekly, Karachi, editor: Mahmood Shaam

20. *Al-Fatah*, Weekly, Karachi, editor: Wahaab Siddiqui

21. *Inqilaab*, Weekly, Muzaffarabad, editor: Wahaab Siddiqui

WRITINGS OF ZULFIKAR ALI BHUTTO

1. *Peace-Keeping by the United Nations*, 1967. Karachi: Pakistan Publishing House

2. *Political Situation in Pakistan*, 1968. New Delhi: Veshasher Prakashan

3. *The Myth of Independence*, 1969. Karachi and Lahore: Oxford University Press

4. *The Great Tragedy*, 1971. Karachi: Pakistan People's Party Publications

5. *Politics of the People: Reshaping Foreign Policy, 1948–1966* Vol. 1 (A Collection of statements, articles and speeches). Edited by Hamid Jalal and Khalid Hasan. Rawalpindi: Pakistan Publications

6. *Politics of the People: Awakening the People, 1966–1969* Vol. 2 (A Collection of statements, articles and speeches). Edited by Hamid Jalal and Khalid Hasan. Rawalpindi: Pakistan Publications

7. *Politics of the People: Marching Towards Democracy, 1970– 1971* Vol. 3 (A Collection of statements, articles and speeches). Edited by

Hamid Jalal and Khalid Hasan. Rawalpindi: Pakistan Publications

8. *Bilateralism: New Directions*, 1976. Government of Pakistan, Islamabad, 1976
9. *Third World: New Directions*, 1977. London: Quartet Books
10. *My Pakistan*. Reproduced by Sani H. Panhwar, Member Sindh Council, 1979. New Delhi: Biswin Sadi Publications
11. *If I am Assassinated*, 1979. New Delhi: Vikas Publishing House.
12. *My Execution*, 1980. London: Musawaat Weekly International

Acknowledgements

For twenty years loving friends have stood by me.

My endless gratitude to Dr Mubashir Hasan who was for me the beginning, middle and end of this process. To Dr Shubbar Hasan and Begum Sylvia Hasan, both of them passed away in the last two years, I owe the mahaul which enabled me to write; for 20 years I enjoyed their loving hospitality in Lahore as my home away from home.

No words are sufficient for my colleague Ruth Zothanpuii who assisted the research, scrutinized each word and blended beautifully with the project.

To Begum Ghinwa Bhutto, who opened for me her library and home at 70 Clifton, my sincerest thanks. And what would I have done if not for the oral history and candid moments shared with me by Mr I.A. Rehman. For the delightful morning and precious wisdom I gained, I offer Mr Ghulam Mustafa Khar my salaams. To Mr Ibrahim Ramay, I am grateful for sharing his father's photograph collection. Thanks to Mr Adnan Adil for his consistent help.

To Rupa Publications team for seeing this book to the end; most of all to Mr Rudra Sharma, who kept me going by his gentle but firm persuasion, I offer my sincere gratitude.

Index